Postmetaphysical Thinking II

Essays and Replies

Jürgen Habermas

Translated by Ciaran Cronin

polity

First published in German as *Nachmetaphysisches Denken II. Aufsätze und Repliken* © Suhrkamp Verlag, Berlin, 2012

This English edition © Polity Press, 2017

Polity Press
65 Bridge Street
Cambridge CB2 1UR, UK

Polity Press
350 Main Street
Malden, MA 02148, USA

All rights reserved. Except for the quotation of short passages for the purpose of criticism and review, no part of this publication may be reproduced, stored in a retrieval system or transmitted, in any form or by any means, electronic, mechanical, photocopying, recording or otherwise, without the prior permission of the publisher.

ISBN-13: 978-0-7456-8214-3
ISBN-13: 978-0-7456-8215-0 (pb)

A catalogue record for this book is available from the British Library.

Typeset in 10.5 on 12 pt Times NR MT by
Servis Filmsetting Ltd, Stockport, Cheshire
Printed and bound in the UK by CPI Group (UK) Ltd, Croydon CR0 4YY

The publisher has used its best endeavours to ensure that the URLs for external websites referred to in this book are correct and active at the time of going to press. However, the publisher has no responsibility for the websites and can make no guarantee that a site will remain live or that the content is or will remain appropriate.

Every effort has been made to trace all copyright holders, but if any have been inadvertently overlooked the publisher will be pleased to include any necessary credits in any subsequent reprint or edition.

For further information on Polity, visit our website:
politybooks.com

Postmetaphysical Thinking II

Contents

Contents

LINGUISTIFICATION OF THE SACRED

In Place of a Preface

The collection of essays published in 1988 under the same title as the present collection[1] dealt with the self-confirmation of philosophical thinking. This remains the theme of the present collection. Philosophy is not a scientific discipline that could be defined in terms of a fixed method or a set subject matter. Philosophical discourses derive their unity instead from the formation of a canon – in other words, from the texts that have been associated with the history of philosophy for two and a half millennia. What philosophy can achieve is therefore an essentially contested question. Nevertheless, this is not an idle question that we can sidestep. For even a form of thought that is not determinate must tie itself down for the time being if it is not to wander around aimlessly.

A cursory examination of our scientific, cultural and social context already tells us that philosophers no longer keep company with poets and thinkers. The role of the sage or seer who – like Heidegger – still claims privileged access to the truth is no longer an option for them. Since philosophy has *also* joined the ranks of modern scientific disciplines, philosophers begin their efforts at persuasion among their peers. Anyone who does not withstand the tribunal of professional criticism is rightly suspected of charlatanism. Today philosophical arguments, too, can expect to be accepted as *prima facie* worthy of consideration only in the context of the established discourses of the natural, social and human sciences, of existing practices of art criticism, legal discourse, and political and public communication. Only in this wider context of intrinsically fallible knowledge can we seek the narrow path on which philosophical reasons still 'count'.

But this search must assume a performative form – that is, by actually engaging in philosophy; metatheoretical considerations remain abstract in the pejorative sense. Anyone who wants to engage in the business of clarifying philosophy's proper role must actually do philosophy. This reflexive circle is unavoidable even for those who still think that it is possible to define a canon of philosophical knowledge. In a recent study, Herbert Schnädelbach tries to persuade his readers that a certain compendium of knowledge comprises 'what one can learn from philosophers'; but in doing so he has to develop his arguments in a philosophical way.[2] Authors for whom the question is problematic rather than one that admits of conclusive answers, too, can differentiate philosophical from other forms of thought only by trying to show what philosophy actually is. For example, I could not justify my recommendation that philosophy should henceforth be conducted only in the mode of 'postmetaphysical thinking' without at the same time arguing for the concept of 'communicative reason'. This is why *Postmetaphysical Thinking II* opens with a systematic section on 'The Lifeworld as a Space of Reasons' (just as the earlier volume began with a corresponding section on the 'pragmatic turn').

I now approach the same theme from an evolutionary perspective, however, because a different constellation has developed over the past two decades. The philosophical scene at the time was dominated by trends towards a return to metaphysics. On the one hand, there were some nuanced attempts to return to speculative ideas in response to the deflationary schools of thought of analytic philosophy – one proposal was to rehabilitate metaphysical figures of thought by drawing directly on classical sources;[3] another was to renew motifs from German idealism by reactivating the post-Kantian problem of self-consciousness.[4] On the other hand, critiques of reason inspired by Nietzsche and the late Heidegger had inspired attempts to recover the dimension of a 'true origin' in a different way.[5] As things now stand, political and historical developments over the past decades have lent topicality to a completely different theme. In the wake of globalization and digitalized communication, the largely secularized societies of Europe are confronted with religious movements and forms of fundamentalism of undiminished vitality both at home and throughout the world.

This development has not only steered the discussion in social science on secularization and social modernization in a different direction; it also poses a challenge for philosophy – in two respects.[6] As normative political theory, philosophy must first examine that laicistic interpretation of secularized state power and religious pluralism which would banish the religious communities from the political public arena and confine them to the private domain. Moreover, in its role as heir to the European Enlightenment, philosophy feels provoked. Insofar as it sees itself as the 'guardian of rationality', what should philosophy make of the fact that religious communities and religious doctrines, in spite of their archaic roots in ritual practices, seem to be asserting themselves at the heart of social modernity as a contemporary, culturally productive intellectual formation? Philosophy cannot fail to be disconcerted by this contemporaneity of religion because a relationship of parity between philosophy and religion would profoundly alter the constellation that became established in the eighteenth century. Since that time, philosophy, in an alliance with the sciences, had either treated religion as an obscure object in need of explanation (as did Hume, for example) or subsumed it under its own concepts as a past but transparent intellectual formation (as from Kant to Hegel). But now, by contrast, philosophy encounters religion not as a past but as a present-day formation, however opaque. What does this mean for philosophy's self-understanding?

The first chapter in the present volume, 'From Worldviews to the Lifeworld', throws light on the change in the constellation formed by philosophy and science. In this essay, the hard-core scientistic self-understanding of philosophy proposed by advocates of a 'scientific worldview' provides an occasion for defending a 'soft' version of naturalism. The new debate over naturalism calls to mind the aspects under which philosophy, as a scientifically imbued discursive understanding of ourselves and the world, differs from the objectifying sciences. Here, in the context of a rough sketch of the emergence of postmetaphysical thinking out of the symbiosis between faith and knowledge, I develop the basic concepts of 'communicative action' and 'symbolically structured lifeworld'.

The following two essays in the first section present a more in-depth account of this communicative approach from an evolutionary perspective. Michael Tomasello explains the development of human communication out of contexts of cooperation in which the participants coordinate their intentions and actions via simple symbolic gestures.[7] Tomasello's socio-cognitive approach emphasizes the intersubjectively shared knowledge that proceeds from gestural communication and makes possible the purposive coordination of actions and intentions. However, the socio-cognitive requirements for realizing shared goals through cooperation can explain the communication only of facts, intentions and requests, not of normative behavioural expectations. Simple requests and expressions of intentions do not have the intrinsic obligatory force of commands or precepts. The intersubjectively shared normative meaning of moral obligation draws on binding energies that cannot be explained in terms of the constraints of cooperation. If the social-pragmatic approach is sufficient to explain the origins of linguistic communication, it must be possible to explicate the meaning of linguistic communication independently of a 'strong' normative consensus about values and reciprocal normative expectations. In any case, the dimension of obligations requires a special explanation.

The hypothesis that language originates in gestural communication directs our attention to ritual practices, which seem to have supplemented everyday communication as an extraordinary form of communication. Even though this form of communication deviates conspicuously from everyday communication in being decoupled from all tangible functional contexts and not referring to inner-worldly objects and states of affairs, it exhibits structural similarities to gestural communication. Durkheim already identified these ritual practices as the source of social solidarity. This suggests the following hypothesis. As gestural communication developed into fully fledged grammatical languages, ritually generated normative binding energies could be captured and explicated in this fully differentiated linguistic medium. At any rate, the illocutionary forces of many regulative speech acts (such as commanding and promising, appointing, putting into force, etc.) can be understood as the result of a conventionalization of meanings of ritual origin through which they become routines. J. L. Austin developed the concept of 'illocutionary force' with reference to examples of institutionally bound speech acts such as baptizing, swearing, praying, proclaiming, marrying, etc., whose sacred background is evident.

As it happens, the evolutionary perspective outlined throws light on two problems in the theory of language that I would like at least to mention in passing.[8] The socio-cognitive hypothesis concerning the origin of language focuses on cooperative relationships as the original source of language. This context of emergence speaks against the widespread intentionalist conception that the meaning of human communication consists in people informing one another about their ideas, desires and intentions. If exchanging symbolic gestures originally served the purpose of pursuing shared goals based on a division of labour, then the meaning of linguistic communication can be explained in terms of the practical need for participants to reach an agreement under the pressure to act. Person A wants to communicate with person B about something, be it about the existence of states of affairs or about intentions, desires and requests to intervene in the world to bring about corresponding states of affairs. Under the pressure to coordinate their actions in ways which promote their goals, it is not enough simply to let the addressee know what is meant. Rather, with her utterance the speaker pursues the illocutionary goal that the listener should accept her assertion as true, take her desire seriously, if necessary accept the correctness of her normative expectations or reproaches, and comply with her requests. For every utterance is addressed to persons who can take a position by answering 'yes' or 'no'. The success of communication is measured by whether the person addressed accepts the claim to truth, truthfulness or rightness raised for what is said as valid (or as sufficient in view of potential reasons).[9]

The second problem I would like to mention concerns the striking asymmetries between the validity claims of truth and truthfulness, on the one hand, and normative rightness, on the other. Taken together with the supposition of a secondary linguistification of the sacred, the hypothesis that there are two equally original forms of communication provides an explanation of these asymmetries. Elementary speech acts can *always* be questioned both as regards the truth of statements (or the existential presuppositions of the propositional contents) and as regards the sincerity of the speakers' intentions (whether these are thematized or implicitly accompany their speech acts). These two cognitive validity claims seem to be intrinsic to language. By contrast, motivationally binding claims to rightness come into play only when speech acts are *embedded* in normative contexts that are already assumed to be obligatory or to be capable of justification.

Normatively 'freestanding' requests and proclamations are authorized by nothing except the justified intention and the rationally intelligible will of the speaker. We understand such speech acts, therefore, when we know the actor-relative reasons for the rationality of the corresponding intentions (and the conditions for implementing them).[10] By contrast, commands derive their binding authority, or declarations their legal force, from a prior normative background that is assumed to be valid. We understand such speech acts only when we know the authorizing reasons which must be drawn from this background. This dependence of normative claims to rightness on their context can be explained in terms of the hypothesis that the binding energies initially generated through ritual are connected only subsequently with the language that arises from everyday contexts of cooperation. This also implies, on the other hand, that we must not attach too much explanatory weight to the linguistification of the sacred.

In the *Theory of Communicative Action*, I made the rash and over-inclusive assumption that the rationally motivating binding force of good reasons, on which the coordinating function of linguistic communication turns, can be traced back *in general* to the linguistification of a basic agreement initially secured through ritual: 'The aura of rapture and terror that emanates from the sacred, the *spellbinding* power of the holy, is sublimated into the *binding/bonding* force of criticizable validity claims and at the same time turned into an everyday occurrence.'[11] In the light of a differentiation between roots of language in communication within and beyond everyday contexts, I now conceive of the linguistification of the sacred differently. Normative contents first had to be liberated from their encapsulation in rituals before they could be translated into the semantics of everyday language. To be sure, the ritual propitiation of the forces of salvation and perdition had always been associated with a semantic polarization between 'good' and 'evil'. But it was only when ritual meanings found linguistic expression in mythical narratives that this psychodynamic opposition between good and evil could become assimilated in everyday language to the binary coding of statements and utterances (as true/false and truthful/untruthful) and develop into a third validity claim associated with regulative speech acts (right/wrong). I mention this speculative hypothesis about how meanings frozen in rituals could be released into language because the development of worldviews can also (though by no means only) be understood as the disenchantment and reflexive dissolution of sacred meanings.

If we follow Michael Tomasello,[12] contemporary languages owe their grammatical complexity to a prehistoric differentiation of gestural languages into propositionally structured languages (though this process of differentiation can be reconstructed only in a hypothetical way). Let us assume, then, that in early human history there was such a period of 'linguistic' communication,[13] albeit communication mediated exclusively by deictic and iconic gestures.[14] It was only the emergence of grammatical languages that made it possible not to base the fragile solidarity of the social collective (as analysed by Durkheim) and the recognition of its normative framework – that is, of institutionalized kinship relations – any longer only on rites, but also to interpret, explain and justify social solidarity and its normative foundation in terms of mythical narratives. After all, the interplay between ritual and myth founds the sacred complexes that continue to exist in highly reflexive forms to the present day. Until the development of a secular, postmetaphysical understanding of self and the world in the modern West, all cultural systems of interpretation developed within such a sacred framework.

I now understand the linguistification of the sacred in the narrower sense that a transfer of meaning from sources of sacred communication to everyday language took place in these worldviews. The achievement of mythical, religious and metaphysical worldviews was to liberate the semantic potentials encapsulated in ritual practices into the language of mythical stories or dogmatically developed teachings, while at the same time processing them, in the light of the contemporary profane knowledge, into an identity-stabilizing system of interpretation. In doing so, the worldviews established a connection between the collective self-understanding of the respective intersubjectively shared lifeworlds rooted in sacred sources, on the one hand, and the empirical knowledge of the world acquired in profane interactions, on the other. They established an internal, conceptual link between the conservative self-interpretation supported by tradition and an understanding of the world subject to continuous revision.[15]

A study of the genealogy of faith and knowledge would be required to make plausible at least the major stages in the reflexive dissolution, sublimation and displacement of semantic potentials originating in rituals – hence, to explain these stages in the development of worldviews. The essays collected in the present volume are not a substitute, but can offer at best some pointers, for such a study. However, the idea of such a still-to-be-conducted genealogy may explain why I think that the continuing contemporary vitality of religious traditions and practices represents a challenge for philosophy.

Hume and Kant mark the end of metaphysics. Philosophy no longer insists on its original Platonic route to salvation through contemplation of an all-encompassing cosmic unity, so that it no longer competes in this regard with religious worldviews. The nominalist revolution paved the way for liberating philosophy from the embrace of religion; it now claims to ground morality and law, and the normative content of modernity in general, in reason alone. On the other hand, the critique of a false scientistic self-understanding of philosophy can highlight the fact that it cannot be reduced to science. In contrast to the objectifying sciences, philosophy still shares with religious and metaphysical 'worldviews' the self-reflexive attitude in which it processes mundane knowledge (now produced and filtered by the institutionalized sciences). It is not directly involved in increasing our knowledge of the world but asks instead what the growing body of empirical knowledge, the knowledge we acquire through interactions with the world, *means for us*. Instead of being reduced to the role of an auxiliary of cognitive science, for example, philosophy should continue to pursue its task of articulating a justified understanding of ourselves and the world in the light of the best available scientific evidence.

There is no reason to question the secular character of postmetaphysical thinking. But the fact that religious communities, through their ritual practice, *maintain* a connection, however refracted and sublimated by reflection, with the archaic origins of the ritualized production of normative binding and bonding energies raises the following question for postmetaphysical thinking: Can we know whether the linguistification of the sacred, which took place over the millennia in the work on myth, religion and metaphysics, has run its course and has come to a close? However, philosophy now faces the task of *continuing* the 'theological' linguistification of the sacred, which was conducted until now within religious teachings, 'from the outside'. For philosophy, 'linguistification' can only mean discovering the still vital semantic potentials in religious traditions and translating them into a general language that is accessible beyond the boundaries of particular religious communities – and thereby introducing them into the discursive play of public reasons.

The reflections and replies included in the *second section* of the book serve as variations on this single theme. They collect evidence for a changed constellation in the relationship between philosophy and science, on the one hand, and between philosophy and religious traditions, on the other. And they exemplify a dialogical relationship to religious interlocutors which could be adopted by a philosophy that is willing to learn, without regarding this dialogue as a zero-sum game.[16] This has obvious relevance for political questions raised by ideological pluralism. Therefore, the *third section* builds on those contemporary discussions which demonstrate that religious communities remain relevant for the democratic legitimization of political rule even after political authority has become secularized. John Rawls's political theory is based on the insight that the secularization of the state is not necessarily synonymous with the secularization of civil society. The question that interests me is what follows for the role of religious communities in the political public sphere.

In constitutional democracies, the relationship between religion and politics is quite clear-cut from a normative point of view. This makes the unhinged responses we are currently witnessing to outbreaks of religious violence, and to the difficulties faced by our postcolonial immigrant societies in integrating foreign religious communities, all the more disconcerting. I do not want to play down the seriousness of these political problems; but what political theory has to say about them is not particularly controversial. Evoking 'the political' is not a convincing remedy for a political system that has become administratively independent and whose power is at the same time being undermined by developments at the global level. But the dispute between secularists and supposed multiculturalists, who accuse each other of Enlightenment fundamentalism or of watering down basic rights, is not a convincing remedy for our predicament either.

Jürgen Habermas
Starnberg, June 2012

I

THE LIFEWORLD AS A SPACE OF REASONS

1

FROM WORLDVIEWS TO THE LIFEWORLD

When we reflect theoretically on our understanding of the world and of ourselves, we speak in terms of worldviews [*Weltbilder*] or *Weltanschauungen*. While the notion of a '*Weltanschauung*' has the connotation of the *process* of comprehending the whole, the concept of a 'worldview' places the emphasis more on the *result* of an interpretation of the world – that is, its theoretical or represen-tational character. Both expressions have the existential significance of something which provides orientation – *Weltanschauungen* and worldviews give us orientation in our life as a whole. This orienta-tional knowledge must not be confused with scientific knowledge even when it claims to represent a synthesis of currently valid research. This explains the distanced tone of the associated terminol-ogy. When 'worldview' and '*Weltanschauung*' are not used merely as pejorative expressions to distinguish philosophy from dubious rivals,[1] the preference is to apply them retrospectively to the 'strong' traditions of the past. Then we mean first and foremost conceptions which can be traced back in one way or another to the cosmological and theocentric worldviews of the Axial Age, also including essen-tial parts of Greek philosophy.

Even today philosophical doctrines still fulfil the function of worldviews to the extent that they have preserved their reference to the world as a whole, to the cosmos, to world history and the history of salvation [*Heilsgeschichte*], and to a process of natural evolution that includes human beings and culture.[2] Such doctrines can be justified as forms of ethical self-interpretation; but the more or less explicit self-interpretation of a particular ethos cannot claim univer-sal validity any longer under modern conditions of the pluralism of worldviews. Moreover, philosophy in the guise of postmetaphysical thinking would also be well advised to refrain from merely producing worldviews. How can it satisfy this requirement without at the same time sacrificing its reference to the whole? Today philosophy as a discipline is disintegrating into the fragments of its hyphenated philosophies by specializing in reconstructing particular competences, such as speaking, acting and knowing, or by reflecting on the *pre-existing* cultural forms of science, morality, law, religion or art. Can these fragments be reassembled to form a whole by taking the focus on the lifeworld as our starting point? The path leading from worldviews to the concept of the lifeworld which I will sketch here suggests that we can arrive at a non-foundational 'non-hyphenated' philosophy after all.

Admittedly, the world of the lifeworld is a different one from that of worldviews. It neither signifies the sublime cosmos or an exemplary order of things, nor does it refer to a fateful *saeculum* or an eon – that is, to an ordered succession of occurrences of relevance for salvation. The lifeworld does not confront us as a theoretical object; rather, we find ourselves *in* the lifeworld in a pre-theoretical sense. It *encompasses* and *supports* us insofar as we, as finite beings, *cope* with the things and events we encounter in the world. Husserl speaks of the 'horizon' of the lifeworld and of its 'function as a ground' for our everyday activities. To anticipate, the lifeworld can be described as the insurmountable, only intuitively accompanying horizon of experience and as the uncircumventable, non-objectively present experiential background of a personal, historically situated, embodied and communicatively socialized everyday existence. We become aware of this mode of existence under a variety of aspects. We become aware of ourselves performatively as *experiencing* subjects who are embedded in organic life processes, as *socialized* persons who are enmeshed in their social relations and practices, and as *actors* who intervene in the world. What is compressed into this compact formula cannot be contemplated like the starry heavens above us; and it is not something that can be accepted as binding truth trusting in the word of God.

When we engage in explicit communication about something in the world, we are operating in a milieu that has always been constructed on the basis of such performative certainties. It is the task of philosophical reflection to bring the most general features – as it were, the architectonic – of the lifeworld to consciousness. Therefore, this philosophical description refers not to how the world in itself hangs together but to the conditions of our access to what takes place in the world. All that is left of the image of the world after this anthropocentric return to the ground and horizon of our being-in-the-world is the empty framework for *possible* factual knowledge.

With this, the analysis of the lifeworld background also loses the orienting function of worldviews, which with their theoretical access to the whole also promise to provide practical insight into how to lead our lives. Husserl nevertheless wants to extract an important practical lesson from the phenomenology of the lifeworld, which he conceives as a strictly descriptive enterprise. Specifically, with this concept he wants to uncover the forgotten 'meaning foundation' of science and thus to preserve knowledge-based society from the far-reaching consequences of objectivism. Today the challenge posed by an excessively scientistic form of naturalism raises a similar question – namely, whether and, if necessary, in what sense the epistemic role of the lifeworld sets limits to a scientific revision of how people understand themselves in their everyday lives.

I would like to test the plausibility of Husserl's thesis of the forgotten meaning foundation in terms of a rough outline of the development of worldviews. With the spread of an ontological world concept and, later, the construction of an epistemological concept of world,[3] European philosophy on the one hand played a central role in the cognitive process of disentangling the objective world of science from the projective objectivization of aspects of lifeworlds which operate in the background. As a secular intellectual formation, philosophy turned its back on religion while simultaneously renouncing strong metaphysical claims to knowledge. On the other hand, while it contributed to the genealogy of a disenchanted and objectivized concept of the empirical world, philosophy suppressed the epistemic role of the lifeworld. Therefore, I am interested in how reflection on this repressed background changes the self-understanding of postmetaphysical thinking.

Anticipating the communicative concept of the lifeworld, I will first explain the difference between 'lifeworld', 'objective world' and 'everyday world' (1). These basic concepts will serve to relate the critique of science to the context of worldview development. The interesting thing about this development is the progressive cognitive liberation of the 'objective world' from projections of the 'lifeworld' (2) and how the resulting problems of the objectivized image of the world of natural science are dealt with by transcendental philosophy (3). This picture is further complicated by the rise of human and social science, which at the same time represent a challenge for transcendental philosophy (4). The bipolar objectivization of our picture of the objective world and a corresponding detranscendentalization of the underlying constituting subjectivity explain why Husserl's critique of science becomes heightened into a dilemma. The complementarity between the lifeworld and the objective world, which we cannot circumvent *in actu*, is connected with a form of

epistemic dualism which conflicts with the need for a monistic interpretation of the world (5). In conclusion, I will briefly examine some
attempts to find a way out of this dilemma (6).

(1) The concept of the lifeworld is based on the distinction between
performative consciousness and fallible knowledge. The unique
character of the attendant, intuitively certain background knowledge
that accompanies us in our everyday routines but always remains
implicit can be explained by the fact that the lifeworld is present to
us only in a performative manner, when we perform actions which
are always directed to something *else*. The fear of losing one's foothold on loose gravel or the feeling of blushing over an embarrassing
mistake, the sudden realization that one can no longer count on the
loyalty of an old friend, or what it means for a long cherished background assumption suddenly to begin to totter – these are all things
that we 'know'. For in situations such as these in which established
routines are disrupted, a layer of implicit knowledge is uncovered,
be it a habitual ability, a sensitivity, a dependable social relationship
or a firm conviction. As long as they remain unthematized in the
background, these components of the performative knowledge thus
adumbrated form an amalgam.

In principle each of these certainties can be transformed from a
resource of social cooperation and communication into a theme,
especially when the normal routine is disrupted and dissonances
arise. Hence, the lifeworld described in phenomenological terms
can also be understood as the background of communicative action
and be related to processes of reaching understanding.[4] Then it is no
longer the conscious life of a transcendental ego that stands at the
centre of the lifeworld horizon, as in Husserl, but instead the communicative relationship between at least two participants, alter and
ego. The lifeworld appears to both participants in communication
as the accompanying, only implicitly present, arbitrarily expand-
able horizon within which each present encounter is localized in the
– likewise only performatively present – dimensions of social space
and lived historical time.

This approach in terms of a theory of communication is well
suited to clarifying the basic concepts of the 'lifeworld', the 'objective world' and the 'everyday world' (a) in terms of which I want to
analyse the development of worldviews (b).

(a) Lifeworld certainties represent a heightened and nevertheless
deficient form of 'knowledge', because they lose their performative
character once they are expressed in assertions. What cannot be
expressed in true or false assertions cannot count as knowledge in

the strict sense. We must place the background knowledge that we have been talking about until now in quotation marks. For what we 'know' in this intuitive way can be made explicit only by transforming it into a description; however, in doing so, the performative character of what is merely 'known' dissolves – it disintegrates, as it were. Interestingly, the only exception to this are illocutionary acts. The illocutionary components of speech acts – such as 'I concede, that I . . .', 'I recommend that you . . .', or 'I am quite certain that p' – express the performative character of what is lived or experienced, of interpersonal relations and of convictions *as such, without explicitly representing it in terms of a proposition,* because in each case the propositional contents expressed with the illocutionary act deal with something else. An embarrassing confession, a piece of friendly advice or a firm conviction can have any content whatsoever. But only in the case of a constative speech act is this propositional content presented as an existing state of affairs. In an expressive utterance, the propositional meaning becomes the content of an experience to which the first person has privileged access and which he or she 'discloses' to others. In regulative speech acts, it becomes the content of an interpersonal relationship that a first person enters into with a second person. All three modalities are reflected in the validity claims of the corresponding types of speech acts, in the truthfulness, rightness or truth claims that speakers raise for first-person assertions, for propositions addressed to second persons or for descriptive statements. Thanks to this triad of validity claims, the performative meaning of subjective experiences, intersubjective obligations and what is objectively meant enters the public space of reasons via linguistic communication.

What is interesting in the present context is the relationship between 'lifeworld' and 'objective world' as reflected in the twofold structure of speech acts. When performing their illocutionary acts, speakers belong to a lifeworld, whereas in using the propositional components of these acts they *refer to* something in the objective world. In communicative action, they jointly assume the existence of this objective world as the totality of the objects or referents existing independently of description about which states of affairs can be asserted. However, this does not mean that statements cannot be made about the lifeworld itself. Those involved can assume a third-person attitude towards their own engagement and, in a *further* act of reaching understanding, thematize a performatively produced communicative relationship – that is, *treat it as something that occurs in the world.* This is because anything that is made into the content of a proposition is thematized as something which is given or exists in the world.

Despite the insurmountable intentional distance from events in the objective world – the gap between the performance and the explicit content of communicative act – it is part of the experience of participants in communication and of their background knowledge that the communication process in which they are currently involved takes place in *the same* world as that to which the referents of the statements they make in the same moment also belong. The lifeworld *as a component of the objective world* enjoys a kind of 'ontological primacy' over the respective current background consciousness of the individual involved, because the performatively present life processes – i.e., experiences, interpersonal relations and beliefs – presuppose the bodily organism, the intersubjectively shared practices and the traditions in which the experiencing, acting and speaking subjects 'always' find themselves.

(b) I will return to the mode of existence of these lifeworlds articulated in symbolic forms and to the objectifying description of 'socio-cultural forms of life'. First I would like to examine the 'picture' we form of this all-inclusive objective world. As long as we are absorbed in *performing* these intentional (linguistic or non-linguistic) activities, we cannot detach ourselves from the lifeworld which is present in the background and forms the horizon within which we adopt an intentional orientation to something 'in the world'. But we can know that this same objective world, viewed from the perspective of a distanced observer, in turn *includes* us, our networks of interaction, and their background side by side with other entities. This shapes our inclusive 'everyday world', the world of common sense. We should not equate this with the philosophical concept of the 'lifeworld', even though the performative traits of the lifeworld also determine the structure of our 'everyday world', the fact that it is centred on us, our encounters and practices, our states of mind and interests. However, the 'everyday world' is inclusive. It includes not only what is familiar in a performative manner but also the perceived and known elements of the natural environment that confront us. The everyday world is not exhausted by the segments constituted by our background knowledge – that is, by the subjective life routines, the social relations and the taken-for-granted cultural beliefs with which we are familiar in the performative mode. The image we form of the 'objective world' – our worldview – is directly shaped by this everyday world.

In our everyday lives, we categorize the things we encounter in the world according to levels of practical involvement. Roughly speaking, we categorize them as persons if they can enter into communicative relations with us; we categorize them as norms, speech

acts, actions, texts, signs, artefacts, and so forth, if they can be understood as things produced by persons; we categorize them as animals
and plants if their self-sustaining and boundary-maintaining character as organic systems compels us to treat them with consideration
(for example, to tend to or breed them); or we construe things as
manipulable objects when we can strip them of all lifeworld qualities
that accrue to them from other domains of experience (for example,
the qualities of a 'tool' or of natural beauty). It is no accident that
the ontology closely allied to everyday life which we find in Aristotle
recalls this practically imbued 'picture' of the 'objective world'.

Clearly, the production of worldviews – of the historically
varying pictures we make of the objective world – starts from the
trivial layers of the everyday world. Whereas the scientific view
of the world takes its orientation from the everyday category of
bodies and comprehends the universe as the totality of physically
measurable states and events regulated by natural laws, the earliest
mythical traditions assimilate almost all events to communicative
relations between persons. If we can believe the accounts of cultural
anthropology,[5] the world reflected in those mythical narratives
has a monistic structure: there is only *one* level of phenomena but
nothing 'in itself' underlying them. Narrated events are structured
as social interactions involving people and animals, but also the
spirits of the ancestors and imaginary natural and original forces,
supra-personal powers and personalized gods.[6] Almost anyone can
communicate with anyone and everything with everything; they
can express feelings and wishes, intentions and opinions, and influence one another.

The narratives give rise to a network of 'correspondences' in
which ritualized actions are also embedded. The dealings with the
mythical powers organized in burial and sacrificial rituals, in ances-
tor worship and natural magic, acquire their self-evidence from this
embedding. In this way, the *performative attitude*, in which a first
person adjusts herself to a second person in order to communicate
with him about something, merges in magical practices with the
objectifying attitude of a technician towards impersonal or supra-
personal forces over which she wants to exercise causal influence.
By communicating *with* a spirit, the sorcerer acquires power *over* it.
The dominance of a single category, namely, that of communicative
action, provides impressive evidence of this.

Clearly, so-called mythical worldviews are not only shaped by the
totalizing features of a centred lifeworld inhabited 'by us'. They are
also imbued with and structured by the performative consciousness
of the lifeworld in such a way that the *distinction between lifeworld
and objective world* built into the grammar of communicative action

and managed practically by those involved in everyday life *merges* in the worldviews of early tribal societies. The categories of action oriented to reaching an understanding structure natural processes in the world as a whole, so that, *from our point of view*, what occurs in the world *is absorbed by the segments of the everyday world constituted by the lifeworld.*

For us today, these mythical origins and the worldview of modern science stand in a peculiar contrast, which suggests that during the development of worldviews the objective world that exists 'in itself' was progressively purified *for the participants* of the surplus lifeworld qualities projected upon it. As we learn to cope with cognitive dissonances that are empirically triggered and mastered, our view of the objective world becomes *disenchanted*. Would an exaggerated scientistic version of naturalism have to have the last word from this perspective? Or can we defend Husserl's thesis that science rests on a forgotten foundation of meaning by arguing that the progressive trend towards objectivization has led to an increasingly extreme polarization between the lifeworld, which is henceforth defined exclusively in formal terms but remains epistemically unavoidable, and a scientific objectified world?

(2) The following, very rough sketch of the development of worldviews is a proposal for how we can understand three caesuras along the path 'from worldviews to the lifeworld' as cognitive advances, each of which led to increasingly disenchanted and progressively more specific perspectives on the objective world. From this selective and correspondingly biased viewpoint, I am first interested in the step which leads from mythical thinking absorbed in the fluctuation of inner-worldly events, as outlined above, to a conception of 'the' world as a whole; I will then examine the distinctive occidental combination of theocentric and cosmological worldviews which leads to a polarization between faith and knowledge; and, finally, I will trace the emancipation of scientific knowledge of nature from metaphysics, which also breaks the link between cosmology and ethics and thus destroys the shared rational basis of faith and knowledge.

Since this account focuses narrowly on the development in the West, and even then would need to fill several books or even libraries, I can address only one aspect of my proposal regarding our topic: How did the conceptual constellations of 'lifeworld', 'objective world' and 'everyday world' shift in the wake of these presumed advances in learning?

With his concept of the 'Axial Age', Karl Jaspers highlighted the fact that, during a relatively short period around the middle of the first millennium BCE, there was a cognitive breakthrough in the world of civilizations that extended from the Middle East to the Far East.[7] The religious doctrines and cosmological worldviews that remain influential up to the present day arose around that time in Persia, India and China, and in Israel and Greece. These 'strong traditions' – namely, Zoroastrianism, Buddhism and Confucianism, Judaism and Greek philosophy – brought about a shift in worldviews from the plurality of surface phenomena linked at the same level through narratives to the unity of the world as a whole conceived in theological or 'theoretical' terms. In monotheism, the cosmic 'order of things' assumed the temporalized form of a teleological order of world ages.

In the meantime, the concept of the Axial Age has inspired a diverse international literature.[8] Of primary interest in the present context is the process by which an *involved* actor became liberated from the cognitive bias that confined her to a representation of the world from the *internal perspective* of someone entangled in mythical stories. The new dualistic worldviews broke with this two-dimensional monism. With the conception of a single God beyond the world or concepts of a law-governed cosmic order, they opened up perspectives from which the world could be grasped as an objectified whole. The reference to the fixed pole of the single creator of the world, to the nomos which holds everything in balance, to the deep underlying reality of Nirvana or of eternal being, afforded the prophet or the wise man, the preacher and the teacher, the contemplative beholder and the mystic, the holy man absorbed in prayer and the philosopher sunk in intellectual contemplation, the necessary distance from the many, the contingent and the changeable. Regardless of whether the dualistic view of the world was more pronounced, as in the salvation religions of Israel and India, or less pronounced, as in Greek philosophy and Chinese wisdom teachings, these intellectual elites everywhere achieved a cognitive *breakthrough to a transcendent standpoint*.

From this vantage point, everything that takes place *within the world* could be distinguished from *the world as such or in itself*. And this perspective on being and humanity as a whole gave rise to that categorical distinction between essence and appearance which replaced the older, expressivist distinction between the spirit world and its manifestations (and in addition undermined the basis of magical conceptions in worldviews). With the differentiation between 'world' and what is 'in-the-world', *the everyday world was demoted to the realm of mere appearances*. This theoretical grasp of essences enhanced the explanatory power of narratives. The conceptual framework was now able to process the mass of practical, natural historical and medical knowledge, including astronomical and mathematical knowledge, which had accumulated in the urban centres of the early civilizations and to integrate it into a coherent whole that could be transmitted.

While myth remained tightly interwoven with everyday practices and did not acquire the self-sufficiency of a theoretical 'image' of the world, philosophical and theological conceptions of an 'objective', all-encompassing world found expression in the worldviews of the Axial Age. *For those involved*, religious or contemplative conceptions of the world as a whole marked the dissolution of the fusion of the 'objective world' with the 'lifeworld' which *we* today read out of mythical worldviews. *From our point of view*, the introduction and subordination of the everyday world *downgraded to a mere phenomenon* takes account of the fact that the performatively present lifeworld, together with the practices and network of cross-references in which they become accessible to communicative actors, is an entity *in* the world like all others.

However, this objectivization exacts a price. The 'lifeworld' as such does not appear in the worldviews of the Axial Age but is merged with the appearances of the 'everyday world'. For believers and philosophers, their own lifeworld operating behind their backs disappears so completely behind the ontotheologically objectivized images of the world that the projective traits which these worldviews continue to *borrow* from the performative consciousness of their vital lived existence in the world remain hidden from them. This can be shown by three aspects of the lifeworld which are reflected in the world of cosmologies and theologies.

- *First*, the cosmos and the history of salvation are depicted in dimensions of lived social space and experienced historical time. As a result, the boundaries of the object world merge with the lifeworld horizon, projected to a superhuman scale, of an inhabitable world centred on us, of which the fleeting appearances of our everyday life in turn constitute only a part. In this architectonic of what Jaspers calls the 'encompassing', the teleological constitution of the world retains the lifeworld character of our everyday dealings with human beings, animals, plants and inanimate nature.
- *Second*, the worldviews of the Axial Age are by no means theories in the sense of a value-neutral description of known facts. The reason for this is that the *theoretical* interpretation of the world is already fused with precepts of the *practical* conduct of life through its strong, value-laden conceptual frame. When the whole is described with the help of such concepts as 'God', 'Karma', 'to

on' or 'Tao', the *description* of sacred history or of the cosmos simultaneously acquires the *evaluative* connotation of an exemplary being [*Seiende*] whose telos has a normative significance for the believers and wise men as something to be emulated. This conceptual fusion of the binding force of normative statements with the truth of descriptive statements is reminiscent of the lifeworld background syndrome, which dissolves only in the course of linguistic thematization and becomes ramified into the different validity dimensions of the corresponding types of speech acts.

- *Finally*, the claim to infallibility with which religious and metaphysical 'truths' appear is also a function of the practical connotations of the theoretical interpretation of the world. Because the various conceptions of the world and of the ages of the world are supposed to be 'cashed out' in paths to salvation or in politically influential models of an exemplary life, theoretical beliefs have to be as convincing and as immune to cognitive dissonances as are ethical-existential certainties. This explains the *dogmatic form of thought* which lends religious and wisdom teachings the shape of 'strong' theories. With the claim to infallible truths, the *performative mode of knowledge* as it were reaches out of the lifeworld into the domain of explicit mundane knowledge.

Insofar as the worldviews of the Axial Age can be described retrospectively as involving an unreflected projection of such aspects of the lifeworld onto the objective world, the structure of the world concept already prefigures the path leading to a possible objectivization. The cognitive development points, firstly, towards a decentred concept of the world as the totality of physically describable states and events, secondly, towards a separation between theoretical and practical reason, and, finally, towards a fallibilistic, but non-sceptical understanding of theoretical knowledge. These vanishing points refer, of course, to our own hermeneutic starting point – that is, to a postmetaphysical understanding of ourselves and the world as this developed from the seventeenth and eighteenth centuries onwards. In order to strip this 'narcissistic' developmental construction at least of the deceptive appearance of necessary progress, I would now have to discuss the historical contingencies which first explain the improbable and unique systematic interpenetration of a cosmological worldview with a theological doctrine – that is, the productive conflation of Pauline Christianity and Greek metaphysics into the twofold shape of Hellenized Christianity and theologically founded Platonism. During the centuries that followed, the discourse on revelation and natural reason contended with the explosive impact of sciences such as mathematics, astronomy, medicine and natural philosophy, each of which observes a logic of its own. However, *the discourse on faith and knowledge* developed its explosive power only with the reception of Aristotle through Arab mediation in the twelfth and thirteenth centuries.[9] In the course of this reception, the opposing concepts of 'faith' and 'knowledge' sharpened their respective profiles in contrast to one another.

However, the shared rational basis of faith and knowledge fell to pieces to the extent that natural philosophy lost its ability to connect up with theology, which nevertheless wanted to keep pace with contemporary science. Aristotle's teleological ontology still contains a semantic potential which was open to a practical connection interpreted in terms of a conception of salvation. However, scholastic nominalism laid the groundwork for an unbiased empirical view of nature and ultimately for nomological empirical science for which the book of nature no longer bears a divine signature; it also prepares the way for a theory of knowledge which correlates the 'nature' of modern natural science with the human mind.[10] This *second orientation* involves an inversion of the burden of proof when it comes to demonstrating the compatibility of religion and science, because henceforth stubborn philosophical discourses develop around the modern empirical sciences and the secular political powers which assert their independence from theology.[11]

Along this line of development, metaphysics, which until then had been contained within the realm of theology, assumed, in the course of the seventeenth century, the form of philosophical systems which received their formative impulses from both epistemology and social contract theory. The world of moving and causally interacting bodies conceived in physicalist terms lost the character of a 'container' of human existence. At the same time, the theoretical knowledge of this world, which is no longer affiliated with practical reason, forfeited its ability to provide practical orientation. For this reason Christian natural law also had to be replaced by human law based on practical reason alone. From that point onwards, philosophy gradually lost interest in its relation to religion. Postmetaphysical thinking concentrates on philosophy's relation to science. This gives rise to a deficit that I cannot discuss in greater detail here.[12]

With the advance to the modern secular and scientized understanding of the world, the conceptual constellation of lifeworld, objective world and everyday world once again undergoes a change. Because the objective world consists of everything about which true statements can be made, Newton's philosophical contemporaries comprehended the world in terms of the mechanistic picture that physics forms of nature as a whole. To the 'world' belong the objects of experience, which stand in a 'natural' – that is, law-governed – relationship with all other things. Mathematics and scientific experimentation succeed the 'natural reason' of the theologian-philosopher in its role as the canonical authority for judging notoriously unreliable everyday experiences. Underlying the sensory phenomena of the everyday world are no longer essences but the law-governed movements of causally interacting bodies.

Having taken the step to the mechanistic concept of nature, the picture of the objective world seems to be freed from objectivized aspects of the lifeworld. But what place does the lifeworld have in this objectivized understanding of the world? The world concept purged of lifeworld projections was introduced not from an onto-logical but, at first, from an epistemological perspective. It is the product of reflection on the conditions of possibility of reliable physical knowledge. This is why the knowing subject represents the counterpart of the objective world. The conceptual dualities of the mentalistic paradigm leave only the niche of representational sub-jectivity for the lifeworld. This retreat leaves behind traces both in the aporetic character of the mental and in the rumblings of practi-cal questions for which, following the split between practical reason and scientized and postmetaphysically deflated theoretical reason, there is now no longer any clear place.

(3) In the course of the seventeenth century, empiricism developed the beginnings of the scientific image of the world which Husserl accused of 'objectivism'. This worldview developed within the para-digm of the philosophy of consciousness and, hence, is haunted by its problems. In order to prepare the argument that, in the mentalist paradigm, the lifeworld is hidden behind the façade of the human mind, I will first explain the aporetic status of the mental (a) and then trace the 'moral unbelief'[13] of the empiricists which provoked Kant's transcendental turn (b).

(a) Following the introduction of the concept of the objective world as the totality of all descriptively ascertainable states and events ultimately explicable in terms of laws, a concept which henceforth became canonical for epistemology, the 'nature of the human mind' becomes a problem. From an epistemological point of view, the subject of knowledge acquired an external status vis-à-vis the world as a whole. As mind, the subject withdrew from the totality of objects of representation. On the other hand, together with its ideas, affective states and actions, it can represent itself as an *object in the world* interwoven with its causal nexus. Therefore, the objective world is not reduced without remainder to the totality of physically explicable phenomena; it also includes the mental phenomena to be explained in psychological terms.

The mental can indeed be regarded *as an object*, but it is accessible only *in the performative mode* as an active and receptive mind. This subjectivity which stands over against the objective world is the antithesis to the mental phenomena encountered in the world. Epistemology conceives of the mind *in actu* as sensing, representing and thinking consciousness and the subject of cognition as a self which can, in turn, subjectively represent the fact that it has representations of objects. Consciousness is inherently bound up with self-consciousness. The extramundane status of these mental states, which are peculiar because they are accessible only in a performative way in the experience of present states of consciousness, remains a thorny issue for the conception of an objectivized world as the totality of causally interconnected bodies. Under the description of mental states and events, the psyche, which is accessible only from the first-person performative perspective, acquires the status of a *temporary* anomaly. But in spite of this status as a *candidate* for scientific explanation, the mental retains a Janus face. To this day, facts of experience alert us to a vexing incompleteness of the objectivizing description of the world.[14]

Seventeenth-century philosophy at first continued to answer the question of the locus of performative consciousness which had been expelled from scientifically objectivized nature, as it were, in metaphysical terms – a dualistic answer in Descartes's case, a monadological answer in Leibniz's case, or a deist answer in Spinoza's case. But, viewed in terms of the mentalist paradigm, these ontological constructions inevitably represent a regression behind the epistemological turn. To the Cartesian objectification of the mind as *res cogitans*, Hobbes opposes a predicative conception of the mental as an activity or performance that we ascribe to a subject, so that mental faculties can be attributed to an organism, hence to a bodily thing: 'Hence it may be that the thing that thinks is the subject to which mind, reason or intellect belong; and this subject may thus be something corporeal. The contrary is assumed [by Descartes], not proved.'[15]

Following Hobbes, empiricism from Locke to Hume seems to provide the more consistent answer when it conceives of the human mind as a 'mirror of nature' located in nature itself and concentrates on the genesis of reliable knowledge.[16] Nature gives rise to sensations in the subject and reflections of itself in its judgements by causally influencing the human sense organs. From the beginning, however, those who were opposed to this conception did not appeal so much to the awkward ontological status of *experiences*; after all, we also attribute the subjectivity of conscious life to animals. But *attitudes* which people can adopt to facts and states of affairs or towards other persons are not subjective experiences which one can have or not have; rather, they are actions which one performs – and which can go wrong. It is this *normative constitution* of the mind to which Descartes already drew attention[17] and to which Kant appeals against Hume when he defines the understanding as a spontaneous faculty of applying rules or concepts.

(b) Kant found another implication even more troubling, namely that empiricism fails to explain the normativity of the mind as regards not only its epistemic but, above all, its moral-practical functions. The picture of the objective world constructed by the understanding out of contingent sensory stimulations consists exclusively of descriptive judgements – that is, of value-neutral factual knowledge. Practical reason can no longer derive moral insights from this objectivating view of the world. Evaluative and normative propositions cannot be justified on the basis of descriptive statements. With this uncoupling of practical from theoretical reason, which was completed by Hume, philosophy is in danger of losing entirely its power to provide practical orientation. In particular, if all mental processes could be explained on the model of physics, it would no longer be possible to derive normative orientations from this kind of knowledge.

However, as persons of flesh and blood, knowing subjects do not simply stand over against the world. When they speak to each other and engage in joint actions, they must be able to orient themselves when dealing with the things they encounter in the world. The community of researchers, as a cooperative association of acting subjects, is also embedded in a context of social and cultural relations. Philosophy had long since ceased to offer a route to salvation of its own. But now even the normative knowledge of the classical teachings of 'ethics' and 'politics', in the reconstructed version of rational morality and rational law, ultimately not only assumed an inferior status vis-à-vis empirical knowledge of the physical world, as already in Aristotle, but its status as knowledge was shaken to the core. Kant responds to this problem of the devaluation of practical knowledge, which, as I would like to show, was provoked by the mentalistic suppression of the lifeworld, by using a revolutionized epistemology to vindicate the cognitive claim of practical reason in postmetaphysical terms.

The peripeteia begins with the fact that Kant probes the constructive accomplishments of the *knowing* subject and interprets its contact with the world no longer in passive terms – taking sensory stimulation as the starting point – but, rather, in transcendental terms. This underlying idea of the constitution of a world of appearances combines elements of dependence with elements of freedom. The knowing subject enjoys the freedom of cognitive legislation of a finite mind which reacts to the contingent sensory constraints of an independently existing world.[18] Although the human mind operates at the level of transcendental consciousness under the guidance of *theoretical* reason, with the recourse to subjective conditions of possible objective experiences Kant gains a noumenal perspective from which he can shield not only the knowing subject but also the spontaneous achievements of subjectivity *as such* from empiricist distortion.

As Kant stresses in the preface to the second edition of *Critique of Pure Reason*, restricting the theoretical use of reason to objects of experience inspired by a critique of metaphysics under the premise of the legislative accomplishments of finite understanding can have the 'positive and very important utility' of disclosing a transcendental level of intellectual spontaneity where the freedom of the will bound up with the practical use of reason also finds its place: 'Thus I had to deny *knowledge* in order to make room for *faith*; and the dogmatism of metaphysics, i.e., the prejudice that without criticism reason can make progress in metaphysics, is the true source of all unbelief conflicting with morality, which unbelief is always very dogmatic.'[19] It is important in the present context that locating the free will in the 'kingdom of ends' first brings a phenomenon into play which can preserve the whole noumenal sphere from an obvious misunderstanding.

With the 'transcendental fact' of the moral law which anchors every deontological morality, Kant appeals to a phenomenologically convincing example of *background knowledge*. The peculiar fact of a feeling of unconditional obligation, which is supposed to bear the entire burden of proof for morality, differs from other, descriptively raised facts in that it can be *thematized only in the performative mode*. The consciousness of duty is nothing other than the knowledge, which is *performatively present* in the language game of responsible agency, of *being obliged* to obey a rationally justified moral imperative. When one chooses the lifeworld as the key to interpreting the freedom of the rational will, the noumenal sphere loses its metaphysical appearance of a ghostly 'hinterworld' (Nietzsche). Only when actually engaging in communicative action can we experience the obligations that we incur with social relations *as such*. Without this performative experience, we would not know what a description of this state of affairs from the perspective of a third person is about. Therefore, the normative meaning of a morally justified behavioural expectation must be sought at the original locus of the phenomenon. The normativity of a moral 'ought' can neither be objectivized speculatively into a command of the natural order of things or into an existing value, nor can it be reduced psychologically to objective states of mind – to pleasure and pain, reward and punishment. The 'idea' of freedom is just one among many ideas. Kant's doctrine of ideas throws general light on a performatively present background which is objectivized only when theoretical reason goes beyond the limits of the legitimate use of the understanding.[20] The distinction between ideas of practical and theoretical reason already anticipates the difference between lifeworld and objective world. On this reading, Kant's doctrine of ideas offers points of contact for the de-transcendentalized concept of reason as world-constituting while nevertheless being situated in the lifeworld as described in terms of the theory of communication.[21]

(4) However, the constraints of the mentalistic paradigm first had to be overcome before the lifeworld could be discovered behind the façade of subjective mind conceptualized in transcendental terms. Although the insights of Humboldt's philosophy of language already point towards a pragmatic 'supersession' of transcendental philosophy,[22] this development of the idea of 'detranscendentalization', starting from Hegel and extending via Peirce and Dewey, and via Dilthey and Husserl, to Heidegger and Wittgenstein, cannot be understood as an internal development driven solely by philosophical problems. Just as philosophy following Galileo and Newton had to cope with the sober gaze of modern natural science on the objective world, after Hegel it had to come to terms with the historical perspective of the humanities and social sciences on culture and society. Just as little as philosophy at the time could evade the question concerning facts of consciousness – that is, the status of mental episodes – could it now ignore the question of how this 'objective' mind, which clearly transcends the human mind, should be conceived and integrated into the causal nexus of events in the world.

Amazingly enough, historical, social and cultural facts began to attract systematic scientific interest only at a very late date. The historical humanities arose from formal doctrines, from the humanistic traditions of poetics, and from historical narratives and theories of language and literature; similarly, the new sciences of the state and society developed out of the classical doctrines of politics and economics. Like the canon of the 'liberal arts' – which themselves reached back to the beginnings of civilizations – these formal doctrines had their origin in professional knowledge. Like grammar, rhetoric and logic, like arithmetic, geometry and music, and even astronomy, liberal arts and formal doctrines developed out of reflection by participants on a *previously mastered* practice. The stance cultivated by the humanities and social science, by contrast, is completely different.

They are no longer interested in achieving reflective reassurance of the rules of an *established* practice – be it of a particular language or of the fine arts and literature, historiography, the art of government or the conduct of a household. Rather, a *methodologically guided* curiosity is now directed to comparing and analysing the diverse cultural forms of life, which, although accessible only from the participant perspective, are used *as sources of data* from the observer perspective and are processed into historical, cultural and social facts. It is this transformation of the participant into the observer perspective that first makes cultural sciences into scientific disciplines in their own right. In contrast to the object domain of natural science, however, the symbolic objects of the human sciences retain an idiosyncratic status. This is because the observer must have already participated in the lifeworld practices, he must have understood them first in the role of a virtual participant, before he can objectivize the practices and products in which they are reflected into data.

There sciences use everyday practical experiences and knowledge, which until then had been recorded only in literature and travel reports, in diaries and chronicles, in business and administrative statistics, in war reports, historical narratives, textbooks, and so forth, either as 'sources' for philologically informed historical-critical research or in order to model domains of data to be gathered empirically and analysed systematically from theoretical points of view. With this advance towards scientific objectivation of those *segments of the everyday world constituted through our background experiences*, the monolithic concept of the objective world, which, under the influence of Newtonian physics, forced itself upon epistemology, becomes even more problematic. Now we must ask again how the conceptual constellation of 'lifeworld' and 'objective world' changed after segments of the lifeworld became objects of research not only under psychological but also under cultural, social and historical aspects.

The phenomena of the everyday world are now subjected to scientific objectivation essentially from two sides.[23] By 'objectivization' is meant an increasingly impartial description of reality based on a progressive decentring of the perceptual and interpretive perspectives centred on our respective lifeworlds. We must not confuse 'objectivization', or *Versachlichung*, with reifying abstraction – that is, with the reduction of natural occurrences in the world to the sole dimension of dealing with manipulable and measurable states and events.[24] Natural science approaches the idea of impartial judgement by stripping the everyday world of its lifeworld qualities and producing counter-intuitive knowledge. The humanities and social sciences, by contrast, must pursue *the same* goal through hermeneutic interpretation and more in-depth reconstruction of everyday experiences and practices.[25] Since then, our image of the objective world has become polarized because the objectivization of everyday phenomena points *in different directions*. Before I return to this further complication for the 'scientific worldview' and the project of a naturalization of the mind, we must trace the final stage of the path leading from the worldviews to the lifeworld. For transcendental philosophy is vulnerable to the criticism of the humanities and social science especially on the interpretation that we decipher the 'kingdom of ends' at the heart of the noumenal realm as a silhouette of the mentalistically repressed lifeworld. How can the fundamental transcendental insight into the normative constitution and law-giving character of the human mind be defended against the empirical evidence of the historical diversity of socio-cultural forms of life? Because the new disciplines deal above all with the specificity and variability of symbolically generated artefacts, forms of life and practices, they seem to provide evidence against the assumption that there is a *single* transcendental legislation.[26] It is not the spontaneous, word-constructing character of the mind that inspires the opposition of the hermeneutic sciences but, instead, the abstract universality and extramundane status which is supposed to set transcendental consciousness apart from the exotic diversity and contingency of languages, cultures and societies.

Philosophy since Herder, Hamann, Humboldt and Hegel responds to this challenge with a critique of mentalism whose central plank is to oppose the intersubjective character of languages, practices and forms of life to the subjectivistic constitution of the human mind. This critique was radicalized by Feuerbach and Marx from the perspective of a philosophy of dialogue and social theory and by Kierkegaard from an ethical-existential perspective. However, historicism, *Lebensphilosophie*, pragmatism and the philosophy of language first ascribed epistemological relevance and relevance for the theory of science to the symbolically mediated practical life contexts of the bodily, social and historical existence of socialized individuals during the latter part of the nineteenth and the early twentieth century. These intellectual movements laid the groundwork for the interpretation of Husserl's concept of the lifeworld by the theory of communication, which allowed the detranscendentalization of active subjectivity without depriving it of its

world-constituting spontaneity and assimilating it to natural processes in the world.

The empirical perspective of the humanities and social sciences on
the changeable forms of culture or 'objective mind' did not place the
constructive character of the legislation of a transcendental subject
in question, but it did problematize its intelligible status as something
withdrawn from events in the world. Heidegger's transformation
of Husserl's phenomenological concept of the lifeworld also shows
that all attempts to detranscendentalize world-constituting subjectivity are condemned to failure as long as the 'ontological difference'
between world disclosure and occurrences within the world precludes
interaction between the *world-forming productivity* of being and the
results of the *learning processes in the world* that this facilitates.
The Heideggerian conception of a transcendental originary power
which announces itself in the transformation of linguistic worldviews
conceived as a history of being, but only at the cost of the disempow-
erment of subjects submissive to being, is not in any coherent sense
'detranscendentalized'. A different picture emerges when 'language'
is not reduced to the semantics of linguistic worldviews but is understood (as Humboldt already understood it) in pragmatic terms – that
is, in terms of the communicative practice of acting subjects who are
capable of learning because they are engaged in discourse and solve
problems. Languages do not merely open up the horizons of a pre-
interpreted lifeworld. While paving the way for possible encounters
with things and events in the world, world-disclosing language does
not always remain ahead of these encounters. On closer examination, linguistic communication instead compels the participants to
take reasonable – that is, autonomous – 'yes' or 'no' stances. Because
linguistic communication proceeds via 'yes' and 'no' responses to
reciprocally raised and criticizable validity claims, participants in
communication are exposed to the objections of opponents and can
also revise their concepts *in the light of reasons* when compelled by
unexpected negative experiences.

This pragmatic notion of language as the medium of a form of
world disclosure *that has to be confirmed in practice and makes room
for learning processes* undercuts the rigid transcendental distinction
between world-constituting activity and constituted events within
the world. The categorizations and perspectives which are advanced
by the linguistic frame are subject in turn to sustained testing in
everyday life *and especially in scientific research*. They are revised
by the participants in problem-solving activities themselves in the
course of these activities. The complementary processes of world
disclosure and learning in the world are interconnected in communicative action and discourse. The communicating subjects are

involved in this interplay, and hence also implicitly in the reproduction of their own lifeworld. Between a lifeworld which makes
communicative action possible and a background exposed to continuous testing, which is confirmed in uninterrupted communicative
action but is also subsequently revised as a result of problematization and learning, there is an incessant circular process in which
the missing transcendental subject does not leave any gap behind.[27]
Although communicative actors are *involved* in the reproduction
and revision of their lifeworld, they nevertheless remain *embedded*
in these lifeworld contexts.

(5) At the end of the path 'from worldviews to the lifeworld' that I
have depicted in broad brushstrokes, our initial question about how
the progressive objectivization of our image of the objective world
should be understood still awaits an answer. Does the reflexive
knowledge of the lifeworld present in performance also prove in the
end to be an illusion that natural science sees through? Or does the
epistemic role of the lifeworld set limits to a scientifically oriented
revision of socialized subjects' operative everyday understanding of
themselves *as learning, rationally motivated persons who act responsibly*? The detranscendentalization of active subjectivity performed
by the theory of communication provides us with the concept of a
lifeworld which remains performatively 'behind the backs' of communicative actors as an ensemble of enabling conditions, though
only as long and insofar as they are involved in forming the relevant
action. The lifeworld background is removed from events in the
world *in principle*. Otherwise lifeworld practices and artefacts could
not be treated as entities in the world or be made into objects of the
human sciences and philosophy. But then what speaks against the
possibility of bringing the performatively present background of
our practices *completely*, thus including the research practices themselves, to the object side, and doing this *in the familiar categories of
the natural sciences*?[28]

It is *bipolar objectivization* which, at the end of the path from
worldviews to the lifeworld, confronts us with a semantically
unbridgeable epistemic dualism – that is, with a divided image of the
objective world. The vocabulary of the human sciences cannot be
connected with that of natural science; statements in the one vocabulary cannot be translated into statements in the other. The human
brain does not 'think'.[29] If the semantic chain breaks, entities on the
one level cannot even be correlated one-to-one with entities on the
other level. From the perspective of the development of worldviews
outlined, this epistemic dualism loses its contingent character.

If we conceive of the objective world as the totality of physically measurable states and events, we are making an objectivizing abstraction in the sense that we strip the natural processes of dealing with manipulable objects within the world of all merely 'subjective' or lifeworld qualities. These processes lose all of the qualities attached to them in a 'projective' way based on *other* practical experiences (for example, as a tool or an obstacle, as poison or food, as shelter or inhospitable surroundings). On the other hand, an interpreter who seeks access to cultural expressions, actions, texts, markets, etc., must essentially engage in the very practices to which the segments of the everyday world constituted through the lifeworld owe their qualities. In the process, the interpreter draws on a prior understanding she acquired *previously* based on an ordinary language – that is, as a participant in everyday communication and as a member of an intersubjectively shared lifeworld.

This methodological connection between the observer perspective in the humanities and social science and the perspective of a participant in antecedent practices explains the peculiar dynamic generated by these disciplines themselves, which necessitates a *different* kind of abstraction from the one involved in natural science – namely, reflection on *underlying general structures* of the lifeworld. The more the social and cultural sciences objectify lifeworld practices in their functional differentiation and their historical and cultural diversity, the more they force these analyses to make a transition from *hermeneutic* to *reconstructive* interpretation and to develop a *formal* concept of the lifeworld as such that can only be acquired through *reflection*.[30] The analytical clarification of the background and presuppositions of communicative action requires a kind of reflection that is beyond the scope of the humanities and social sciences. The *only* experiential basis for this genuinely philosophical inquiry, as I tacitly assumed when I introduced the formal pragmatic concept of the lifeworld, is the *performative consciousness* of speaking and communicating, cooperating, experiencing, calculating and judging subjects who intervene in the world.[31]

Husserl correctly recognized that the progressive scientific objectification of the everyday world necessitated the disenchantment of nature and the formal characterization of the lifeworld. Within the horizon of the lifeworld, the human and natural sciences find their own modes of access to their respective object domains. But the detranscendentalization of the lifeworld also reveals the *dilemma*. On the one hand, the *dual perspective* of the natural and the human sciences is at odds with a deep-seated intuition: even a concept of the 'objective' world that has been deflated to a presupposition of communication still has a *unifying* function. Even in everyday communicative practice, the formal-pragmatic assumption of a world of objects that exists independently of description and is identical for all observers suggests unity and connection in the multiplicity of entities. Reason is 'dissatisfied' with a form of ontological dualism that erupts within the world itself and is not merely epistemic in nature. On the other hand, the bipolar objectivization is the result of a stubborn worldview development: that semantically secured dual perspective is deeply anchored in the lifeworld and sets conceptual limits to the naturalistic self-objectification of the human mind.[32] Under a naturalistic description, regardless of how accurate, a person would not be able to recognize herself as a person in general or as this individual person (as 'herself'). For this reason, the paradigmatic natural sciences would be able to redeem the claim to provide a monistic description, even if such were possible, only by way of elimination, hence through exclusion, not by translating the self-understanding of persons into an objectifying language. But would they then still provide an inclusive description of everything in the objective world?

(6) Those who in the final analysis accord natural science a monopoly over socially recognized empirical knowledge respond with compatibilist arguments when confronted with the dilemma that, while assuming an objective world compels us to describe the latter in monistic terms, epistemic dualism prevents us from providing such a description.[33] They want to uncouple empirical knowledge over which natural science claims a monopoly from the understanding of self and world centred on the lifeworld. I do not need to repeat my objections against this position here.[34] Others search for the constitutive conditions of empirical knowledge in the lifeworld taking the object domain-specific basic concepts of physics, biology, psychology and the humanities as their guide.[35] An epistemological link is then produced via world-disclosing theoretical languages, methodologies, and lifeworld practices between the 'segments of the world' that correspond to specific object domains. This strategy builds on Husserl's science-critical question but at the same time rids itself of the baggage of a transcendental primordial ego through the recourse to lifeworld practices.[36] But how can the world-projecting practices themselves still be conceived as something which occurs in the world? Because the projected possibilities of truth can prove themselves only with reference to contingent natural processes that we experience, we must assume that our practices and these processes themselves are somehow interconnected. This connection becomes apparent when our projects fail; without this confrontation we could not learn anything about the world.

Anyone who rejects the ontological question raised by the

epistemological turn as incorrectly formulated, but at the same time does not want to project the levels of language into reality itself in the manner of Nicolai Hartmann's ontology of levels of reality, must come to terms with the pluralism of some deeply anchored world-disclosing perspectives; then the world itself disaggregates into the particularism of segments of the world that are relevant for the lifeworld.[37] From a neo-pragmatist perspective, we encounter natural processes under different functional aspects of our 'coping' with the world which vary with vocabularies and practices.[38] But those who are not content with simply insisting on such a detranscendentalized, but *divided*, epistemic situation must not capitulate before the black hole represented by the ontological question of the origin and existence of the lifeworld.

Most of the options available here lead us onto speculative paths. Thus one can take the peculiar ontic groundlessness of the lifeworld as a starting point for retranscendentalizing and deepening the transcendental difference – either to supplement the deflated post-Kantian philosophical understanding of self and the world with a religious interpretation of the world[39] or to advocate a post-Kantian metaphysics which starts from an analysis of self-consciousness and dares to take the step towards a cosmically expanded consciousness.[40] For those who are uneasy with this return to the motifs of the 'strong' traditions rooted in the Axial Age, there is, if I am not mistaken, only one alternative – namely, the attempt to outdo the detranscendentalization of performing subjectivity once again through a weak form of naturalism.[41]

The recovery of religious experience, of religious-metaphysical thinking in terms of unity, and of scientistic naturalism are not the only ways we can try to reconcile epistemic dualism with ontological monism. On the proposed reading in terms of a theory of communication, the transcendental spontaneity of active subjectivity withdraws into the lifeworld practices through which the reproduction of the lifeworld is interwoven with the results of learning processes within the world. To be sure, this circular process can also be exemplified by processes in social space and historical time. But this detranscendentalization is not radical enough to break out of the self-centred reconstructive analysis of general structures of possible lifeworlds in another direction – that of the evolution of socio-cultural forms of life as such. What we are describing, after all, is the structures of linguistic communication and its background of which we are aware only in performance and which can be accessed only through reflection from the perspective of a participant in lifeworld practices. We describe these structures with the help of rational reconstructions of general competences of knowing, speaking and acting subjects. The learning processes of a socialized mind are facilitated primarily by the interplay between the intentional relation to the world, reciprocal perspective-taking, the use of a propositionally differentiated language, instrumental action and cooperation.

In conclusion, I would like at least to mention the heuristic question – namely, that of the possibility of an empirical theory with which a mind thus characterized can reconstruct its natural historical genesis in such a way that it can recognize itself in it.[42] Perhaps the perspective of a 'natural history of the mind' suggests itself because we can focus on the natural conditions of emergence of a relation of complementarity between lifeworld and objective world only under the epistemic conditions of this complementarity. From an evolutionary perspective, the general structures of the lifeworld as described by philosophy seem to provide the empirical initial conditions for accelerated cultural learning processes. Our task would then be to identify the constellation of features that satisfy these conditions based on natural history and to explain them in terms of a process of natural evolution conceived in turn as a 'learning process'. It would then have to be possible to 'explain' the general structures of the lifeworld which have been reconstructed reflexively – that is, 'from the inside' – like the emergent properties of an initial constellation described in empirical terms.

Such an investigation, which is conducted in the archive of nature rather than in the laboratory, would thus have to be guided by a comprehensive theory of learning. However, this should not be conceived in a reductionist way such that we would have to make concessions from the beginning concerning 'our' performatively acquired understanding of cultural learning processes.[43] Until the theory acquires sharper contours, however, it remains unclear in what sense we can speak of 'emergence' and 'explanation'. The analyses of the increase in complexity of basic concepts observed at the linguistic levels of the life sciences, psychology, and the cultural sciences could play a heuristic role for such a natural history of the mind, which would enable us to connect the explanatory perspective 'from above' with that 'from below'.[44] Any such enterprise is, of course, in danger of merely dressing up a metaphysical natural philosophy in postmetaphysical garb.

2

THE LIFEWORLD AS A SPACE OF SYMBOLICALLY EMBODIED REASONS

(1) Although language serves the purposes of both representation and communication, the pragmatic role of reasons can be explained in terms of the communicative use of language. Reasons are statements with which one speaker responds to the 'why' questions (or negative stances) of another speaker: 'Why did the Polish president's airplane crash on its approach to the Russian airport?' or 'Why do you insist on objecting to the tax assessment?' or 'Why did you attack him so aggressively?' We can answer such questions with a causal explanation (referring to causal factors), a normative justification (appealing to justifying rules) or a psychological explanation (citing justifying circumstances and motives). Everyday communication seems to be the natural context for using reasons. But did not philosophy, which has taken 'giving reasons' as its defining theme since Plato, identify scientific practice as the privileged locus of explanations and justifications?

Take a question such as 'Why do you think that conventional safety inspections of nuclear facilities are inadequate?' The addressee may respond by referring to a newspaper article concerning the report of an expert commission; but if he is addressed in his role as an expert, then his answer will be based on test series, complex calculations, probability arguments – in short, on scientific analyses of the results of measurements conducted in laboratories far removed from everyday practice. Does this mean that reasons are more at home in scientific texts than in everyday life? This conjecture is misleading. In scientific texts which *represent* reflections and results, the pragmatic role inherited as it were from everyday practices by reasons in scientific practice is effaced – specifically, the role of the *discursive exchange of reasons* which throw light on something obscure, that is, which remove the perplexity caused by disconcerting and opaque events or actions.

Reasons provide people who are in need of orientation with clarity concerning opaque or puzzling conditions which are disturbing because they open up a breach in the horizon of a totality which we understand in a preliminary way, however vaguely – and possibly even wrongly. Reasons restore the epistemic relationship to a familiar world which has been disrupted by failure to understand something. Even when they revolutionize our understanding of the world, they still repair a disruption of our naïve relation to the lifeworld. This 'confidence-building' function of reasons, their role in restoring familiarity, tends to be obscured by institutionalized research, which places the fallibility of knowledge on a permanent footing. The true locus of reasons is in discursive practice, whether it be the elliptical forms of everyday communication or the professional practices of law, politics, science, etc. At any rate, everyday life and expert cultures are not separated by an impermeable barrier within the space of reasons;[1] on the contrary, reasons circulate between the wide riverbed of everyday communication and the narrower channels formed by discourses among experts.

However, concentrating on scientific discourses not only suggests a false separation of reasons from the lifeworld; it is also misleading because it focuses too narrowly on our epistemic relation to the world and leads to a one-sided specification of the pragmatic role of reasons. Reasons not only serve to provide people in need of orientation with clarity about the world – and to provide clarification about people and their motives as things we encounter in the world. In performative, practical relations between people, questions concerning reasons have a completely different function from filling gaps in our understanding of the world: reasons help to avoid or to cement fissures in the chain of socially established interactions. In everyday communication, reasons serve primarily as a lubricant ensuring smooth cooperation. What reasons both enable and repair is the connection between the practical intentions of one participant and those of another – hence, the social networking of actions. This functional context is not primarily a matter of rendering intelligible those events in need of explanation and those actions in need of justification that we encounter in the world but, instead, of explaining or justifying in reflexive terms the propositional attitudes of another person to the world or of criticizing them. The reasons of relevance for interaction explain to one person why another person has the beliefs, intentions and feelings which she has.

Interestingly, these reasons do not normally exert their effects by being expressed in the form of explicit explanations or justifications but instead operate in the background. Every speech act which expresses a belief, a feeling or an intention, every request and every promise is *tacitly connected with a whole semantically interlinked series* of reasons. Most utterances remain opaque or ambiguous unless the speaker shares some *implicit prior knowledge* with the hearer. Let us imagine the following scene: with a mute gesture, his index finger pressed to his lips and his eyes fixed on the door to the adjoining room, someone tries to deter his brother from entering the bedroom because a friend is resting in there. The return from a strenuous journey and the normative reason for not disturbing someone who is exhausted can remain unspoken, because both are part of the implicitly shared background knowledge.

This knowledge stabilizes the flow of everyday communication like a kind of shock absorber. But the horizon of unspoken certainties also involves a potential for negation that can be activated at any time; certainties also depend tacitly on a mode of assuming-to-be-true or assuming-to-be-right which points to reasons in case what is said is problematized. Therefore, reasons in communication processes have the double-edged function of bedrock that provides support *and* of loose gravel – they can support a consensus but can just as well unsettle it. Speech acts, indeed *all* intentional actions, are embedded in a space of interlinked reasons that is for the moment unclear. Because the status of a linguistic utterance depends on reasons, with each of his utterances a speaker accepts a corresponding normative burden. With the semantic content – that is, the conventionally regulated 'how' and 'what' of what is said – the speaker implicitly settles on certain kinds of reasons and on certain implications and, as a result, incurs duties to account for himself towards the other participants in communication.[2] Reasons imply certain determinations on the part of those who support them; and they challenge the addressee, who is supposed to accept them, to take a rational stance – that is, one based on reasons.[3]

The assumption or thematization of reasons that presumably count for both sides is part of the pragmatics of communicative language use. This widespread mode of communication is marked by the participants' intention to reach an understanding about something in the jointly assumed objective world within the context of shared background knowledge.[4] Here the speaker raises a validity claim for the content of his utterance to which the hearer can take a 'yes' or a 'no' stance. Which validity claims can even play a role here is shown by the aspects under which we can object to speech acts *as a whole* in each case. We can call into question the *truth* of assertions, the *legitimacy* or *reliability* of requests or promises, or the *truthfulness* of confessions or expressions of subjective states and feelings. These validity claims express an internal relationship between the semantic content and potential reasons. This explains why understanding language is already interwoven with the practice of *reaching understanding* and hence also with the practice of asking for and offering reasons. Understanding a speech act also involves knowledge of the kind of reasons with which a speaker could redeem under the given conditions the validity claim which she raises for what she has said.

While the analysis of *speech acts* is directed to linguistic communication as such, the study of *communicative action* is concerned with this communicative process only insofar as the latter enables the connection between the action plans of the participants, hence social interactions. Actions 'can be connected' if the options open to the participants in interaction are harmonized in such a way that their themes and practical intentions can be interlinked within restricted social spaces and historical times. In communicative action this connection is established through the binding or bonding effect of validity claims which are in fact recognized. Here, the rationally motivating force of a speech act offer springs not from the validity of what is said but from the guarantee which the speaker implicitly assumes for the redeemability of her validity claim and which is effective for coordination.

(2) The role of reasons in communicative action has brought us a step closer to the topic of the lifeworld as the space of symbolically embodied reasons than the confidence-building function which reasons play in the epistemic relation to the surprises sprung by a contingent environment. The reasons which are in a state of flux at the level of communication become *solidified* in the cultural traditions and institutionalized practices that are part of the lifeworld background in the context of everyday communication.[5] This is a matter of a higher-level consolidating embodiment; for the reasons that enter into such traditions and norms are themselves already symbolically embodied. Therefore, I would like to begin by discussing the most elementary symbolic embodiment of semantic contents of all. Specifically, reasons can feature for the first time in propositional differentiated language because speech acts qualify as reasons only thanks to the logical connections between propositions. Only descriptive or expressive or normative propositions can assume the pragmatic role of causal or psychological explanations and normative justifications. But in what dimension does symbolic embodiment occur as such? How the medium of the embodiment of symbolic contents functions can be studied already below the level of complexity of a propositionally differentiated language in

the use of individual symbols, for example simple communication by means of expressive gestures. Charles Sanders Peirce's semiotics drew attention to iconic and deictic signs, to heraldic animals, national flags, steeple cocks, etc., which symbolize contents even though they lack any explicit propositional contents.[6]

I speak of a linguistic symbol when a sign is used by at least two competent users *with the same meaning* in order to communicate with one another about something in the world. The use of elementary gestures can already fulfil the normative meaning of a communication even before reasons *explicitly* come into play.

Recall the scene mentioned above: someone looks silently at the door to the adjoining room and makes a gesture intended to admonish the individual entering the room not to disturb the person who is sleeping there. If this communication is to be successful, then the following conditions at least must be fulfilled: (i) based on intentional bodily movements, a pointing gesture and a gesture, those involved (ii) enter into the relationship between a speaker and an addressee who adjust to each other from the 'I' and 'you' perspectives respectively; (iii) they connect this interpersonal relationship with their own intentional relation to a state of affairs in the world (iv) by jointly relating to the same state of affairs through their gestures, (v) whereby the hearer, based on shared prior normative background knowledge, concludes that the communication of the state of affairs is intended as a request (not to disturb the individual who is sleeping). 'In virtue of', or 'thanks to', intentionally generated body movements, the individuals involved enter into a communicative relationship with each other and, based on these gestures, jointly refer on the same state of affairs. Of course, here we are dealing with competent speakers who already know what a symbol is and know the meaning of these specific gestures.

What does this knowledge involve? Practical knowledge of how a publicly perceptible physical movement is understood as a gesture that has the 'same' meaning for several persons enables us to distinguish two intentional attitudes which are interconnected *in the act of using and understanding the gesture*: in making a *communicative use* of the symbol, the participants enter into an interpersonal relationship with each other by relating to each other reciprocally as second persons; at the same time, they make *a representative use* of the symbol by directing themselves intentionally to an object or a state of affairs in the objectifying attitude of an observer. Like a catalyst, the material element, the sound or the bodily movement, triggers the interconnection between the socio-cognitive and the more narrowly cognitive performance: the gesture is the public element and the intentions of the participants meet in the perception of the gesture.

Prompted by the shared perception of this catalyst, the respective attitudes of the participants to something in the world are communalized by each taking the perspective of the other, so that *shared intentions* – hence shared perceptions and intentions – can arise. By entering into an interpersonal relationship, the participants reciprocally adopt each other's perceptual perspectives on something in the world and in this way create a store of shared knowledge.

In his ingenious experiments in developmental psychology, Michael Tomasello has shown that this very triadic relationship is already involved in interactions with pre-verbal infants. It is produced between the participants in communication and the object about which they communicate by symbolically linking the vertical reference to the world with the horizontal relationship to the other.[7] Children around the age of one follow the pointing gesture of reference persons and use their own index finger to draw the attention of others to certain things and to share their perceptions with others. In the functioning of these simple gestures Tomasello discovers the socio-cognitive core of the pragmatic presuppositions of linguistic communication. At the horizontal level, the mother and the child adopt each other's intention through the direction of gaze, giving rise to a social perspective from which both direct their attention to the same object in the vertical direction. With the aid of pointing – soon also in combination with mimicry – children acquire intersubjectively *shared* knowledge of objects that are jointly identified and perceived. Shortly thereafter the pointing gesture is supplemented by imitative gestures which represent properties of objects, including objects that the child cannot currently see. Out of these two elements there later develop expressions for the two components of the proposition, reference and description.

Here we can see in the nascent state how gestural communication first gives rise to the *objectifying* reference to something in the world by way of an *intersubjective* interconnection between the respective viewpoints and perceptions. Only through the decentring adjustment of the reciprocally assumed perspectives does the world gradually lose the characteristics of an environment perceived in an 'egocentric' way.[8] As a result, the child achieves the distance from the world that we associate with the intentionality of references to and attitudes towards objects and states of affairs. Tomasello's comparative studies between children and chimpanzees provide in addition the contrasting foil against which the phylogenetic origins of human communication can be made out.[9] Chimpanzees do not seem to be able to break out of the constraints of their self-referential viewpoint, which is steered by their respective subjective motivations. They are indeed highly intelligent and can act intentionally, they are able to understand the intentions of conspecifics and correctly assess the spatial difference between their locations, and they can even draw practical inferences from this. However, they cannot enter into those *interpersonal* relationships with conspecifics which would enable them to socialize their cognition in symbolic form. (One need not be a 'lingualist' to assume that cultural learning replaced the genetic evolutionary mechanism only with the acquisition of language.) From a social-pragmatist point of view, the decisive evolutionary achievement of *Homo sapiens* is the ability to adjust to a conspecific in such a way that both can pursue the same goals, and hence can cooperate, in the gesturally mediated reference to objective states of affairs.

However, the critical role of gestures for the emergence of the triadic relationship is not exhausted by the catalytic function in producing intersubjectively shared knowledge. That may be true of the initial stages; but only the following step, *the conventionalization of the use of signs*, turns the sign substrate itself into the bearer of meanings. Only the regular association of the shared knowledge with those sounds and bodily movements that initially elicit joint attention and shared knowledge in a catalytic way leads to the symbolic embodiment of semantic contents. We can distinguish two socio-cognitive preconditions for the symbolization of contents: without the intervention of the intentional but jointly perceived gestural utterance, the relationship to the other cannot be coordinated with the intentional attitude to something in the world; and, unless the shared knowledge becomes permanently associated with the gesture which leads to the coordination of these two intentions on both sides, the semantic contents cannot find symbolic embodiment.[10]

(3) The mentalist expression 'shared knowledge' conceals the *world-disclosing and world-constituting* function performed by symbolization, which must be distinguished from its *socio-cognitive* function. Thus far we have examined the socialization of a form of cognition that is already highly developed among primates from the perspective that the use of gestures is necessary to interconnect reciprocally interchangeable perspectives with an intentional – i.e., objectifying – distancing from the pressure of the environment. Gestures qualify for this role among other things in virtue of their public character as expressive movements which can be perceived as physical elements by all those involved. But, as soon as these gestures are used on a regular basis and develop into conventional bearers of intersubjectively shared knowledge, they acquire the stubborn character of objective cultural phenomena vis-à-vis the mind of the individual subject. They give rise to a public space

of prior interpretations in which participants in communication encounter one another. This capacity to found publicity reveals the fictive power of the symbolization that gives rise to a shared life-world. Ontogenetic evidence also confirms this moment of poiesis. Children not only learn to understand symbols *but also confirm their symbolizing activity as such through play*. What has always fascinated psychologists about young children's play behaviour is the creation of 'as-if' scenarios. When a two-year-old amuses herself in interactions with adults by using a pencil as if it were a toothbrush, she is consciously switching between levels of reality, where one 'represents' the other symbolically.[11]

This reading emphasizes the independent status that conventionalized gestures acquire as signifiers or repositories of intersubjective knowledge. Accordingly, based on the *understanding* of the gesture that stands for something in the world, a shared perspective on this thing, and intersubjective knowledge of it, develops between the participants in communication.[12] Understanding a gesture does not require a complex calculation of the consequences of reciprocally recognized intentions. This conception avoids the difficulty of a mentalist explanation, which presupposes a complex stage of reflection as an initial condition for using symbols. On the mentalist account, the participants would already have to be able to acquire recursive knowledge, and thus meta-representations, of each other.[13]

Chimpanzees do not exhibit the type of communication which opens up a shared objective world within the horizon of an intersubjectively shared lifeworld through the use of symbols with identical meanings. But going beyond egocentric attachment to the lifeworld to an intersubjectively shared, jointly interpreted world is connected with a further operation of symbolization over and above gestural communication. When shared knowledge becomes detached from the subjective mind, the mental acquires independent form not just in linguistic communication, because the latter is not the only way in which conscious operations become externalized. Linguistic communication also provides the basis for the development of other forms of objective spirit, such as oral traditions, family structures, habits and customs. With traditions and established norms, a publicly accessible space of symbolic objects arises. Ontologically speaking, these peculiar objects first acquire existence in the communicative utterances, actions and artefacts of socialized participants in communication and agents. For the latter, the network of practices and traditions forms a performatively present and intersubjectively shared background whenever they relate intentionally to each other and to something in the objective world. In short, the mind externalizes itself not only in the use of symbols for communicative purposes but also in normative structures of the lifeworld which the members share with each other, like their language, through implicit background knowledge.

How this symbolizing activity goes beyond the symbolic embodiment of semantic contents is shown by the distinctive *binding effect* of traditions, roles and institutions. To be sure, the conventionalized use of symbols already marks the development of the normative consciousness inscribed in all rule-governed behaviour as such – specifically, knowledge of the difference between right or rule-conforming and wrong or deviant behaviour. But the normativity manifested in observing linguistic conventions is weaker than the authority expressed in the exemplary claim of traditions and in the obligatory character of normative behavioural expectations.[14] We must distinguish between the cognitive guiding force of grammatical and logical-semantic rules and the power of institutions to control emotions and bind motivations. The source of this strong normativity of right or wrong social action is not already contained in the use of linguistic symbols oriented to reaching understanding itself.[15] For the interpersonal binding energy of obligations and entitlements must not be confused with the appellative character of requests or demands in the sense of a unilateral expression of will. From the perspective of a version of social pragmatics that explains the use of language exclusively in terms of the cognitive requirements for efficient coordination of action, the transition from imperative demands to strong valuations and normative behavioural expectations remains a void.[16]

(4) In my view, this void can be filled from a phylogenetic perspective if we consider a form of communication different from, though related to, the use of iconic gestures, namely, ritual communication. Anthropologists report that tribal societies exhibit an abundance of ritual practices which take place on very different occasions. Structurally speaking, these practices exhibit similarities to the gesturally mediated communication that we have considered thus far. However, there is one striking difference between these two forms of communication. Rites are not connected directly with the functional contexts of social cooperation. Research in cultural anthropology teaches us that the mimetic skills of our ancestors were not exhausted by everyday gestural communication but also found expression in the modelling of striking objects and processes, in dances, pantomimic representations, sculptures, paintings, monuments, and the like.[17] Ritual communication is distinguished from other iconic representations, however, by its peculiar self-referential character: it does not refer to a jointly identifiable 'something in the

world', even though this is precisely what constitutes the novelty of symbolically mediated communication. Rather, it is turned away from the everyday world and remains in a peculiar way self-enclosed. It is precisely this lack of a referent in the everyday world which lends it the character of *extra-ordinary* communication.[18]

Consider what is involved in a ritual dance. While the rhythmic movements in the communal execution of the practice express commonality of intentions, spur the participants on to reciprocal imitation of gestures and mutual perspective-taking, and apparently trigger an intersubjectively shared experience, the third arrow of the triadic semiotic structure points nowhere – at any rate, not as long as we try to identify an object or state of affairs in the *objective* world as what is experienced and intended. The dimension in which we seek the missing referent is apparently the evolutionarily new dimension of communal social life itself which is first produced by symbolically mediated communication. I understand ritual behaviour as an answer to the problems to which *the socialization of the individual* gives rise at this level of communication. From the social-pragmatic point of view we regard gestural communication as a new, evolutionarily advantageous form of intelligent cooperation. But this socialization of intelligence must have had an impact on how behaviour was coordinated. The first gesture that gives rise to an identical meaning for ego and alter liberates subjective consciousness from its egocentric shell. Insofar as individual contents of consciousness are simultaneously externalized and socialized through the symbolization of meanings, the monadic consciousness of the one conspecific opens itself up to that of the other. This entry into the public world of symbolic forms does not only mark the overcoming of a form of cognitive egocentrism. In addition, the socialization of intelligence goes along with a revolution in the way behaviour is coordinated – with a switch-over to symbolically mediated interaction among group members who have to cope *in a cooperative way* with the contingencies of the world within the horizon of their shared lifeworld. This cognitive challenge goes hand in hand with a psychodynamic one.

The contrast with the 'egocentric' form of life of chimpanzees highlighted by Tomasello stresses an upheaval in social relations which must have drawn the individual into the maelstrom of a communicative *communalization of his motives*. We can imagine this socializing revolution exercising a pincer pressure of *simultaneous socialization and individualization* on the individual's consciousness. On the one hand, with the new form of communication through symbols used with identical meanings, the onus of coordinating action falls increasingly on communicative action, and hence on the shoulders of the individuals *themselves*; on the other hand, individuals become aware that the reproduction of their own lives depends essentially on *collective* self-assertion, hence a functioning system of social cooperation. The complex social organism must have confronted individual members as an overwhelming, all-consuming power and, simultaneously, as a one which protects and guarantees survival and security for the first time. The new form of communicative communalization gives rise to a structural tension between the self-assertion of the individual and that of the collective and demands that this tension between conflicting imperatives be stabilized. If ritual practice now serves the purpose of ensuring the cohesion of the social group which is exposed to permanent risk and maintains a precarious balance, it is natural to assume that the strong normativity of behavioural expectations springs from this extraordinary form of communication.

From the beginning there seems to have been a complementary relationship between communication in ordinary everyday and out-of-the-ordinary contexts. While the one proceeds from contexts of cooperation and leads to the socialization of intelligences, the other responds to a tension between the imperatives of individual and collective self-assertion resulting from the communalization of motives. Everyday communication generates the weak normativity of a language logos which transcends the subject and makes the human mind receptive to reasons; communication with the powers of salvation and misfortune[19] gives rise to and renews the strong normativity of social solidarity. Once gestural communication has developed in the context of everyday cooperation into full grammatical speech, both forms of communication become open for propositions and their narrative interconnection – in other words, for reasons. Thus research in anthropology encounters rituals almost exclusively in the light of explanatory myths. At any rate, solidarity-founding rituals, together with mythical interpretations of self and the world, form a sacred complex which has survived up to the present day in a transformed guise.

Mythical narratives at first reflected the norms of the kinship system in the cosmos as a whole and justified them in narrative terms. At the same time, however, new experiences from dealing with the social and natural environment were processed discursively in everyday communication. In the long run, apparently, mythical explanations were not able to withstand the pressure of cognitive dissonances generated by the encounter with pragmatic mundane knowledge which had withstood the test of successful action. Reasons develop a dynamic of their own. This antagonism between profane knowledge and the sacred complex suggests that the emergence of the sacred complex can be explained in functionalist terms: the connection with ritual practices also has a protective function for myths which explain the world in the narrative terms and are exposed to the criticism of profane mundane knowledge. This is because this iconic form of gestural communication is impervious to reasons formulated in a propositionally differentiated language simply in virtue of the structural disparity between these two levels of communication.

Nevertheless, I conjecture that this antagonism between profane experiential knowledge and the worldviews attached to the sacral complex functioned as a driving force of cultural learning processes. This brings me back to the issue of the higher-level symbolic embodiment of reasons beyond discourses. This consolidating embodiment of reasons in culture and society first sheds light on the lifeworld as the space of symbolically embodied reasons.

(5) In all societies there is a tension-laden correspondence between reasons *bound* in traditions and *enshrined* in institutions, on the one hand, and reasons which are *released* in communication and float freely, on the other. Reasons develop their simultaneously problematizing and problem-solving force in the exchange of speech acts in communication; but, from the standpoint of social stability, the ever-present risk of dissent that lurks in the ability to say 'no' turns everyday communicative practice into an uncertain and quite costly mechanism for integration. In fact, *every* society restricts the negating potential of the reasons available in each case in the form of cultural traditions and norms, even if it is initially the good reasons which are preserved in this way. The *dogmatization* of teachings taken to be true and exemplary and the *institutionalization* of behavioural expectations taken to be good and right are two mechanisms of a higher-level, consolidating embodiment of reasons that restrict the flow of the discursive exchange of reasons by channelling it.

Cultural traditions and corresponding mentalities constitute *the* segment from the horizon of shared and symbolically stored background knowledge which, even though open to thematization, should nevertheless remain beyond the reach of radical problematization. Traditions ensure the transmission of that knowledge which a culture singles out as proven, excellent and authoritative. A prime example of the tradition-forming mechanism is the kind of educational canon which took shape already in the early literate cultures of the Near East. At that time 'classical' works acquired canonical validity by the fact that the contents were placed beyond the reach of criticism and discursive change by conserving their wording as literally as possible.[20] In this way, the informed selection of a corpus

of good and relevant works led to their immunization against critical objections. To this day, the formative power of all traditions
resides in the fact that selected core elements of a store of knowledge
are shielded from being problematized by questions and objections.

Thus *culture* moulds and perpetuates communicative actors'
understanding of themselves and the world across large expanses
of time through a binding selection of interpretations; it embodies reasons by dogmatizing stores of knowledge. At the same time,
society embodies reasons for action by subjecting behavioural
expectations to norms, which in turn condense and stabilize the
networks of communicative action across social spaces in the horizontal dimension.[21] The practical reasons that support the validity
of the norms have to be internalized in order to become effective for
behaviour; this holds even for the foundations of state-sanctioned,
and hence enforceable, law. Unlike the epistemic authority – in
the broadest sense – of traditions, the normative binding power
of customs and the imperative force of institutions and systems
of rule become anchored through socialization processes – that is,
through the implicit 'formative' influence of social environments on
the motivational structures of adolescents. Through internalization,
the supporting values and normative reasons of a society literally
become embodied in the personality structures of its members.

Of course, these values which have become solidified into dispositions are connected with corresponding cultural traditions, because
the framework of social norms remains embedded in the justifying
context of the understanding of self and world of the social collectivity. Reasons are also embodied in the objects of material culture and
can often be read off from functions or reconstructed from construction plans. To the dogmatization and institutionalization of reasons
there corresponds the *materialization of reasons in artefacts* as a
third higher-level mechanism of embodiment. These three modes
of cultural, psychosocial and material embodiment of reasons are
constitutive of the lifeworld context in which the communicative
actors find themselves. In this way, the metaphor of the space of
reasons acquires a concrete meaning which goes beyond mastery of
the inferential relationships stored in the linguistic vocabulary.

Cultures and societies conserve good reasons. But good reasons
can be replaced by better reasons in the light of different conditions
and new insights. This is what underlies the internal dynamics of
learning processes. In some epochs, cognitive dissonances accumulated to such an extent that cumulative learning processes triggered
an advance by invalidating a whole *category* of conventional
reasons and revolutionizing the dominant social understanding of
self and the world. I would like to mention just two large-scale

examples of such cognitive advances. The first one I have in mind is the revolution of worldviews during the Axial Age. This occurred around the middle of the first millennium BCE in China, India, Israel and Greece and marked the emergence of those metaphysical and religious worldviews which overcame magic and magical thinking and invalidated the explanatory power of myths, and which have preserved their ability to shape civilization up to the present day.[22] The other example comes from a development in the West, namely, the so-called nominalist revolution in thought in the High Middle Ages. This marked the beginning of the devaluation of metaphysical modes of thought and explanation in terms of essences, which served in turn as a kind of detonator for the major cultural and scientific innovations of Western modernity.[23] However, these examples should not suggest the Whig image of an inexorable, linear rationalization of our understanding of ourselves and the world. Although there is also evidence for the socio-evolutionary assumption of a successive dissolution and communicative release of potentials that are, as it were, encapsulated in the sacred complexes,[24] here 'dissolution' does not mean evaporation. Evidently, discursive practices which subject controversial utterances to the unforced force of the better argument ultimately operate within a horizon of impenetrable and opaque experiences which can be represented iconically but cannot be completely grasped and explained in discursive terms.

Only with the development of a grammatical language, hence with the differentiation of propositional contents from the holophrastic expressions of gestural communication, can reasons emerge as such. In the single-word sentences of children – for example, the exclamation 'Fire!' – the three modes (communicating this occurrence, expressing fear at the sight of it and the call for help) still form a syndrome, whereas in grammatical language the propositional contents become detached from their possible modes of use and become discursively available as such. With this decisive step towards explicitly processing reasons, however, we have not entirely left the meaning syndromes familiar from gestures and iconic representations behind us as a thing of the past. The domain of symbolically expressed meaning continues to extend beyond the sphere of linguistically expressed meanings interwoven with reasons. In other words, the space of reasons is embedded in a non-verbalizable or pre-predicative horizon of meaning. It is limited by a zone of non-linguistic representations and practices whose meaning can indeed be commented upon, though it cannot be exhausted discursively. Emil Angehrn has analysed images, music and dance as media which involve such an extralinguistic embodiment of meaning.[25]

Theology does not derive support exclusively from the statements of sacred texts either; it remains dependent on and moves within the foundation of belief of religious communities which preserve the context of the transmitted word in their liturgical practice and religious observances. For even when sacramental actions are exposed to hermeneutical interpretation within the framework of highly developed theological doctrines, their meaning is accessible only from the perspective of participants who engage in the ritual practice itself. As agnostic members of largely secularized societies, we have lost access to this archaic source of solidarity. We may ask whether we must take religion seriously in a philosophical sense as a contemporary intellectual formation, where by 'religion' I understand religious observances in connection with conceptions of redemptive justice.

Interestingly enough, despite the fact that even professional art critics run up against similar limits of discursive explication when they try to grasp in words the content of symphonies and paintings, of architectural forms, designs and ornaments, of ballet performances or sculptures, we do not pose this question with regard to modern art. Aesthetic experience can be circumscribed and explicated in conceptual terms, but it *cannot be expressed without remainder* in explicit judgements. Although art criticism also operates like exegetical hermeneutics which seeks to penetrate the text, in the end it has to be content with evocative, eye-opening commentary which awakens an intuition.[26] Clearly, highly developed aesthetic forms of expression, such as music, dance, pantomime, painting and sculpture – including the onomatopoeic echoes without which fictional literature, and especially the evocative power of poems, would be inconceivable – remain rooted in a *symbolic, but non-linguistic mode of communication*. Ritual practices also employ the iconic media of artistic representation in a similar way. They develop a wealth of aesthetic effects, but they live on as an archaic element within the ensemble of highly developed aesthetic forms. In contrast to the arts, which have become autonomous and are in the meantime associated with discursive art criticism, rituals as such, even if they are commented upon in mythical narratives, do not yet seem to be infected with the spirit of language – unlike, for example, instrumental music, which for Adorno exhibits a mute 'resemblance to language'.[27]

In short, reasons and discursive thought are central to mind insofar as its operation depends on language and, above all, they constitute the vehicle of the learning human mind; nevertheless, the space of symbolically embodied meaning still extends into a peripheral zone of sediments of meaning that goes beyond the domain of explicitly accessible reasons.

3

A HYPOTHESIS
CONCERNING THE
EVOLUTIONARY MEANING
OF RITES

When sociologists or anthropologists speak of 'religion' today, they are using the term in an inclusive sense that encompasses all possible religious beliefs and practices insofar as they involve a confrontation with extraordinary forces of salvation and misfortune.[1] The Californian guru and the Native American medicine man command the same interest as the Old Testament prophets or the Chinese wise man. When we speak as educated laypersons of 'religion', however, we have in mind first and foremost the major world religions which Max Weber studied and Karl Jaspers traced back to the Axial Age. The term 'Axial Age' stems from Jaspers's conception that the middle of the first millennium BCE represented an 'axis' around which the rotation of world history accelerated, as it were. During the comparatively short period from around 800 to 300 BCE, cognitive revolutions occurred independently of each other which gave rise to those 'strong' religious doctrines and metaphysical world-views that remain influential to the present day.

This period marked the emergence of 'religion' in the sense of a 'founded' doctrine and practice out of mythical narratives and ritualized practices in ways that can be traced back to the teachings of a historical figure: Zoroastrianism in Iran, monotheism in Israel, Confucianism and Daoism in China, Buddhism in India and (with the proviso that it lacked deeper roots in the cult of the polis) Greek metaphysics. These 'religions' assumed the form of canonized scriptural doctrines that left their imprint on entire civilizations. Holy books formed the rationalizable and institutionalizable cores around which both the dogmatic elaboration of sophisticated traditions and the influential organization of worldwide religious communities could crystallize. Karl Jaspers highlights the striking fact that cosmological worldviews and world religions emerged at approximately the same time in world history in order to oppose the pluralistic thesis that the major Eurasian civilizations emerged at the same time in history to the Eurocentric fixation on Jerusalem and Athens.

The focus on this revolutionary break in the mode of thinking must not mislead us into adopting a one-sided, intellectualistic view of religious and metaphysical worldviews. The cognitive break-throughs to points of view anchored beyond – or at the foundation of – the world, to moral universalisms, and to new conceptions of salvation and redemptive justice were, indeed, prodigious achieve-ments. But these teachings also preserve the archaic unity of myth and rites, because religious interpretations of the world preserve the archaic unity with ritual practices by transforming them and making them compatible with a higher level of reflection. Without this proper core, the religions would not have been able to stub-bornly affirm their status in contrast to secular thought up to the present day. Through their rootedness in the sacred complex, they remain connected with an archaic experience to which all other cultural sensors and sectors have lost access in the course of social modernization. I would like to explore the relationship between myth and rites in an attempt to localize this experience of dealing with the 'sacred' over the course of human development and to sift out its core meaning. A cursory examination of the relevant theories in anthropology leads me to the conjecture that ritual prac-tices may have involved the reworking of the buried phylogenetic experience of a shift in forms of social life from innate, species-specific behavioural patterns to symbolically mediated patterns of communication.

I The Sacred Complex

If we want to understand the sacred complex, we must draw upon anthropological observations of modern tribal societies from which we can make inferences, at best, to Neolithic forms of life extending back to the eleventh millennium BCE. The more recent literary tes-timonies and archaeological remains of the more accessible archaic civilizations were already based on the reconstruction of an older fund of myth and rites. The processing and *literary* elaboration of this prehistoric fund took place during the period from around 3000 BCE onwards in the context of state-organized societies. It was informed by an emerging historical consciousness and responded to the interests of ruling dynasties. However, the origins of the sacred complex extend much further back than even the Neolithic period. The oldest rock paintings discovered in Australia that permit inferences to cultic worship sites are estimated to be 50,000 years old, whereas the first attested burial by *Homo sapiens* is circa 100,000 years old. The oldest discoveries of jewellery also date from this period. The indestructible material of these pearls, however, reminds us that even more ancient mythical stories and ritual actions expressed in the more ephemeral media of speech, song and dance must have disappeared without trace.[2] Therefore, there are plausible speculations that the sacred complex has even earlier origins extending back before the archaeological findings into the period of the evolution of *Homo sapiens* and *Homo neanderthalensis* from the older *Homo heidelbergensis* (from over 300,000 to 100,000 years ago).

Mythical narratives and ritual practices belong together, even if they no longer occur together in every historical case. Mythical narratives are in many cases what first provide us with the key to understanding rites. Of course, such 'translations' involve a transfer of semantic contents into a medium of communication of a different stage of development (or even the superimposition of a more recent stage of communication on an older one). With ritual practice we associate the meaning of warding off danger and surmounting crises, including the existential experience of death. Burial rites seem to assuage the awakened consciousness of the finite nature of human existence. The idea of the soul or spirit escaping from the lifeless body revokes the definitive character of the almost incomprehensible and unendurable prospect of having to take leave of those closest to us. The idea of a polymorphous 'spirit' endowed with superhuman powers, which can also be present while remaining invisible, seems to provide a semantic link between mythical narration and ritual invocation and, in general, the ritualized treatment of 'higher' or 'superhuman' forces.

Mythical narratives often preserve in the medium of a fully developed language some of the meaning that rites already express *performatively* in visible gestures and images – that is, in their own iconic representational forms of music, dance, pantomime and body painting. Narratives spell out what may originally have been the independent meaning of ritual behaviour – warding off misfortune and invoking propitious forces – both as regards mastering critical situations (whether natural disasters, famines, epidemics or enemy attacks) and as regards guaranteeing functions critical for survival (the hoped-for rain, a sufficient harvest, the restoration of health, etc.). The unmistakably archaic character of ritual practices and their need for translation raise the question of whether rites and myths developed simultaneously with the emergence of *Homo sapiens* endowed with the ability to speak, or whether ritual behaviour is an even earlier phenomenon than the evolutionary threshold represented by the development of a grammatical language.

II Myth and Ritual Practices – World Disclosure and Staging

To my knowledge, the ongoing controversy since the early nineteenth century over whether myth or ritual is the prior formation is still awaiting a conclusive resolution.[3] The pliant narrative form explains why myths are inherently suited to providing reports and explanations, and thus to processing observations of the natural and social environments at the cognitive level. Since narratives provide the grammatical form for organizing complex occurrences into wholes, we regard them primarily under the aspect of *representation* unless it is a matter of providing systematic classifications of observations of nature or cosmological explanations of the origin of the world. We encounter rites, by contrast, primarily under the *performative aspect* of the execution of precisely schematized and repeated actions. In this context the semantic contents remain implicit despite the pronounced expressive character of the symbols and images employed. For, regardless of verbal exclamations and interspersed phrases, ritual practices are essentially symbolic actions which display an iconic level of propositionally undifferentiated communication bound to interaction.

However, juxtaposing myth and rites in this way does not do justice to the psychodynamic role of worldviews. In his analysis of myths, Lévi-Strauss rightly highlights intellectual curiosity as a motive for such conceptual systematization of observational knowledge.[4] But in the process of recounting their mythical narratives to each other and enacting them communally, participants simultaneously reassure themselves of their collective identity. The collectivity contemplates itself in its worldview, specifically in its social structures and simultaneously as an integral component of the natural environment. The fact that the collectivity relates to itself in narrating myths first explains why mythical stories reflect features of its culture in the image of its natural environment. In a controversy with Jean-Paul Sartre's *Critique of Dialectical Reason*, Lévi-Strauss explains the totalizing tendency of primitive thought as being motivated by the assimilation of what is strange and unknown to what is familiar.[5] It is this motivation to secure the identity of the collectivity, and not intellectual curiosity alone, that first explains the conceptual link between the binary classifications of natural occurrences and the classifications of kinship relations, the spatial organization of social life, the mode of production, and so forth.[6]

Because mythical narratives do not just process observations and express something about the visible world but also reflect the psychodynamics of coping with risks which arise within the world, there is a bridge leading from myth itself to rites: 'Myth is not just a statement but an action.'[7] The myth of the New Year made famous by J. G. Frazer, according to which the ritual slaying of the old king sustains the seasonal cycle of vegetation and the return of the spring, is just one example of the close relation between mythical narration and its enactment. We need to keep both aspects in view: 'framing', hence, the world-disclosing power of mythic language on which Lévi-Strauss's investigations throw light, goes hand in hand with 're-enacting', with the periodically recurring 'performance' of the myth.

III The Intrinsic Meaning of Ritual Behaviour

It would be unproductive, however, to conceive of ritual behaviour merely as an accompaniment of myth. From the perspective of communication theory, rites represent an earlier stage of symbolic expression by comparison with mythical narratives.[8] The media of communal dance and song, mime and pantomime, body painting, jewellery and cultic objects (masks, emblems, coats of arms, ornaments, etc.) permit iconic representations or imitations that do not require any further explication. If we want to discover the original meaning that the sacred complex had for the participants, we must follow the traces back to these meanings *encapsulated in rites themselves*.

When I review the anthropological theories developed over the past century, I find it striking that most of the explanations of rites already presuppose a mythically articulated and narratively accessible world peopled by specific spirits and gods. This holds for explanations of rites as attempts to influence the favour of superhuman powers by magical means and for the derivation of rites from the sacrifice of persons or things (an example being René Girard's theory of the scapegoat mechanism). In my view, the elementary rituals of gift-giving and exchange already studied by the Durkheim disciples Henri Hubert and Marcel Mauss are more informative because these practices in a sense express their own meaning. These rituals, perhaps starting from the exchange of women, establish relations of reciprocity between kinship groups and thereby reinforce social relations of solidarity, or at any rate of non-violence.[9]

Sacrificial rites could have developed out of such profane exchange rituals. The reciprocity founded and renewed through the exchange forges a social bond between potential rivals.

This brings us closer to the intrinsic meaning of ritual behaviour which Émile Durkheim, still the most important interpreter in this area, was pursuing. He understood rites as self-referential practices that stabilize the cohesion of social groups,[10] and he was the first to ascribe an intrinsic meaning independent of any narrative explanation to ritual practice. Strictly speaking, he explored the meaning of ritual practices from two points of view: the self-thematization of society and the production of the binding force of normative expectations. According to Durkheim, on the one hand, rites reflect existing social structures; on the other, in enacting the ritual self-representation of society, the members of a collectivity reassure themselves of their identity and thereby invest interpersonal social relations with normative force.

I would also like to recall another classical theory – that of Arnold van Gennep. His well-known studies of initiation rites regulating the transition from one status to the next, whether at birth, at the threshold to adulthood or in marriages or burials, represent an important supplement to Durkheim's analyses.[11] The ritualized transition from one life cycle to the next also lends itself to an analysis under the two aforementioned aspects of the self-thematization of society and the creation of normative obligations. For example, when the adolescent is accepted into the circle of adult men, he learns the social roles attached to the new status. In enacting the prescribed ritual forms he in a sense encounters a relevant segment of society, namely, the roles assigned to male adults, and simultaneously acquires the dispositions to meet the corresponding normative expectations. The initiation pre-empts the danger that the continuity of social integration could break down at the threshold between successive generations – and that the normative binding forces would be weakened as a result.

Especially informative as regards the meaning of the sacred, however, is the aspect under which van Gennep interprets the three phases involved in status transitions: the initiation, which represents a profound change in identity for the individual concerned, is staged as a death and social rebirth. The new moment introduced by van Gennep is the transition through a stage of segregation from the community during which the candidate's membership is in suspense, as it were, so that his social existence expires temporarily – that is, until the rescuing act of reintegration through which he is accepted into a new status. This intermediate stage of segregation, of being cast out into a social no man's land, recapitulates the extreme experience of the fathomlessness of an existence that, by being thrust into the helplessness and isolation of a segregated organism relying on itself alone for its survival, becomes aware that it is completely reliant on the support of a social network. In developing my hypothesis, I take my orientation from a generalization of this experience.

The simulated experience of complete exclusion and alienation makes the individual aware not only of a *specific* social role change, and hence of the structure and dynamics of the particular society into which the novice is being initiated. The situation confronts him, rather, with an experience implicit in the socialization process as such, one implicit *in the mode of socialization itself*: the adolescent cannot secure his identity over the course of a long period of rearing and dependence by clinging to a *status quo ante*. He has the exemplary experience that he can recover and maintain himself as a regenerated self only through self-renunciation.

In the meantime, research in cultural anthropology has to my knowledge thrown additional fruitful light on rites, but without refuting the central insights of Durkheim and van Gennep. Max Gluckmann and Victor Turner, for example, shift the emphasis from the renewal of social solidarity to containing and stabilizing enduring social tensions. Functionalism conceives of ritual behaviour as a mechanism for securing the cohesion of the group. And, since Clifford Geertz's culturalistic turn, ritual practices are regarded as a kind of code in their own right which structures social relations. This conception of ritual practices as constituting an independent language has led Wilhelm Dupré to revive the romantic tradition going back to Herder, Hamann, Humboldt and Hegel which understands the human being as an *animal symbolicum* (Cassirer). Dupré construes the universal phenomenon of the sacred found in all primitive societies as a form of self-referential communication about the revolutionary innovation involved in the use of world-disclosing symbols with the same meaning. He construes rites, in turn, as an original form of self-reflection of early societies.[12] But now, according to Dupré, the sacred simultaneously provides a 'language' for communication about the existential presuppositions of a symbolically constituted form of life – hence, about themes such as birth and death, the fragility of social relations, the exhaustibility of material and natural resources, and the vulnerability of body and soul. These conditions are 'ultimate' in the sense of being inalterable: 'The turn to the ultimate . . . is thus interwoven with the phylogenetic process of hominization.'[13]

IV The Hypothesis

I would like to radicalize this ontogenetic reflection into the phylogenetic hypothesis that the sacred complex reflects the mastering of a problem that arises once the evolution of primates crosses the threshold to a new level of symbolically mediated communication and interaction. The origin of language represents a caesura in the evolution of the human species. The old idea that grammatical language originated in gestural communication has acquired a surprising topicality in recent research. Therefore, it seems plausible to assume that this form of communication reveals a family relation between this early form of everyday communication and the extra-ordinary language of rites which is specialized in dealing with the powers of salvation and misfortune. Both cases involve a form of mimetic behaviour or iconic representation which suggests a comparison between ritualized communication and ordinary gestural communication. But how should we understand the division of labour between forms of communication one of which has its origin in contexts of cooperation while the other is decoupled from everyday functions? The studies in anthropology mentioned briefly tend to support the conjecture that rites are a response to the susceptibility to disruption of the new evolutionary stage of social life founded on *symbolically mediated communication*.

But in order to identify and explain the problem to which rites could have been the solution, we must first make clear what constitutes the evolutionary innovation in the use of linguistic symbols.

V Communicating with Someone about Something

According to the present-day view, mutation and selection regulate the adaptation of each species-specific configuration of the gene pool to changed environmental conditions. With the evolution of a species that learns to speak, this mechanism of natural evolution is superseded by constantly accelerating cultural learning processes. Cultural learning abilities are the result of a cognitive advance which is clearly bound up with the socio-cognitive switch-over of signal behaviour to the use of symbols.[14] The ability to address signals to conspecifics is also observed among primates; in brief, the innovation consists in the *reciprocal* use of symbols that acquire *the same* meaning for different users. What is new is the creation of a space of *intersubjectively shared* semantic contents through communication. In contrast, our highly intelligent relations the chimpanzees do not seem to be able to break out of the constraints of their self-referential viewpoint steered by each individual's subjective motives. It is the step out of this 'egocentric' field of vision of still self-enclosed primate consciousness into the public domain of a shared world that gives us some inkling of the relevance of the transition to a new symbolically mediated form of interaction.[15]

What sets linguistic communication apart is the *interweaving of a horizontal relation* between *speaker and addressee* with a *vertical relation to objects or state of affairs* that proceeds from this shared basis. The interpersonal relation between those involved is interwoven with a reference to something in the objective world that not only points in the same direction but is also intersubjectively *shared*: the participants communicate *uno actu with one another about something*.[16] Thus, the decisive evolutionary innovation cannot be read off directly from the linguistic product itself, from its grammatical form and semantic contents, but from the *pragmatic framework conditions* for a conventionalized, hence fallible, use of linguistic symbols. The conventionalized exchange of gestures is sufficient for symbolically mediated communication with a 'language-like' character. This does not yet call for mastery of a grammatical language. The semantic content expressed, for example, in interjections, single-word sentences or childish gestures consists – as in the exclamation 'Fire!', which simultaneously refers to an occurrence, expresses fear, and calls for help – of a syndrome of three elements which are still connected: the perception of an episode or state of affairs in the world, the expressions of subjective moods or emotions, and the associated imperatives and behavioural expectations addressed to others.[17] Only as such elementary gestures or holophrastic conventions become interconnected by grammatical rules do the two decisive differentiations which set our grammatical language apart arise in the course of phylogenesis or ontogenesis: the development of the structure of propositions composed of referential and predicative expressions and the differentiation of the propositional components from their illocutionary use.

The decisive point in the present context is that even straightforward gestures can found a shared semantic space for a communication community only when they are used in such a way that

- the reciprocal adoption of the perspective of the other gives rise to an interpersonal relation between ego and alter (in the form of an I–thou relation); and that
- the communicative intention towards a second person is first fulfilled in the intersubjectively shared intention directed to something in the world (whereby the latter first acquires the objectivity

of an independently existing world that is supposed to be the same for everybody).

The assumption that these two anthropological achievements – intersubjectivity and objectivity, which in turn depend on the use of symbols – emerge simultaneously is supported, among other things, by the observation that neither the visual eye-contact typical for addressing second persons nor the use of pointing gestures is customary among primates. Apes cannot look one another in the eyes and thus are not 'second persons' for each other. Moreover, primates never disinterestedly direct the attention of a conspecific to an object in their surroundings, either by pointing to it directly or by pantomimically imitating its characteristic features; otherwise they would express the assumption of a shared objective world through pointing and mimicry, as one-year-old children already learn to do.[18] Michael Tomasello and his collaborators have attempted to show through ingenious experiments involving human children and young chimpanzees that the triadic reference of the intersubjectively shared intentions of speakers and hearers towards something in the objective world is a human monopoly.[19]

Chimpanzees are extraordinarily intelligent animals who are able to act intentionally, to understand the practical intentions of others, and to draw practical inferences. The striking cognitive difference between the ways in which chimpanzees and human beings communicate with each other is that these primates use their phenomenal capabilities exclusively in self-referential strategic ways to realize their own objectives by manipulating conspecifics. They are incapable of forming an interpersonal relationship with reference to a shared goal in the objective world. They cannot cooperate in the sense that several conspecifics coordinate their actions in order to achieve a common goal – as is required, for example, in hunting big game. They lack both the shared intention and the reference to the world that would be necessary to represent in an anticipatory way cooperation involving themselves and others – that is, to conceive of it as a project.[20] This does not mean, of course, that chimpanzees have not developed a rich social life regulated by emotions. But, at the conscious level of intentionally influencing their conspecifics, they lack a cooperative orientation. Life within the group is regulated by evolutionarily older mechanisms.

VI The Development of the Hypothesis: Ordinary and Extra-ordinary Communication

Ritual practices can be understood as a variant of gestural communication; they also represent a mimetic form of communication which gives rise to a shared world of symbolic meanings. In the rhythmic motions of dance, different modalities of iconic representation become fused with one another.[21] However, ritual behaviour differs from other iconic representations in its peculiar self-referential character: rites do not refer to a jointly identified 'something in the world'. The third arrow of the triadic structure points nowhere – at any rate, as long as we try to identify an object or state of affairs in the visible, objective world as what is experienced and intended. The referent of this self-enclosed communication is not something palpable but is instead situated in another dimension. The disruptions to which ritual practices respond arise from within the social collectivity and are specifically bound up with the susceptibility to disruption of a communicative form of socialization.

The gestural communication that arose in contexts of cooperation is in the first instance a response to challenges of a cognitive kind. With the opening to jointly interpreted empirical events placed at a distance, the receptive human mind is exposed to an overwhelming flood of information which must be processed. In each case, the new must be integrated into already known contexts. However, only to the extent that the representational function of language became detached from contexts of social cooperation and that grammatical language became differentiated did the human mind confront the challenge of processing the overwhelming wealth of observations in the – as Lévi-Strauss admiringly observed – quasi-scientific form of mythical worldviews. However, the entry into the public world of symbolic forms is not only a cognitive challenge. The change-over from interactions steered by emotions and triggered by signals among conspecifics who, in acting intentionally, remain trapped in their egocentric perspectives to interactions among group members who have to cope *cooperatively* with empirical contingencies represents another challenge. This requires a revolution in how behaviour is coordinated. The changeover to cooperation amounts to a revolution in the individual's relations to his social environment, in the course of which egocentric consciousness is drawn into the communicative socialization of individuals who are becoming aware of their own intentionality.

This revolution exerts the pincer pressure of simultaneous socialization and individualization characteristic of symbolically structured forms of life on the individual's consciousness. While the onus of coordinating action falls increasingly on communicative action, and hence on the individuals' own consciousness, the latter become aware that the reproduction of their own lives depends essentially on collective self-assertion and effective social coordination. In this dependence on the shared objective mind, however, subjective consciousness also becomes aware of itself *as* individual consciousness. Thus, the individual must have encountered the complex social organism simultaneously as the threat of an overwhelming, consuming force and as the promise of a redemptive force which guarantees survival and security. From the perspective of the individual, the power of the collectivity had to be simultaneously repelled and kept intact.

The crisis experience of being suspended without support between an existence under the sway of the collectivity which nevertheless has to be 'accomplished' individually is built deeply into the reproduction of social life and into the ontogenetic development of each individual. It found a literary echo in Rousseau's description of the social contract as an act of individual self-alienation and simultaneous self-assignment of the individual to society. This figure of thought is instructive insofar as the social contract refers to that layer of basic norms which bring about a legitimate settlement of the conflict between the individual and the community. The normativity of the obligating force of such rules of action goes beyond the inherent weak normativity of linguistic conventions. If we are looking for a generator of this strong normativity that binds motives for action, ritual behaviour presents itself as a plausible candidate.

Durkheim described ritual practices under the aspects of the regeneration of social solidarity and of the self-thematization of society. Our analysis reveals a surprising connection between these two aspects. That rites do not refer to something in the world can be explained by the fact that they process a self-referential theme, namely, a crisis intrinsic to the processes of social integration which breaks out in pressure situations. According to my proposal, in the evolution of our species this crisis can be traced back to the changeover in cognition and the coordination of action from the pre-linguistic to the linguistic level of communication, whereby the socialization of intelligence goes hand in hand with an individuating socialization of the cooperating subjects themselves. This explains the conflict inherent in the socialization of the motivational structures of individuals. In any cooperating community there is a tension between competing and yet complementary imperatives – that of the self-preservation of individuals on one side and that of the survival of the collectivity on the other – which is held in check, but not mastered once and for all, through the evolutionarily new normativity of an institutionalized order which imposes obligations on everybody. The tension is structural in nature and requires an ongoing balancing between individual and collective imperatives of self-preservation. In view of this precarious balance, which is in constant need of stabilization, rites can be understood as those social practices from which the normativity that grounds solidarity originated in the early periods of social evolution.

Every destabilization of the delicate internal balance of society calls forth a practice in which the individual members reassure themselves of their dependence on the powerful collectivity. This kind of reassurance assumes a self-referential form because the referent is not something visible in the world to which one can point with one's finger. According to my hypothesis, the referent, the higher powers which are invoked, arose with the transition to a new level of communication and to a corresponding socialization of cognition and motivation. The socialization of intelligence leads to the institution of the new authority of the transsubjective language logos; simultaneously, the dialectical process of individual socialization assumes the form of creative destruction which condemns the old identities to extinction. The individuating effect of the linguistic mode of socialization turns the latent problem of striking a precarious balance between individual and community into a permanent problem.

VII The Transformations of the Sacred Complex

If we conceive of the ritual regeneration of social solidarity as an answer to disturbances in the precarious balance of social integration, a possible explanation also ultimately suggests itself for the emergence of the sacred complex, hence for *the subsequent connection* between myth and rites. Whether myths merely decipher the meaning of rites or arose completely independently from them, in the first instance they fulfil the cognitive function of world interpretation. This is why they are not immune to cognitive dissonances that arise when they clash with mundane knowledge. They cannot permanently shield the coherence of their interpretations against contradictory experiences. Therefore, when it comes to their further role in confirming collective identity and solidarity, they are more part of the problem of social integration than its solution. Therefore, connecting mythical narratives and ritual practices in such a way that the mythical contents are staged and enacted, as it were, was certainly functional. But, given the fundamentally irreconcilable conflict between the functions of rendering the world intelligible and of confirming a collective identity, this linkage could in the long run have only a postponing effect. At any rate, during the Axial Age the major world religions undermined the foundations of myth by superseding magical thought and abolishing (or inverting) sacrifice.[22] And in the meantime this religious-metaphysical thinking has had in turn to make its peace both with the claims to knowledge of the institutionalized sciences and with the claims to legitimacy of the secularized authority of the constitutional state. On the other hand, ritual practice has survived, albeit in a transformed guise. The sacred complex has not disintegrated and religious traditions have preserved their vitality in their symbiosis with the liturgical practices of worldwide religious communities. Their members can even lay claim to a privilege. Religious communities, in performing their rituals, have preserved the access to an archaic experience – and to a source of solidarity – from which the unbelieving sons and daughters of modernity are excluded.

II
POSTMETAPHYSICAL THINKING

4

THE NEW PHILOSOPHICAL INTEREST IN RELIGION

A Conversation with Eduardo Mendieta[1]

EM: *Over the last couple of years you have been working on the question of religion from a series of perspectives: philosophical, political, sociological, moral and cognitive. In your Yale lectures from the autumn of 2008, you approached the challenge of the vitality and renewal of religion in world society in terms of the need to rethink the link between social theory and secularization theory. In those lectures, you suggest that we need to uncouple modernization theory from secularization theory. Does this mean that you are taking distance from the dominant trends in social theory in the West, which began with Pareto, continued through Durkheim, and reached their apogee in Weber, and thus also from its explicit and avowed Eurocentrism?*

JH: We should not throw out the baby with the bathwater. The debate over the secularization thesis in sociology has led to a revision especially in respect to prognostic statements. On the one hand, the system of religion has become more differentiated and has limited itself to pastoral care – that is, it has for the most part lost *other* functions. On the other hand, there is no global connection between societal modernization and religion's increasing loss of significance, a connection that would be so close that we could expect religion to disappear. José Casanova, for example, has developed interesting new hypotheses in the still undecided dispute over whether the religious United States or the largely secularized Western Europe is the exception to a general development trend. In any case, we must expect that the world religions will remain vital at the global level.

In view of the consequences of which you speak, I consider the programme of the group around Shmuel Eisenstadt and its comparative research on civilizations to be promising and informative.

In the emerging world society, and concerning the social infrastructure, there are, as it were, by now only modern societies, but these appear in the form of multiple modernities because the major world religions have exerted major power to shape culture over the centuries, a power they have not lost entirely by any means. As in the West, these 'strong' traditions also paved the way in East Asia, in the Middle East, and even in Africa for the development of cultural structures that confront each other today – for example, in the dispute over the correct interpretation of human rights. Our Western self-understanding of modernity emerged from the confrontation with our own traditions. The same dialectic between tradition and modernity is repeating itself today in other parts of the world. There, too, societies and cultures fall back on their own traditions to *confront* the challenges of societal modernization rather than to *succumb* to them. Against this background, intercultural discourses about the foundations of a more just international order can no longer be conducted one-sidedly, from the perspective of 'first movers'. These discourses must become habitual under the symmetrical conditions of mutual perspective-taking if the global players are to finally bring their social-Darwinist power games under control. The West is one participant among others, and all participants must be willing to be enlightened by others about their respective blind spots. If there is one lesson to be learned from the financial crisis, it is that it is high time for the multicultural world society to develop a political constitution.

EM: *Let me come back to my original question: If we can no longer explain modernization in terms of secularization, how then can we speak about societal progress?*

JH: The secularization of state power is the hard core of the process of secularization. I see this as a liberal achievement that should not get lost in the dispute among world religions. But I never counted on progress in the complex dimension of the 'good life'. Why should we feel *happier* than our grandparents or the liberated Greek slaves in ancient Rome? Of course, some people are luckier than others. Like a ship on the high seas, individual fates are buffeted by an ocean of contingencies. And happiness is as unjustly distributed today as it ever was. Perhaps something has changed in the course of history in the subjective *coloration* of existential experiences. But no progress alters the crises of loss, love and death. Nothing mitigates the personal pain of those who live in misery, who feel lonely or are sick, who experience tribulations, insults or humiliation. This existential insight into anthropological constants, however, should not lead us to forget the historical variations, including the indubitable historical progress that exists in all those dimensions in which human beings can *learn*.

I do not mean to dispute that much has been forgotten in the course of history. But we cannot *intentionally* revert to a stage prior to the results of learning processes. This explains the progress in technology and science, as well as the progress in morality and law – that is, the decentring of our ego- or group-centred perspectives when it comes to resolving practical conflicts in non-violent ways. These social-cognitive kinds of progress already refer to the further dimension of the increase in reflection – that is, the ability to step back behind oneself. This is what Max Weber meant when he spoke of 'disenchantment'.

The (for the present) last socially relevant advance in the reflexivity of consciousness can in fact be traced back to Western modernity. In early modernity, the instrumental attitude of the state bureaucracy towards a form of political power which was largely bereft of moral norms represented such a reflexive step, as did the instrumental attitude, which appeared around the same time, towards nature objectified in accordance with methodological principles, which first made modern science possible. I am thinking, of course, primarily of steps of self-reflection which gave rise, in the seventeenth century, to social contract theory and autonomous art, in the eighteenth century to rational morality and the internalized religious and artistic forms of expression of pietism and romanticism, and, finally, in the nineteenth century, to historical enlightenment and historicism. These cognitive advances had widespread effects – and cannot be easily forgotten.

It is also in connection with these influential advances in reflection that we have to view the progressive disintegration of traditional popular piety. Two specifically modern forms of religious consciousness emerged in addition: on the one hand, a form of fundamentalism that either withdraws from the modern world or turns aggressively against it; and, on the other, a reflective form of faith that adopts a relation to other religions and respects the fallible insights of the institutionalized sciences as well as human rights. This faith remains anchored in the life of a congregation and should not be confused with the new, de-institutionalized forms of fickle religiosity that have withdrawn entirely into the subjective domain.

EM: *For over two decades already, you have been arguing for an enlightenment of philosophical thinking in terms of 'postmetaphysical thinking'. You have characterized postmetaphysical thinking in terms of the rearticulation of reason as procedural – that is, thoroughly linguistified – and at the same time historically situated, which has led to the deflation of the extraordinary. Postmetaphysical thinking, thus, is parsimonious, fallibilistic, and humble in its claims. In your recent work, however, you claim that postmetaphysical thinking forces us to take the next step – namely, the post-secular step. You talk about a 'post-secular world society' as a sociological condition, as a socio-cultural fact. In what sense, then, is post-secular reason catalysed by social developments and in what sense is it the result of the inner dynamic of postmetaphysical thinking?*

JH: Your question alerts me to a terminological ambiguity. The widespread fashion of distinguishing all kinds of new phenomena from familiar phenomena merely by the preposition 'post' has the disadvantage of indeterminacy. Postmetaphysical thinking as I conceive it also remains secular in a situation depicted as 'post-secular'; but, in this different situation, it may become aware of a secularistic self-misunderstanding. It seems I should have guarded against the misleading equation of 'postmetaphysical' with 'post-secular'.

In considering Kant to be the first 'postmetaphysical' thinker, I simply follow a convention. His 'transcendental dialectic' ends the bad habit of applying the categories of the understanding, which are tailored to inner-worldly phenomena, to the world as a whole. This devaluation of essentialist statements about nature and history as a whole is one of the far-reaching consequences of the 'nominalist revolution' of the High Middle Ages and early modern thought. The anthropocentric turn towards the world-constituting achievements of subjectivity or language – that is, the paradigm shift to the philosophy of consciousness and the philosophy of language – can be traced back to this revolution as well. Already in the seventeenth century, the objectifying natural sciences led to the separation of practical and theoretical reason. This separation in turn provoked the attempts of social contract theory and rational morality to justify obligations and worldviews on the basis of practical reason alone, rather than from the 'nature of things'. Finally, with the emergence of the human sciences in the early nineteenth century, a historical mode of thought became established which – up to a point – devalues even these transcendental approaches. Furthermore, the results of hermeneutics confront us with a split in our epistemic access to the world: the lifeworld that discloses itself to our understanding only as (at least virtual) participants in everyday practices cannot be described from the natural-scientific perspective in such a way that we could recognize ourselves in this objectifying description.

The sciences emancipated themselves from the guidelines of philosophy in *both* directions: they condemn philosophy to the more modest business of retrospective reflection on, first, the methodological advances of science and, second, the presumptively universal features of those practices and forms of life which are without alternative for us, even though we find ourselves in them as a contingent matter. In other words, the place of the transcendental subject is taken by the uncircumventable universal structures of the lifeworld in general. Along the paths of a *genealogy of modern thought*, which I have merely sketched here, a differentiation took place to which the strong, metaphysical claims fell victim. We can also think of this differentiation process as a process of selecting those reasons that alone still 'count' for postmetaphysical thinking. By contrast, the statements concerning essences typical of metaphysical contemplation of the cosmos and the categories of reasons that metaphysical thinking could mobilize have been *prima facie* devalued.

The expression 'post-secular', by contrast, is not a genealogical but a sociological predicate. I use this expression to describe modern societies which must assume that religious groups will continue to exist and that different religious traditions will remain relevant, even if the societies themselves are largely secularized. Insofar as I use the predicate 'post-secular' to describe, not society itself, but a corresponding change of consciousness within society, it can also be used to describe a change in the self-understanding of the societies of Western Europe, Canada or Australia which are largely secularized. This is the reason for your misunderstanding. In this case, 'post-secular', like 'postmetaphysical', refers to a caesura in the history of mentalities. But the difference is that we use the sociological predicate as a description from the observer's perspective, whereas we use the genealogical predicate from the perspective of someone who shares in the goal of self-understanding.

I choose the discussion about the secularization thesis only as a starting point for a question that aims to clarify the self-understanding of postmetaphysical thinking. For the nominalist revolution had a further implication, namely, that, in the seventeenth century, theology lost the connection with contemporary science that Aristotle's philosophy of nature, with its teleologically structured worldview, had offered it. Since then, philosophy has sided with the sciences and more or less ignored theology. At any rate, since that time the onus of proof between religious and secular arguments has been reversed. Even the philosophers of German idealism, who *assimilated* the heritage of the Judeo-Christian tradition, simply took for granted their authority to assert what is true and false in religious contents. They too still considered religion to be essentially a configuration of the past. But is it?

Besides *empirical* evidence that religion remains a *contemporary* intellectual formation, philosophy finds *internal* grounds for this in its own history. The long process of translating essential religious contents into the language of philosophy began in late antiquity; we need only think of concepts such as the person and individuality, freedom and justice, solidarity and community, emancipation, history and crisis. We cannot know whether this process of appropriating semantic potentials from a discourse that at its core remains inaccessible has *exhausted* itself or whether it can be continued. The conceptual labour of religious writers and authors such as the young Bloch, or of Benjamin, Levinas and Derrida, speaks in favour of the continuing productivity of such a philosophical effort. And this suggests a change in attitude in favour of a dialogical relationship open to learning with *all* religious traditions, and a reflection on the position of postmetaphysical thinking *between* the sciences and religion.

This reflection has a twofold thrust. On the one hand, it turns against a secularist self-understanding of philosophy that aspires to merge with science or to become a science itself. Every assimilation to the sciences cancels the reflective dimension that distinguishes philosophy's task in forming a self-understanding from research. The methodologically oriented sciences direct themselves without mediation to their object domains, thus without reflexive verification of the inevitable contribution of science's own research practices to its results. They have to pretend to look upon the world from nowhere. This self-forgetting is acceptable. It becomes a problem only when philosophers dress up as scientists and surreptitiously totalize the object domains of the sciences – that is, extend them to the world as a whole. For the 'nowhere' that is then still assumed without reflection, and from which hard-core proponents of scientism project their naturalistic worldview, is nothing but the clandestine accomplice of the vacant 'divine standpoint' of metaphysics.

On the other hand, we should not blur the difference between what it means to take something to be true in the domains of faith and knowledge respectively. Even if thinking about the post-secular situation should lead to a changed attitude towards religion, this revisionism should not alter the fact that postmetaphysical thinking is a secular form of thought and insists on the distinction between faith and knowledge as two essentially different modes of taking-to-be-true. I repeat: the term 'post-secular' can be applied, at most, to the situation in which secular reason enters into a relationship with a form of religious consciousness that has become reflexive. The dialogue between Jaspers and Bultmann can serve as an example of such a relationship.

EM: *In your manuscript 'The Sacred Roots of the Axial Age Traditions', you offer us a sweeping and synoptic overview of anthro-*

pological and social theory in order to explore the relationship between myth and ritual. You set out to demonstrate that symbolic interaction has its anthropological roots in ritual practices. While you acknowledge the difficulty of acquiring archaeological evidence for the priority of ritual to mythological narratives, you do seem to argue that the propositional dimensions of linguistically mediated interaction go back to the evolution of ritual, which, at the very least, we know antedates their symbolic representation in the form of cave paintings. Are you suggesting that before humans became Homo sapiens, *we were* Homo ritualis?

JH: You are referring to a chapter of a work in progress.[2] In it, I take up an old theme again in the light of new investigations: the origins of language – that is, of the use of symbols that have the *same* meaning for the members of a collective. During the vast expanse of time during which *Homo sapiens* evolved, our ancestors must have had the use of symbols at their disposal, at the latest, when groups organized their cooperation and social coexistence by means of symbolically generalized kinship relations – that is, when they lived together in families. In kinship systems, all parents, uncles and children are assigned *the same* status as parents, uncles and children. Since grammatical languages have a complex structure that – *pace* Chomsky – cannot have emerged overnight, today we assume instead (or, better, again) the existence of a prior level of gestural communication which was not yet propositionally differentiated. And, evidently, the ritual practices we know from cultural anthropology belong to this level, even if they are distinguished from everyday communication between a sender and a recipient by their strangely circular and self-referential structure. Thus there is reason to believe that, in terms of developmental history, ritual is older than mythical narratives, which require a grammatical language. Be that as it may, this time I am interested in the complex of ritual and myth, not for the purposes of social theory (as in the *Theory of Communicative Action*) but because ritual survives in the communal cult practices of world religions. When we ask today what distinguishes 'religion', in this narrower sense of the still formative 'strong' traditions, from other worldviews, then these practices are the answer.

Religions do not survive without the cultic practices of a congregation. That is the 'unique distinguishing feature' of religions. In modernity, they are the only configuration of spirit or intellectual formation that still has access to the world of experience of ritual in the strict sense. Philosophy can recognize religion as a *different* and yet contemporary intellectual formation only if it takes this archaic element seriously, *a fortiori* without devaluing it. After all, ritual has been a source of social solidarity for which neither the enlightened morality of equal respect for all nor the Aristotelian ethics of virtue and the good life provides a real, motivational equivalent. This of course in no way precludes the possibility that this source, preserved for the time being by religious communities and often used for politically questionable ends, will one day run dry.

EM: *In this same manuscript you make the following claim:*

> *I would like to examine whether the common origin of metaphysics and monotheism in the revolution of worldviews of the 'Axial Age' also transforms the perspective from which postmetaphysical thinking encounters religious traditions which continue to make their voices heard effectively in debates over the self-understanding of modernity. Perhaps the self-understanding of philosophy in relation to religious traditions, and to the phenomenon of faith and piety in general, would change if it learned to understand the contemporary constellation of postmetaphysical thinking, science and religion as the result of a learning process in which 'faith' and 'knowledge' (at least viewed from the perspective of their history in the West) have engaged one another. Admittedly, we pursue this genealogical trace as modern 'Western' contemporaries.*

There are actually several claims here, but I want to ask you about only two in particular. On the one hand, are you claiming that postmetaphysical thinking deceives itself if it does not acknowledge its common origins with monotheism – in other words, that self-reflexive thinking must acknowledge its common roots with the great Axial Age religions?

JH: The narrow secularistic self-understanding of a 'scientific' philosophy that sees itself exclusively as the heir of Greek philosophy and as a natural adversary of religion involves a certain self-deception. It is wrong in several respects. First of all, it fails to recognize the religious character of the Platonic origins of philosophy: the ascent to the ideas is a genuine path to salvation, which sets Greek philosophy apart, as we can also see in Pythagoras or Empedocles, as a phenomenon parallel to other East Asian cosmologies and religions (such as Confucianism and Buddhism). However, philosophy never took root in the ritual practices of the Greek polis, and with Aristotle it soon took on a worldly and scientific orientation. This may explain why the path to salvation through contemplation could merge with the Christian path to salvation in the monastic culture of the Middle Ages – most readily, of course, in Christian mysticism.

Secondly, the narrow secularistic self-understanding suppresses the conceptual traces, mentioned above, left in philosophical thought by the monotheistic traditions via the symbiosis of Greek philosophy with Pauline Christianity. The nominalist revolution in medieval thought paved the way for the emergence of modern science, for humanism, and for the new epistemological and rational-law approaches, as much as for Protestantism and the secularization [*Verweltlichung*] of Christianity – that is, for what the Catholic Church originally understood by 'secularization'. (Chuck Taylor has recently emphasized this in his study *A Secular Age*.)[3] Insofar as these complex developments can also be understood as learning processes from which no reasonable path leads back to a point prior to them, our self-understanding simply *expands*.

By the way, such an *expanding* genealogy means that the alternative presented by Carl Schmitt and Hans Blumenberg is pointless. The political and intellectual formations of modernity are not *merely* a result of secularization which *remains* dependent on its theological roots – for, in that case, we would not have *learned* anything. Nor is the thinking that since then has operated under the premise *etsi deus non daretur* (i.e., 'as if there were no God') merely a result of the separation from the theological heritage to which it remains in opposition. For the levels of this genealogy that have been critically overcome are subsumed as such into the postmetaphysical self-understanding that sees itself as a result of learning processes. Consciousness-raising critique goes hand in hand with redemptive memory.

EM: *The second question that is suggested by your claim has to do with how postmetaphysical thinking that has, through self-reflexivity about its origins, overcome its secularistic mentality is related to a modern, rather than a Western, attitude. Do you consider the formation of postmetaphysical thinking which has overcome this perspective as an achievement that is relevant only to the West or as an achievement that has universal human relevance?*

JH: This alternative is perhaps a little too simple. Again, it is only secularism that misleads philosophy into understanding itself as science. Philosophizing is a scientific activity; but when we attach the predicate 'scientific' to philosophical argumentation we do not mean that this generalizing activity of philosophy in forming a self-understanding can be *reduced* to science. The royal road in philosophy is self-reflection. That is why it is a discipline but not a 'normal' science alongside other sciences. And this is why it is not equally indifferent to comparable philosophical attempts at self-understanding in *other* cultures. On the other hand, of course, self-understanding regarding postmetaphysical thinking also aims at the differentiation of an intercultural 'space of reasons'.

In this, however, we must distinguish carefully between, on the one hand, philosophical analyses – that is, proposals concerning the correct understanding of the kind of reasons that today can *prima facie* expect to 'count' interculturally – and, on the other, the arguments that are actually used in the corresponding intercultural attempts at self-understanding, which provide the material, as it were, for such a retrospective philosophical analysis. To this extent, you are right: the attempted reconstruction of postmetaphysical thinking is a metaphilosophical proposal which should apply not only to the Western but to the contemporary way of thinking in general. Like all other philosophical contributions, this one is also exposed to critical discussion among disciplinary peers. On the other hand, when we *participate* with such a self-understanding in intercultural discourses about some *specific* political or legal topic, we assume the stance of 'second persons' towards participants from other cultural backgrounds. Then we do not conduct ourselves as philosophers who want to discover the characteristics of presumptively universally acceptable reasons but, instead, direct our attention to the problems to be solved *themselves*. In this *performative* role, we may also, of course, learn from intercultural debates that some aspects of our reconstruction of postmetaphysical thinking may be informed by Western biases and are in need of correction. After all, fallibilist consciousness is integral to postmetaphysical thinking itself.

EM: *You return to Karl Jaspers's genealogical theory of the Axial Age, partly because in his proposal that we find a global, rather than a restrictively Eurocentric, approach to the cognitive accomplishments of humanity. Indeed, the Axial Age allows us to think of cognitive and cultural accomplishments in terms of a global learning process that belongs to the human species as such, and not only to one civilization. Reading your recent texts, one is left with the strong impression that you assume that we are on the threshold, or perhaps in the thick, of something like a new Axial Age. Is the rise of a 'post-secular world society' an anticipation or expression of a new Axial Period?*

JH: Simplifying greatly, the worldview development of the Axial Age exhibits an advance in reflection in three dimensions: historical consciousness develops with the dogmatization of a doctrine that can be traced back to founding figures; interpersonal relations can be grasped as a whole and judged in accordance with universalistic moral principles from a transcendent viewpoint internal or external to natural processes in the world; and the consciousness of personal responsibility for one's own life develops because individual fates become separate from those of the collective. This can also be described as a process of differentiation of lifeworlds that goes hand in hand with an increase in social complexity: a reflexive relation to traditions and to social integration develops which now reaches beyond kinship groups and even beyond political borders; the relation of individuals to themselves also becomes more reflexive. A further cognitive advance in the *same* dimensions can be observed in modern Europe. The awareness of contingency and the anticipation of the future become more acute, egalitarian universalism in law and morality becomes more radical, and individualization becomes more pronounced. At any rate, we still draw our normative self-understanding from this advance (occasional short-winded, fashionable denials to the contrary).

Even though there are certain evolutionary thresholds, we should not, of course, view this as a linear development. The postcolonial encounter with other cultures during the twentieth century brought to our attention the wounds of colonization and the devastating consequences of decolonization, and thus also the shocking dialectic of higher-level reflexivity. Today we are in transition to a multicultural world society and are struggling over its future political constitution. The outcome is completely open. To me, global modernity looks like an open arena marked by disputes from the standpoints of different paths of cultural development over the normative structuring of more or less shared social infrastructures. It is an open question whether we will succeed in overcoming the atavistic condition of the social-Darwinist 'catch as catch can', still dominant in international relations, to the point where unbridled and wild global capitalism can still be tamed and channelled in socially acceptable ways.

EM: *I would like to take the bait of that critical reference to unchained and rapacious capitalism, but that is a topic for another conversation. You argue that postmetaphysical thought must be critical of secularist seductions, and that a way of holding in abeyance such a temptation is to approach the question of religion as a 'contemporary intellectual configuration' that cannot be properly understood if it is observed solely from the epistemological standpoint. In order to overcome this 'cognitivistic' reduction of religion, you turn to the study of ritual and myth, and you write: 'Today when the members of the religious community perform their ritual practice they seem to be seeking assurance of a source of solidarity that is no longer accessible by any other means.' Can it not be claimed that non-religious citizens have been able to engage in 'ritual practices' that are non-religious, and in which they can find assurances of solidarity? Take, for instance, the practices of volunteering to do voter registration, or political canvassing, marching on Washington, working in soup kitchens, visiting inmates in prisons, helping build houses for the homeless. There is a plethora of non-religious 'rituals' – let us call them 'civic rituals' – that can be said to give all citizens access to this sense of solidarity that you think religious citizens alone have access to.*

JH: In his book *After Progress*, Norman Birnbaum has described the religious roots of the motivations driving those socialist and progressivist movements in the US and Western Europe that contributed to shaping the social history of the West for more than a century, until the collapse of the Soviet regime. These social movements were, according to their own self-understanding, thoroughly atheistic. One could speculate that, in this sense, civic involvement, even among non-religious citizens, in many cases preserved some of the edifying and disburdening character of participation in the Sunday worship of a congregation. As we know, volunteerism is one of the outstanding features of political culture in the United States. What volunteerism reveals seems to be less the similarity between religious and civic *ritual* than the enduring potential to motivate of a religious socialization that often remains effective at an unconscious level.

I am not a supporter of the widespread fashion among sociologists of applying the very specific concept of ritual to any form of repetitive behaviour whatsoever. On the contrary, the rituals described by anthropologists seem to derive their power to generate solidarity essentially from those ideas and experiences which are grounded in a very peculiar form of communication. The latter is distinguished, in the first place, by the *lack of a relation to the world* of a self-referential form of communal practice that circles around itself and, in the second place, by the *holistic semantic content* of an undifferentiated, not yet propositionally articulated use of different iconic symbols (such as dance and song, pantomime, jewellery, body painting, etc.). I stick to my assertion that, today, only religious congregations keep open the access to archaic experiences of this sort through their cultic practices. These experiences remain closed to those of us who are tone deaf when it comes to religion; we have to be content with aesthetic experiences as a highly sublimated substitute. This analogy led Peter Weiss to seek political hope in an 'aesthetics of resistance' – that is, in the eye-opening and solidarizing power of forms of art that 'spill over into life'. Even if this hope, which was inspired by surrealism, has faded in the meantime, it would of course be foolish to trust *blindly* in the power of religion to motivate opposition to the destruction of solidarity by neoliberalism. As we know, the motivational powers of religion give rise to highly ambivalent political effects. Constitutional democracy is not compatible with all forms of religious practice, only with non-fundamentalist ones.

EM: *You have been arguing that the secularistic ideology of modern constitutional democracies deprived their public spheres of semantic contents that are indispensable to the moral health of their polities. For this reason, you advocate greater tolerance, or even an accommodation within the public sphere, of the kinds of arguments that religious citizens could make. Now, from the perspective of the US, your call for a post-secular public sphere is in fact very reminiscent of what already takes place. What if I were to say about your proposal for a post-secular public sphere what Rorty said about Rawls, namely, that his political liberalism was the philosophical-political articulation of the political practices of US citizens? In other words, what your theory expresses is a very local practice, namely, the kind of civil religion and acculturation through denominational identification that is unique to the US.*

JH: I understand how this impression could arise. My criticism is directed against the laicist understanding of the separation of church and state. This reflects a European view of the ethics of democratic citizenship. In your country, in which the president publicly prays in office, a criticism informed by *the same principles* should aim in the opposite political direction. In my view, the position that the political influence of religious voices should not be subject to any formal constraints, which enjoys widespread currency among our American colleagues, blurs the boundaries without which a secular state cannot maintain its impartiality. There must be guarantees that the decisions of the legislator, the executive branch and the courts are not only *formulated* in a universally accessible language but are also *justified* on the basis of universally acceptable reasons. This excludes religious reasons for decisions about all state-sanctioned – that is, legally binding – norms. Apart from that, I do not believe that secular citizens can learn anything from fundamentalist doctrines that cannot come to terms with the fact of pluralism, with the public authority of science, and with the egalitarianism of our constitutional principles. On the other hand, you are right that the political cultures of our various Western societies are already so different that these universal principles governing the public role of religion – and, in general, what we in the West call the 'separation of church and state' – would have to be specified and institutionalized *differently* in each local context.

EM: *Now, in your essay 'What Is Meant by a "Post-Secular Society"? A Discussion on Islam in Europe', in your recent book* Europe: The Faltering Project, *you refer to three phenomena that can explain the change in consciousness that you call 'post-secular'. First, the way in which the global media continually impress upon global subjects the ceaseless role of religion in fostering both conflict and reconciliation; second, the ever-growing awareness of how religious convictions shape and direct public opinion through their interventions in the public sphere; and, third – and this is where I want to focus my question – by the way in which 'European societies' have not yet made the 'painful transition to postcolonial immigrant societies'.[4] Are you suggesting, then, that post-secular consciousness could lead to a postcolonial type of citizenship, in which citizens are linked as equals, regardless of their race and religious convictions?*

JH: There certainly is a connection between the emergence of post-secular consciousness and the new migration flows that pose two fundamental problems for nation-states. First, the naturalized immigrants from a different culture must be integrated socially and economically, and they must be given space to affirm their collective identity. Second, non-naturalized, in part illegal aliens who do not enjoy citizenship rights have to be put on an equal footing with national citizens, at least when it comes to their civil legal status. This problem arises today, for example, in the United States in relation to the reform of the health-care system, which was originally supposed to include illegal residents as well.

    Classical immigrant societies cope better with the first problem than European societies that opened themselves primarily either to immigrants from their own colonies (for example, Great Britain and France) or to foreign workers (for example, Germany). In European societies, which are much more homogeneous – also when it comes to religion – constitutional principles have up to now been applied in the light of the respective national cultures. However, increasing cultural and worldview pluralism explodes this fusion. We learn that the abstract legal principles which promise all citizens equal rights have to be detached from what the majority culture hitherto implicitly took for granted. One example is the verdict of the German Constitutional Court about crucifixes in the classroom. Instead of banning minarets, a more wide-meshed political culture has to develop and grow beyond the respective majority culture, so that *all* citizens can find a place in it. The other problem is caused by the uncontrolled influx of economic immigrants and refugees. If I am not mistaken, all states have difficulties with the legalization of 'back-door' immigration. Logically speaking, your proposal concerning postcolonial citizenship would point to an unlimited right to asylum for immigrants of all kinds. Even disregarding the xenophobic reactions ('the boat is full') that are common everywhere, I would not consider such a proposal to be feasible, if only for economic reasons. Rather, this burning issue directs our attention to the development of a more just international order. The constitutionalization of international law would promote a political constitution for the multicultural world society and thus enable a global domestic politics that could tackle the root of worldwide migratory flows – that is, not merely combat the results of immigration but the causes of emigration. As a general rule, people do not emigrate for pleasure and out of pure thirst for adventure.

EM: *You have been leading a seminar here at Stony Brook University in which we are studying the works of Carl Schmitt, Leo Strauss, Johann Baptist Metz and John Rawls. I wonder if you can share with us your own goals in studying some thinkers who (with the exception of Rawls) are as far as anyone can be from your own philosophical intuitions and positions.*

JH: I am interested in whether one can give an innocuous meaning to the normatively charged concept of 'the' political, despite the various misuses of its metaphysical and theological connotations.[5] *Pace* Derrida, the concept of 'the' political no longer seems to find any reasonable place alongside the concepts of the 'political system' and 'politics' used in social science. In a descriptive sense, this concept refers first to the symbolic field with whose help the early societies organized as states formed an image of themselves. 'The political' refers to the symbolic representation and collective self-confirmation of those early civilizations that differ from tribal societies, which are integrated through *spontaneous, quasi-natural* mechanisms, by, among other things, the turn to a reflexive political, and hence *conscious*, form of social integration. The evolution of a new complex of 'law' and 'political power' gave rise to a completely new need for legitimation at that time: it is by no means obvious that one person, or a handful of persons, can make decisions that are collectively binding on all. Only by establishing a convincing connection between political authority and religious beliefs and practices could the rulers be assured of the law-abidingness of their peoples. While the legal system is stabilized by the sanctioning power of the state, political rule has to draw on the legitimizing power of sacred law in order to be accepted as just. It is in this symbolic dimension that the legitimizing alloy of politics and religion takes shape to which the term 'the political' can be properly applied. 'Religion' derives its legitimizing power from the fact that it has roots of its own *independent of politics* in notions of salvation and misfortune [*Heil und Unheil*] and in corresponding practices of dealing with redemptive and protective forces [*heilsstiftende und Unheil bannende Mächte*].

But we owe the first *conceptions of 'the political'* to the nomos thinking [*Nomosdenken*] of Israel, China and Greece and, more generally, to the articulatory power of the metaphysical and religious worldviews which emerged at that time. The reference to a divinity beyond the world or to the immanent vanishing point of a cosmic law liberates the human mind from the grip of the narratively ordered flood of events controlled by mythical powers and makes possible an individual quest for salvation. Once this transformation occurs, the political ruler can no longer be perceived as the manifest *embodiment* of the divine but only as its human *representative*. As a human person, he is henceforth also *subordinated* to the nomos against which all human action is measured. Finally, in the West there developed the improbable constellations that made possible both the ascent of Pauline Christianity to the Roman state religion and the productive confluence of theology with Greek metaphysics. Only in terms of these historical contexts can the mode of thought geared to the concept of 'the political' be explained whose threads Leo Strauss and Carl Schmitt were able to pick up and develop in different ways. The former took his orientation from Greek political philosophy and Christian natural law, the latter from a form of political theology which has left profound traces in the Christian West since the days of Augustine.

However, these highly developed conceptions of 'the political' had lost their 'setting in life' under the completely transformed conditions of the modern period. Nevertheless, Strauss wanted to keep open the dimension of the political even under modern conditions by drawing directly on classical natural law, while Carl Schmitt identified in the sovereign rule of the early modern state a reformed structure of the unifying power of 'the political'. From his historical standpoint of an 'epoch of statehood' that was coming to an end, he wanted to renew the concept of the political under conditions of authoritarian mass democracy. In my view, both conceptions failed, though we must be careful not to confuse Schmitt's clerical fascism with Strauss's admirable hermeneutical revival of classical natural law. However, the concept of 'the political' retains a peculiar pertinence in the face of the challenge posed by 'post-democratic' developments which displace politics, understood as a possible means for actively promoting an egalitarian and inclusive form of societal integration, from public consciousness. This too may explain the subliminal topicality of Strauss and Schmitt, whose theories are being appropriated uncritically even on the left and, in this crude form, often enough poison political thought.

By the way, it is no accident that I am taking up this topic under conditions in which voices of protest are being intimidated into paralysed silence. I am astonished by the absence of any kind of spontaneous protest against the glaring social injustice of multibillion-dollar bailouts of banks at the expense both of future taxes and rising unemployment and of the public and private impoverishment especially of those social classes, sectors and domains of life that are in most urgent need of government services.

This is why I wanted to examine in our joint seminar with reference to the counter-example of John Rawls's political liberalism whether, after all, we can still attach a rational meaning to the evocative concept of 'the political' under the sober conditions of liberal constitutional democracy. To at least hint at this thesis, we need a clear grasp of an implication of the fact that the secularization of the state must not be confused with the secularization of civil society. As long as religious traditions and organizations remain vital forces in society, the separation of church and state in the context of a liberal constitution cannot result in the *complete* elimination of the influence of religious communities from democratic politics. To be sure, the secularization of state power demands a constitution that is neutral among worldviews; and it requires that the collectively binding decisions structured by the constitution should be impartial towards competing religious communities and ideological groupings. But a constitutional democracy, which explicitly *authorizes* citizens to lead a religious life, may not at the same time discriminate against these citizens in their role as democratic co-legislators. For a long time this air of a paradox has stirred up *ressentiment* against liberalism – unjustly, unless one equates political liberalism with its laicist interpretation. The liberal state may not censure the expressions of religious citizens already in the political public sphere – that is, at the root of the democratic process; nor can it control their motives at the ballot box.

In this respect, how a liberal political community understands itself as a collective should not remain unaffected by the pluralism of worldviews in civil society. To be sure, the content of religious expressions has to be translated into a generally accessible language before it can make it onto official agendas and flow into the deliberations of decision-making bodies. But religious citizens and religious communities remain influential precisely where the democratic process *originates* in the encounter between religious and non-religious sections of the population. As long as politically relevant public opinions are nurtured by this reservoir of the public use of reason on the part of religious and non-religious citizens, it must be part of the collective self-understanding of *all* citizens that democratic legitimation achieved through deliberation is *also* nourished by religious voices and debates stimulated by religion. In this sense, the concept of 'the political' which has been *shifted* from the state to civil society retains a reference to religion even within the secular constitutional state.

EM: *As a follow-up, I have been pleasantly surprised to hear in our seminar discussions that you have a different take on Schmitt vis-à-vis Strauss, on the one hand, and Metz, on the other. There are, as you expressed it, two forms of political theology: one that is anti-Enlightenment and another pro-Enlightenment. Could I say, then, that Metz's version of political theology embodies the kind of post-metaphysical religious enlightenment that you advocate in your own political philosophy? Is Metz your ideal religious post-secular dialogue partner?*

JH: That is a bit too simple, but it is not entirely mistaken. Metz's great merit is to have thematized the sensitivity of postmetaphysical thinking to time without succumbing to contextualist fallacies and in such a way that the theme can serve as a bridge to contemporary theology. A younger generation of Catholic theologians has emerged in Germany, in part through Metz's influence, which no longer shares the view expressed by the pope in his Regensburg speech. Its members begin their theological reflection, as it were, *after* Kant's critique of reason, and hence do not lament nominalism as the gateway to modernity's history of decay. Rather, they also recognize in postmetaphysical schools of thought the learning processes from which the corresponding ways of thinking emerged.

5

RELIGION AND POSTMETAPHYSICAL THINKING

A Reply

I am indebted to Craig Calhoun, Eduardo Mendieta and Johann VanAntwerpen for their initiative in inviting a select group of outstanding colleagues to engage in an informed discussion of my scattered works on the theme of 'Postmetaphysical Thinking and Religion'.[1] The results of a vibrant conference are helpful to me as an author because the interesting objections and proposals, coming in the midst of my work on a pertinent project, confront me with new ideas, alert me to overhasty assumptions, and force me to clarify my thoughts. On the other hand, the fortunate circumstance that a birthday with a zero provided an occasion for discussing ideas *that are still in flux* also has its drawback. The participants had to refer to a position that is not yet sufficiently developed. Therefore, I am entirely responsible for the need for explanation, which I would like to meet as far as is possible within the scope of a brief response. I owe a major debt of gratitude to my colleagues for their attentiveness and their patient reading and, above all, for their (in certain cases renewed) willingness to engage in a detailed debate.[2]

I 'Stages' of Religious Development

The contemporary developments that have provoked a controversy which has continued for two decades over the relation between religion and social modernization are not the focus of – though they do provide an important stimulus for – my renewed engagement with the prominence currently enjoyed by religious movements and traditions. José Casanova[3] is one of the most inventive among those sociologists who from an early date argued forcefully for revising the hypothesis, which long dominated the discipline (and to which I at the time also adhered), that the progressive modernization of society and the continued viability of religious communities stand in a zero-sum relation. I find his theses, which he recapitulates here, as impressive as his responses to critics.[4] But I lack the expertise to offer more than this impression of the dispute among the experts.

I use the expression 'post-secular' as a sociological description of a shift in consciousness in largely secularized or 'unchurched' societies which have in the meantime adjusted to the continued existence of religious communities and expect religious voices to be influential both in the national public sphere and on the global political stage. In the present context, Casanova is concerned not so much with the empirical claim that secularistic consciousness is on the wane in such societies. He is interested more in the empirical refutation of the secularist conception itself and denies that religious convictions and practices are essentially expressions of a historically obsolete stage of consciousness. He also finds me suspect in this respect because he interprets my philosophical use of the term 'postmeta-physical' as an attempt to justify a form of secular thought which, even though it rejects naturalistic reductions of the human mind and its cultural objectifications, nevertheless refuses to recognize religion as a contemporary intellectual formation. This misunder-standing can be explained by the fact that José Casanova is critical of the 'consciousness of stages' [*Stadienbewusstsein*] that *also* finds expression in secularistic consciousness. But not *every* attempt to uncover learning processes and advances or 'stages' in the geneal-ogy of worldviews – as articulated in the huge variety of cultural traditions – leads *eo ipso* to a questionable devaluation of religious forms of thought informed by a philosophy of history.

For me, whether religious communities will remain viable in the future is an open question, and in this regard I find Casanova's extrapolations, conducted under the heading of 'global seculariza-tions', entirely plausible.[5] In my view, those religious interpretations of the self and the world that have adapted to modern social and epistemological conditions[6] have as much claim to belong to the legitimate discourses of modernity as the contemporary compet-ing approaches of postmetaphysical thinking. Religious traditions differ from philosophy in their mode of belief and in how they justify taking-to-be-true, but above all in the fact that the ritual practices of a religious community provide a stabilizing anchor for faith. It is precisely the historical 'simultaneity' of the forma-tions of secular thinking and of religious consciousness, which in the meantime have diverged into polar opposites, that leads me to explore the shared genealogy of postmetaphysical thinking and the major world religions. For what still sets philosophy apart from the objectifying sciences today is the self-referential question about how we as human beings should understand ourselves (and how 'modernity' should be understood). I would like at least to mention why I consider an evolutionary perspective in terms of 'stages' in the development of worldviews to be fruitful. In Casanova's view, contingent changes in the external 'conditions of faith' are sufficient to explain historical thresholds such as the emergence of the major world religions in the Axial Age or that shift in the religious self-perception of European societies that Taylor locates in the Reformation era. I do not believe, however, that the structural transformation of religious worldviews and of the corresponding ritual practices can be explained entirely in terms of *accommodations to changed social environments*. Rather, they can be traced back also, and perhaps primarily, to *internal* learning processes that respond to cognitive challenges though they are triggered by social upheavals. At the turn to the third millennium of the pre-Christian era, literate cultures emerged within the first societies organized as states and exerted considerable pressure to change on the oral traditions of tribal origin.[7] The organization of religious worship became the preserve of the state and was made to serve the legitimation of royal rule. At the same time, the mythical narratives were brought into conformity with the political hierarchies in such a way that the centralized pantheons of the gods mirrored political reality. In spite of the pressure to adapt that these profound ruptures in social development exerted on traditional myths and tribal rituals, neither the cognitive structure of mythical worldviews nor the magical mode of thought and ritual underwent significant change over the following two millennia.

It was the well-known metaphysical worldviews and world religions which arose around the middle of the first millennium in China and the Indus Valley and in Israel and Greece that first made the breakthrough to a transcendent point of view, whether in the guise of a monotheistic deity or of a cosmic law. This cognitive advance (to which Robert N. Bellah has devoted a comprehensive study)[8] cannot be adequately explained as an accommodation to changes in the social conditions under which religious communities deal with forces of salvation and perdition [*Mächte des Heils und Unheils*]. The new worldviews instead represent productive answers to cognitive challenges. Only the moralization of '*Heil*' and '*Unheil*', of propitious and unpropitious forces, which had hitherto appeared *within* the world, into a God or godhead who *transcends* the world as a whole could satisfy the minds of prophets, monks, hermits and wise teachers whose moral consciousness revolted against the irresponsibility of capricious gods. They had in the meantime developed new moral sensibilities and standards when faced with the suffering inflicted on the broader population by the repressive and belligerent authorities in the ancient empires. At that time, the educated classes of the first literate civilizations had developed a consciousness of history and a reflexive approach to texts. These intellectuals had also accumulated technical and organizational expertise as well as mathematical, astronomical and medical knowledge. This mundane knowledge inevitably came into conflict with mythological explanations and magical practices. The cognitive dissonances could be resolved only within the more encompassing theological or cosmological conceptual framework of one or other of the Axial Age worldviews. Moreover, the sublimation of the sacred into a transcendent power went hand in hand with distinct paths to salvation, which in turn involved an ethical reinterpretation of the traditional rites and the abolition (or, later on, the inversion)[9] of the magical meaning of sacrifice.

With his insightful remarks on the history of concepts, José Casanova traces the subsequent development of worldviews in the West through which Pauline Christianity entered into a symbiosis with Greek philosophy during the Roman Empire. I found only one aspect of his terminological clarification of the expression 'secular' problematic. In reference to the late Roman imperial period, when the majority of the population continued to make sacrifices at the numerous altars to their deities, while the Christian minority refused to observe the official political rites that were binding for all, Casanova describes how the pagan majority and the Christian minority perceived each other as follows: 'The Christian sacred was the pagan profane and vice versa.'[10] Aside from the fact that those who had a Greek education, and who as Epicureans or (as in Cicero's case) Stoics made fun of the popular religion, constituted a third party,[11] this description implies a relation of symmetry between Christians and pagans that did not exist. The Christian category of 'heathenism' not only expressed rejection of 'idolatry' and polytheism but also betrayed a radical repudiation of a concretistic mode of thought which remained fixated on natural events in the world also when it came to religious conceptions. On the other hand, for the pious worshippers of the Roman gods, it was utterly incomprehensible why the God of the Jews and Christians should not be regarded as comparable with Jupiter, as were Zeus and the other Oriental high gods.[12] This asymmetry is an example of the cognitive transformation that the mode of faith and devotional practice underwent in response to cognitive challenges which cannot be adequately explained in terms of *changed social conditions of belief*. It is the Christians themselves who exhibited something akin to a consciousness of stages by comparison with the 'heathens'. Perhaps the dubious sense of superiority felt by secularists towards religious faith even represents a continuation of the attitude of the early Christians towards paganism. In order to criticize this stance, however, one need neither deny nor play down the importance of stages in the development of religious consciousness.

The transition to modernity constitutes a watershed in the development of religion in the West similar to the Axial Age. Here, too, the internal dynamic of knowledge played an important role. For in the High Middle Ages the Church and theology initiated developments in canon law with the 'papal revolution'[13] and in science with the 'nominalistic revolution'[14] which escaped their control and in the end exploded the framework of both Christian natural law and Aristotelian natural philosophy. With the stubborn moral orientation of the modern legal system and the stubborn empirical orientation of the modern sciences, there developed profane forms of knowledge which retroactively influenced their theological and metaphysical origins. At first sight, it seems as though both the autonomy of morality, rational law and modern science and the secularization of political authority triumphed with the philosophical assault on the waning authority of the Church and of religion in general. On closer consideration, however, these complex developments involved just as many cognitive challenges for the secular philosophical as for the theological side. It is certainly true that theology gradually broke the connection between the message of redemption and the cosmological worldview of the Greeks and absorbed the results of philological criticism of biblical sources, while the Church had to learn to make its peace with the secularized constitutional state. But philosophy underwent an equally profound change when it entered into an alliance with science and the secular state. For its part, it had to revise the metaphysical heritage in the light of an all-pervasive fallibilism and to distance itself from the 'strong' theoretical claims of the teleological view of Greek metaphysics.

Religious consciousness which 'reformed' itself ('reformed', that is, in a non-confessional sense) and postmetaphysical thinking which developed a 'critique of reason' (in both senses of the genitive case) without becoming defeatist[15] are in the final analysis *complementary* answers to *the same* cognitive challenges of the Enlightenment, which was nourished by secular sources of knowledge. This complementarity establishes a contemporaneity between the two intellectual formations which precludes the devaluation of religion along secularistic lines as long as theology can understand its task as being to interpret a vital faith rooted in some form of worship of a religious community. For in this way it upholds under modern social conditions the connection to an archaic source of social solidarity to which secular thought no longer has access.

For secularly minded individuals such as ourselves, only aesthetic experience still contains trace elements from this largely dried-up source. On the other hand, postmetaphysical thinking can claim the advantage that it operates in a universe of unreservedly justifying discourse *that is open to all equally*. Understood in this way, post-metaphysical thinking does not fit the phenomenologically rich, but insufficiently differentiated picture of a philosophical understanding of the self and the world 'devoid of transcendence' that Charles Taylor sketches under the heading of the *immanent frame*. With the moral law, Kant had already explicated a moral point of view that ties the judgements of practical reason to a *transcendence from within*. The theory of communicative action detranscendentalizes the Kantian ideas of reason when it explains the success of linguistic communication in terms of the discursive redemption of validity claims; however, these claims, although they are raised locally, point to a *context-transcending* validity.[16] I am convinced that human forms of civilized social life can neither be established nor maintained without this kind of self-transcendence that creates distance from occurrences in the world.

II Why a Secular Translation of Religious Potentials at All?

Maria Herrera Lima[17] is so well acquainted with my work and develops such a judicious and multifaceted critique that I will be able address only a couple of aspects here.[18] Moreover, her remarks on social evolution and on the legacies that we discuss under the heading of 'secularization' concern a topic to which I will return.[19] I, too, prefer to use the expression 'profane' in a neutral sense to refer to the 'worldly' – i.e., non-religious – spheres of life, for the simple reason that the development of religious worldviews was repeatedly driven forward by the assimilation of pragmatic knowledge. Here, I must confine my remarks to the issue raised by Maria Herrera with the wonderful quotation from Adorno, which affords me an opportunity to clarify the underlying issue. Adorno's ambiguous formulation that 'nothing of theological content will persist without being transformed; every content will have to put itself to the test of migrating into the realm of secular, the profane',[20] touches on several issues. One is whether religion 'survives'; another is whether semantic contents can be detached from religious traditions and acquire independent significance for the social integration of democratic societies as such. Without being able to make predictions, my assumption is

- that, under the premises of postmetaphysical thinking, we do not have any reason to deny the possibility of a *continued* 'migration of theological contents into the secular, the profane'; and
- that it depends on our (admittedly tentative, empirically more strongly or weakly supported) diagnoses of the present whether we regard such a transformative assimilation or translation as desirable.

The first part of this statement presupposes a Hegelian perspective on the history of philosophy, albeit a deflationary one corrected in the light of Jaspers's concept of the Axial Age. We have to be able to draw on past examples of the migration of theological contents into profane cultural domains. However, the source of Maria Herrera's misgivings is more the substance of the claim. If I am not mistaken, she interprets Charles Taylor's description of the state of religious consciousness in our secular age[21] as asserting that, in what appears as 'the other' (even though this has in fact long since been assimilated), modernity encounters only itself. But if faith has also merely become an option in the wake of the expressivist turn 'from obedience to pleasure', there is no reason to assume that semantic potentials *which have not yet been exhausted* remain valid in such assimilated religious communities. I do not have a lot to contribute to the empirical assessment of the relevant phenomena. Yet the impact of the most recent stage of 'individualization' on the evaporation of religious substance may be relativized if we choose a somewhat broader historical horizon.

In the development of religion, the differentiation into public worship of the gods, on the one hand, and the privileged relation of individuals to particular deities, on the other, can be traced back to the era of the Babylonian and Assyrian empires and to ancient Egypt. The next stage of individualization is reflected in the moralization of the sacred and in the corresponding routes to salvation of the Axial Age religions. Finally, a further advance in the subjectivization of piety was accomplished in the West by Protestantism, especially by the pietist movements that flourished from the end of the eighteenth century onwards. Thus, when it comes to evaluating the 'new' de-institutionalized religious movements of the present, it is not easy to distinguish between a continuation of this trend towards a deepening and spiritualization of religiosity and its opposite, the trivializing trend towards mere self-realization and inner-worldly 'human flourishing'. Maria Herrera reserves the term 'internal secularization' for the latter trend towards a self-centred ethos. Only if we could keep these trends apart and measure their relative empirical weights could we gauge Maria's objection that the religious potentials have been 'used up', as it were. If this assumption were correct, religious tradition would forfeit the very solidarity-founding element of a communal practice of religious worship that sets it apart from all other cultural formations in the modern era. A religion that had lost the capacity to organize the encounter with the sacred in the form of rituals and survived only in fleeting forms of religiosity would be indistinguishable from other ethical forms of life.[22] So far, I can find no convincing evidence for a comprehensive development in this direction.

More interesting is the doubt about the second part of the above statement. Even assuming that religious traditions contain buried semantic contents that, in the modern age, have not yet been absorbed by critical reasoning on crises, by conceptions of moral universalism, or by different ethical interpretations of autonomy, ego-identity, individuation, and so on, why should we, as secular members of contemporary societies, take any interest at all in this heritage? The general analysis of contemporary developments according to which the resources of social solidarity are drying up in the course of the accelerated functional differentiation and the increasing autonomy of social subsystems is far from providing new and startling insights. This diagnosis is as old as sociology itself. The associated suspicion motivated programmes in social theory from Émile Durkheim and Max Weber up to Talcott Parsons and needs to be qualified in ways that I cannot address in the present context. This much seems plausible, however: the systemic problems of the emerging multicultural world society, with its national upheavals and international conflicts, have not yet been mastered. For the time being, they outstrip the integration and steering capacities of the nation-states and especially the established forms of coopera-tion in democratic countries, and thus suggest that an old topic has acquired renewed relevance. Moreover, history teaches that in modern societies only social movements bring the relevance of new challenges to the attention of a broader public. They force new issues onto the political agenda and implicitly shift the parameters of the range of values defining the spectrum of what can be per-ceived as topics that call for political treatment. As is shown not only by the first half of the twentieth century, social movements are certainly ambivalent; but without the pressure for innovation they exert, new normative patterns do not emerge either. Where did their motivations come from? Looking back over the progressive, socialist movements to which Western countries ultimately owe the containment of class conflicts by the welfare state, authors such as Norman Birnbaum discover the *unacknowledged* motivating role played by religious socialization which could still be taken for granted at the time.[23] Also in societies marked by high levels of individualization which reward primarily the economic success, opportunistic competition for power and self-realization – and thus the egocentric mindsets – of their 'achievers' and consumers, many children have the good fortune to grow up in families in which they acquire a finely tuned moral sensibility. Maria Herrera makes the correct empirical observation that, in moral matters, religious citizens behave no differently from members of non-religious groups. But the question that interests me is not situated at the level of individual actions and motives. At the level of cultural resources, the normative self-understanding of modernity is expressed primarily in the scientific orientation to truth, the egalitarian universalism of law and morality, and the autonomy of art and criticism. The question I want to ask is the following: Is the potential of this admirable and, let us hope, resilient Enlightenment culture sufficient under conditions of rapidly increasing social complexity to motivate the kind of collective action, of action *in social solidarity*, which is required in times of crisis if social movements are to develop?

I am far from being able to answer this question, but I have my doubts. Maria Herrera is quite right to focus on them, but she does not address the precise point I have in mind. Assuming that the Kantian ethics of duty (however this is interpreted) reconstructs the intuitive kernel of conceptions of political justice that are justified 'from reason alone', and thus that it captures what we can legally and morally expect from each other in terms of self-criticism and understanding in cases of conflict, then the *political* deficiency of that kind of individualistic approach towards rational morality becomes apparent.[24] This should not be confused with a general motivational deficiency. In an attempt to avoid this error, I would first like to distinguish the two deficiencies more clearly, beginning with the *motivational deficiency* usually bemoaned by critics of Kant.

Ideally, someone acting responsibly is aware that she finds herself in a culturally defined 'space of reasons' and that she should be equally open to reasons *pro* and *contra*: she should form her practical judgement by weighing up relevant reasons (in the moral case, ones based on universalizable interests). Then the person who is forming a judgement must *make* the reason that tips the scales in cognitive terms *her own*. If my will is to be determined by reasons, then moral insight must be supplemented by the volitional moment of agency. 'I could have acted otherwise', but it is 'up to me' whether

I act on the better reasons. Because Kant had too much confidence in the power of good reasons to motivate and attached too little importance to the volitional moment of making good reasons one's own, the deontological approach is open to the objection that rational will-formation 'lacks the power to motivate'. I do not find this objection convincing. It is the task of philosophy to explain what it means to examine something from the moral point of view. But philosophy cannot take responsibility for the cultural traditions and processes of socialization, or for the institutions, that must *anchor* the moral point of view in the hearts of acting subjects.

The *political deficiency* I have in mind is instead a result of the individualistic orientation of all modern ethical conceptions. There are good reasons why rational morality recognizes only duties that are addressed to the conscience of the individual and require him or her to act responsibly. In a well-ordered democratic polity, this orientation to duties is completely sufficient as long as it is a matter of routinely responding to problems through reforms. But in times of crisis, when the existing institutions and procedures are no longer able to cope with the pressure of problems, the parameters of the established range of values must first undergo a change.[25] Achieving this requires collective action in Hannah Arendt's sense, namely, joint action that gives rise to communicative power. An ethics of justice is not tailored to *solidary* action of this kind, however; thus it cannot make solidarity *per se* into a duty but can only hope that solidarity will arise as a consequence of individuals fulfilling their duties. I don't want to be misunderstood on this subtle point: there are good reasons why rational morality appeals only to the individual's capacity to bind her will by moral insight; no rational morality can *extend* this appeal to pluralistic collectivities as such – that is, to collectivities composed of individuals who must remain capable of taking independent 'yes' or 'no' stances.

To be sure, with every supposedly valid moral norm we associate the presupposition of rational consensus that could be achieved among all potential addressees of that norm; but the act of making good reasons one's own – that is, the moment of moral agency – could be *socialized* only at the cost of the autonomy of the individual. Interestingly, the practice of religious communities bridges this *fault line of the individual facilitation* of solidarity in advance in the shared belief in the promise of a '*redemptive*' or '*liberating*' justice. Since the Axial Age, this belief has found expression in religious traditions and in corresponding practices of encountering the sacred. This additional dimension of justice must not be confused with the eudaemonistic dimension of an ethics of the good or the good life. The redemptive moment of the impending kingdom of God, or the liberating moment of release from the cycle of rebirths, is not exhausted in personal happiness; rather, *against the background of a widespread awareness of crisis*, it acquires the meaning of a collective fate that affects humanity as a whole. In this process, the sense of crisis was more the triggering condition than itself the force for social integration.

Under the heading of 'Progress versus Providence', Karl Löwith interpreted the philosophies of history of the Enlightenment and the nineteenth century as attempts to appropriate the religious way of dealing with crises in secular terms.[26] These speculations, including the underlying assumptions of the Marxist philosophy of history, have long since been exposed as involving the transposition of the teleology of traditional natural law from the natural sphere into the dimension of history. And the rather ambivalent political potential of this approach is clear to everyone. However, this has not dissuaded some contemporary philosophers – for example, Jacques Derrida – from attempting to recover the religious motif of 'critique and crisis' at a different level of reflection.[27] If we take Derrida's proposal for a 'fiduciary administration' of religious contents by a 'reflected faith' at its word, then it is merely a contemporary version of the old idea of a 'religion of reason' on which the numerous 'positive' religious traditions are supposed to converge. By contrast, Adorno's insight that any theological content that is supposed to achieve universal acceptability in modern pluralist societies 'must migrate into the secular, the profane', requires strict observance of the boundary between the discourses of faith and knowledge.[28] I can reassure Maria Herrera that a 'translation' conceived in postmetaphysical terms can by no means be purchased at the cost of returning to the unity of a 'substantive' concept of a reason embodied in history or nature. And I regard it as an open question whether the political deficiency of rational morality *can* be counterbalanced through a continuing philosophical appropriation of unexhausted religious contents.

III On the 'Secularization Debate' within the Humanities in Post-War Germany

Under the heading of 'Political Theology' to which Carl Schmitt lent currency, Maria Pia Lara[29] takes up a topic that recalls the historical connection between religion and politics.[30] This tradition gave rise to the strong concept of 'the' political that certain contemporary postmodern theorists, following Claude Lefort, contrast with constitutional 'politics' and the 'policies' pursued by the actors within the 'political system'.[31] After the secularization of political authority had dissolved the symbiosis between religion and politics, this religiously connoted concept was set free, as it were, for a quite different constellation. Today the term is used in connection with Hannah Arendt's concept of communicative power to refer to those spontaneous and inspiring counter-currents that can emerge within civil society and the public sphere against a highly bureaucratized form of politics. The political-theological heritage of the concept inclines us to ask what religious traces 'the' political has left behind in contemporary post-secular society. However, I do not want to address this question again in the present context.[32] Maria Pia Lara mainly addresses a debate that touches on Carl Schmitt's theory of the 'transposition' of theological concepts into concepts of modern political theory but essentially concerns another topic, namely, the self-interpretation of Western modernity in relation to the ancient European traditions, be they Greek or Christian. This controversy has nothing to do with the secularization thesis in sociology. It does not concern how 'secularization' is understood in social theory but focuses instead on the contribution of the humanities to clarifying whether monotheism has bequeathed anything at all to modern thought and, if so, what. This controversy addressed by Maria Pia Lara provides a suitable backdrop for a rough sketch of my own interpretation of these legacies.

Karl Löwith (1897–1973) initiated the debate with the first German edition of his work *Meaning in History* (1949), which was published in 1953 under the title *Weltgeschichte und Heilsgeschehen* and was one of the most influential books for my generation. Carl Schmitt's (1888–1985) *Politische Theologie* had already appeared in 1922, but with his 1970 sequel *Politische Theologie II* he garnered renewed attention for a position he continued to develop during the 1920s and 1930s. Both authors dramatized the interpretation of modernity as a history of decline from a perspective they shared with conservative thinkers of the same generation such as Leo Strauss and Martin Heidegger. For all of these thinkers, 'secularization' was a pejorative term – though, of course, this was all that they shared (quite apart from their sharply contrasting political biographies). The diagnoses of the present offered by Karl Löwith, the emigrant, and by Carl Schmitt, the Führer's 'crown jurist', focus attention on different periods in the history of ideas under different aspects.

For Löwith, the kind of historical thinking that began with Judaic eschatological thinking and became secularized, via Christian speculation on the ages of the world, in the philosophies of history of the Enlightenment, represented on the whole an ill-fated deviation from the proper cosmological thought of classical Greece. On this interpretation, the modern notion of progress exposes secularized versions of the history of salvation in general as the fatal turn to the erroneous historical consciousness of the modern mind. It is not secularization as such that points the development in the wrong direction; but secularization first reveals the dire consequences of the breakthrough to monotheistic belief in a 'God in history'. For the committed Catholic Carl Schmitt, by contrast, 'secularization' is something more than merely a catalyst. For Schmitt, the expression acquires its pejorative connotation from the unjust expropriation of the legal power of the Christian ruler by the revolutionary forces of the liberal bourgeoisie and socialism. From the perspective of the history of salvation adopted by political theology, Roman-Christian imperial rule since Constantine and the Christian kingdom of the early modern European states amalgamate into a *saeculum*; and the continued existence of this Christian *saeculum* had been placed in question, from the French Revolution onwards, by the secularization of political authority – that is, by the dissolution of the divinely ordained symbiosis between politics and religion. Carl Schmitt was sympathetic to Donoso Cortés's radicalization of the counter-revolutionary interpretation of history according to which atheism congealed into sheer violence, especially in the anarchism of a Bakunin.

However, in Carl Schmitt's view, a supposed structural similarity between basic concepts of theology and the conceptual frame of early modern public and international law lend the term 'secularization' the additional but, in this case, conservative meaning of the preservation of a Christian continuity through transformation. From the nostalgic historical perspective of a twentieth-century constitutional lawyer on the disintegration of the early modern system of sovereign territorial states, the secularization of divine omnipotence into the conception of state sovereignty of classical international law had also acquired a redemptive significance. On Carl Schmitt's interpretation, the unity of 'the political' preserved in the sacred aura of the medieval emperors had had a chance of surviving under modern conditions only in the guise of the absolutism of Christian kings to which Hobbes erected a monument with his *Leviathan*. This redemptive continuity was supposed to have come about through the secularizing assimilation of the medieval pattern of legitimacy into the divine right of absolutist rulers. For a thinker of the younger generation, Hans Blumenberg (1920–1996), it was precisely this alleged continuity that represented a prime instance of the 'delegitimation of the modern age'. Blumenberg vehemently opposed Carl Schmitt's view on secularization in his work *The Legitimacy of the Modern Age*.[33] To the traditionalist Catholic reading he opposed the thesis that there was a sharp discontinuity between religious and secular thought. Against Schmitt (and against Löwith), he affirmed the independent legitimacy of a modern age that draws upon its own resources in overcoming the ancient European traditions.

The key issue in this controversy is whether the anthropocentric turn during the early modern period should be recognized or rejected. Concerning the 'transfer' of eschatology into the profane 'ledger' of progress, for example, Blumenberg asserts: 'the crucial question is still whether this situation [i.e., the eschaton] is to be brought about immanently or transcendently, whether one can achieve it by the exertion of one's own powers or has to rely for it on a grace that cannot be earned.'[34] In response to the traditionalist critique that the self-empowerment of a finite mind goes too far and should be brought back under the sway of divine authority, Blumenberg appeals to the self-consciousness of an autonomous mind backed by scientific and technological successes which relies exclusively on rational self-preservation. According to Blumenberg's interpretation, the appearance of continuity is merely a reflection of the unsatisfied interest in solving philosophical problems with which the modern mind has to wrestle once again under different premises, because theology bequeathed these problems without solving them. Secularization is not reflected at the semantic level in a 'conversion' of theological contents into secular ones. Rather, the backlog of still smouldering problems leads simultaneously to the systematic devaluation and a merely metaphorical employment of a theological vocabulary that brings the new answers under the sway of the old questions. And because Blumenberg fears that this involves the danger of obfuscating the new, he prefers to speak in terms of a 'reconfiguration' [*Umbesetzung*] rather than of a 'conversion' [*Umsetzung*] of inherited concepts.

The post-war German debate on secularization continued to be shaped by the polarizing controversy over the 'value' or 'worthlessness' of modernity to which Maria Herrera also alludes. The controversy over the 'legitimacy' of the modern age was by no means confined to the political sphere to which Carl Schmitt attached primary importance. Blumenberg more generally resists the idea of a 'cultural debt' that modernity supposedly has to discharge to its religious past. Today, this dividing line has completely lost its relevance. One can instead identify cognitive and even moral-cognitive learning processes reflected in cultural traditions and worldviews without having to claim superiority for the actual moral behaviour or the ethical forms of life of later generations. I cannot discern anything like 'progress' in a form of personal moral *action* that is always tied to particular contexts, and certainly not in the complex dimensions of the 'not-misspent life' – and to try to make descriptive comparisons between such factors over long historical spaces of time strikes me as absurd. The claim that the decentring of our perspectives when it comes to mundane knowledge or making considered judgements on issues of justice exhibits progress is a different matter. Examination of the long rhythms of such learning and progress in knowledge reveals cognitive developments that bear on changes in the patterns of valid argumentation, in the standards in terms of which propositions are justified, and in general in the dispositions to respect the 'burdens of reason' (Rawls).

These changes have become so natural for later generations that they are assumed to be irreversible. Blumenberg appeals to this characteristic of learning processes when he insists, contra Carl Schmitt, that the rationalism of the Enlightenment is no longer in need of justification *as such*.[35] This is why, when translating semantic contents from religious traditions into secular language, the question doesn't even arise as to whether the secular side makes itself dependent on the theological side when it raises claims to validity. If Blumenberg had not been fixated in a negative way on the monotheistic doctrines, he could have been more relaxed in his response to Schmitt's and Löwith's narratives of decline. But none of the three parties to the debate took into consideration Jaspers's concept of the Axial Age, which had affirmed the co-originality of monotheism and Platonism and the structural similarity between them. Otherwise Löwith and Schmitt would hardly have been able to propagate the wholesale return either to the cosmological thought of the Greeks or to the eschatology of the Church Fathers, and Blumenberg would not have felt any need to wrestle with the objection that theology in fact accommodated itself to the advances of modern sciences without having to join with modern philosophy in making the anthropocentric turn. Blumenberg misunderstood the nature of the learning processes out of which modern philosophical thought and a 'reformed' religious consciousness evolved simultaneously. This *simultaneity* enables them to enter into a dialogue in which postmetaphysical thinking can aspire to 'translate' theological contents without having to confront the question of the relative 'value' of the one or the other side.

It is odd, by the way, that Blumenberg did not address the question of the secularization of political authority, since this process is at the heart of Carl Schmitt's denial of the legitimacy of the modern age. Morality, law and politics remain blind spots in Blumenberg's justification of the independence of the modern age.[36] The fact that the constitutional revolutions of the late eighteenth century were inspired by ideas of social contract theory is an example of the dialectical appropriation of a religious heritage that gainsays Blumenberg's alternative according to which modernity is either the heir of tradition and remains dependent on it or repudiates tradition and thereby achieves its independence. On the one hand, aside from Stoic sources, human rights owe their egalitarian universalism to the secular translation of Jewish and Christian ideas of the equal worth of every person in the eyes of God; the egalitarianism and universalism of social contract theory would be unthinkable apart from the anthropocentric reversal of the world-transcending viewpoint of the Last Judgement into the moral point of view which transcends all partial standpoints from within the world. On the other hand, without this transformation it would not have been possible to overcome the limits to which the mutual toleration of religious communities is subject wherever the believer's perspective remains centred on the absolute truth of the teachings of his own community. Blumenberg closed his mind to the fact that the legitimacy of the modern age, conceived as a result of learning, reaches beyond the achievements of modern science to include the moral justification of the principles of the constitutional state. The insight into the twofold character of learning processes as both 'extending' and 'overcoming' also prepares the ground for the modernized concept of *the* political to which Maria Pia Lara appeals to ensure that religious voices are accorded a legitimate place in the post-secular civil society of constitutional states.

IV   What is Meant by a 'Genealogy' of Postmetaphysical Thinking?

The post-war debate just discussed is fundamentally hampered by its narrow focus on free-floating connections in the history of ideas which are considered in isolation from their broader social and cultural contexts. The Axial Age revolution in worldviews and the separation between secular and religious thought in modern Europe represent caesuras in the genealogy of postmetaphysical thinking and at the same time stages in social evolution. The societies of the ancient empires were organized as states and were highly stratified. Their urban centres first enabled those forms of profane knowledge to develop which provided the impetus for critically overcoming mythical worldviews in certain more peripheral regions during periods of social upheaval. And, as research in sociology has shown, it was only with the emergence of the modern administrative state and the capitalist mode of production that the impetuses towards an increasing autonomy of law and politics, of science and philosophy, and of art and criticism from the church and theology gained momentum. This process was driven forward by the decentring effects of the differentiation of functionally specialized subsystems, and the new forms of knowledge to which it gave rise reacted back upon religion.

Amy Allen[37] offers a useful clarification from a Foucauldian perspective of the concept of 'genealogy' that informs my attempt to reconstruct the prehistory of postmetaphysical thinking. From the point of view of *rational reconstruction*, my aim is to show that this history can also be represented as a sequence of solutions to problems, whereas the *genealogical perspective* reveals the contingent historical constellations that made the actual learning processes possible. Imre Lakatos, for example, attempted to reconstruct paradigm shifts in the history of science in an analogous way.[38] This undertaking differs in several respects from Nietzsche's understanding of 'genealogy'. In the first place, it is not guided by the *subversive intention* of undercutting the repressive features of a dominant mode of thought. From my point of view, today there is no alternative to the postmetaphysical mode of doing philosophy. However, the genealogy that leads from the modern age, via the symbiosis of Greek metaphysics with Christianity, back to complementary origins in the Axial Age should serve as a corrective to a particular self-understanding of philosophy that is dominant in the profession, and by no means only among hard-core naturalists. Thus it is guided by the *problematizing intention* of enlightening *secular* thought concerning the Enlightenment's blinkered secular*istic* self-understanding.

Amy Allen is right to ask in what sense this undertaking belongs to the category of *vindicatory*, and hence justifying, genealogies. It is certainly not vindicatory in the apologetic sense that it seeks to provide a *genetic* justification of the validity of the now generally accepted postmetaphysical patterns of argumentation by tracing it back to its *origin* in unquestionably valid religious and metaphysical conceptions of the world. For in that case we would have *learned* nothing as regards our philosophical understanding of ourselves and of the world since the nominalist revolution. On such a false premise it would not be possible (as Pope Benedict XVI suggests in his Regensburg address) to identify any learning processes in those discourses on epistemology, rational natural law and morality that began at that time. In this respect I agree with Blumenberg that the postmetaphysical thinking to which these discourses gave rise operates 'without a ground' insofar as it *creates* the building blocks of its 'ground of validity' from its own resources, instead of *borrowing* them from some traditional authority. An act of *insight* that arises from working through good reasons and is not contradicted by better arguments for the time being does not need *additional* genetic justification.

The intended genealogy does not have a justificatory function but instead a critical one. It is supposed to foster reflexive awareness of the contingency of the context of emergence of the background premises of the kind of theoretical and practical knowledge that for the present may claim rational acceptability. This contextual awareness is generally expressed in the fallibilistic self-interpretation of science and philosophy, because it keeps us alert to the possible context-dependence of *prima facie* universal propositions. This fallibilistic consciousness seems to be especially relevant in intercultural discourses. The genealogy of one's own pre-understanding fosters a willingness to decentre this background and to engage in mutual perspective-taking, a disposition which every party must bring to such a discourse. The awareness of context acquires a special importance that goes beyond this fallibilism, because the genealogy of worldviews alerts postmetaphysical thinking to the fact that philosophy and religion have shared roots. Insofar as the genealogy throws light on the divergence between the secular and the religious intellectual formations – and on the complementary relation between the two that evolved in the course of this differentiation – it can present philosophy with a balance sheet of its learning processes and promote an awareness of how the two sides could *complement* each other through dialogue.

The *problematizing intention* of the undertaking focuses historical attention on the *internal* cognitive dynamic which, where appropriate, can render intelligible the complementarity between postmetaphysical thinking and 'reformed' religious consciousness as the result of learning processes. In this undertaking, portions of the political and social context play the role of contingent boundary conditions. The fact that *countervailing* processes resulting from the repressive influence of theology and the Church on culture and society are excluded from this spectrum of topics may give rise to the suspicion that this amounts to a trite 'Whig' history of progress. Only a perspective on social evolution that is sensitized to the dialectic of enlightenment would also reveal the reverse process, which, as Amy Allen rightly warns, should at least be kept in mind. Before I address the question implied by the title of her contribution,[39] I would first like to clarify two terminological misunderstandings.

'Neo-paganism' is the name adopted by an intellectual current in the Weimar period. Its adherents followed Nietzsche in arguing that monotheism was at the root of contemporary alienation and that this malaise could be healed through a return to the healthy sources of mythical thought. During the 1930s, this reading of Nietzsche also inspired Martin Heidegger, who had previously turned his back on the 'system of Christianity'.[40] From that time onwards, Heidegger sought to return to the pre-Platonic origins of ontotheology in order to recover an 'original truth' from Presocratic sources.[41] My critique of 'neo-pagan' thought is directed against the levelling of the cognitive advance from 'myth to logos' which took place during the Axial Age not just in Israel and Greece, and against forms of 'thinking in terms of origins' that seeks to reanimate supposed mythological 'truths' from the reflective standpoint of modernity.[42]

My second clarification concerns the expression '*context-transcendent*'. When used with reference to validity claims, it was meant to have the meaning of *transcending*; the emendation proposed by Maeve Cooke captures the performative meaning of the act of exceeding all contexts that is *executed* when such claims are made. In science (as already in everyday communication), when we make declarative or normative assertions we unavoidably raise claims to truth or rightness within the respective local contexts which assert a validity that goes beyond, and thus is independent of, all contexts.[43] However, thematizing such contexts, which initially remain in the background, can promote an awareness of fallibility among the participants, because making explicit potentially qualifying background assumptions broadens the spectrum of objections against the claimed universal validity. Bringing implicit qualifying contexts of emergence to awareness generally leads to the enlargement of the previously accepted perspective.

What conclusions should we draw from the reflective experience that we are repeatedly forced to correct context-bound assertions? Should we generalize this experience into the higher-level claim that all presumptively universal validity claims must be restricted to social and temporal contexts? Then we have to confront the question of the meaning of the validity of this claim. Or must 'we', when we assert that something is true, adopt the standpoint of 'everyone' and hope that the reasons which we find convincing also in the final analysis convince everyone else? Who has the final say? The objectifying (and, in this case, self-objectifying) gaze of the scientist or the performative perspective of the philosopher who knows that the self-referential process of forming a self-understanding cannot be reobjectified without becoming drawn into a meaningless and endless regress? This brings me to Amy Allen's *principled contextualism*. Her proposal is that we should subject the results of our learning processes, as reconstructed by genealogy, to a further contextualization at a metatheoretical level. Adopting a bird's-eye perspective, we should, for example, relativize the methodological atheism of postmetaphysical thinking or the egalitarian universalism of rational law and morality into something that is binding *only* 'for us' in our historical context. However, this supposed objectivity misunderstands the *irreducible* self-referentiality of genealogy. We cannot have good and, hence, context-independent reasons for taking the knowledge derived from our learning processes to be true while *simultaneously* relativizing the scope of its validity for *additional* genealogical reasons. My objection is aimed at the postulate of an unsurpassable 'view from nowhere'. The whole thrust of postmetaphysical thinking was to deconstruct the divine standpoint which by definition has the last word. Its place is taken by the impartiality of the practice of argumentation among participants to which there is no alternative. Abstracting from the participant perspective that we adopt with every truth claim is required for the objectifying sciences, but it is not allowed in the case of the self-referential philosophical process of contributing to the best available and most reasonable self-understanding.

Foregoing self-reflection for the purposes of objectification is even less an option for a genealogist who knows that she is situated within and speaks from contexts when she defends what she has learned from her reconstructive descriptions – for instance, the premises of postmetaphysical thinking – against objections. On the other hand, she would fail to take these reconstructions seriously if she did not assume for the time being that, in justifying her reconstructions, she had liberated herself from all contexts that could limit the validity of her statements. Her fallibilistic consciousness tells her that this *assumption* is not without risk, because she cannot immunize her convictions by appealing to a divine standpoint. No 'observer perspective', however neutral, can provide the appropriate meta-level for testing the premises of postmetaphysical thinking further, but only the horizontal exchange of pro and contra arguments, first within the discipline and then if possible also in intercultural debates that may compel 'us' to adopt an enlarged 'we-perspective'. Such discussions will be more productive the greater the cultural distance between the background assumptions of participants (and the more successfully they in turn have been in similar attempts to reconstruct the origins of their own cultural background).

Finally, with her point about having one's cake and eating it, Amy Allen addresses the problem that changes in religious consciousness that we describe from a secular point of view as learning processes might appear in a completely different light in the self-description of religious communities. Wouldn't even a, let us assume, successful genealogy of postmetaphysical thinking describe the modern relation between faith and knowledge in an asymmetrical fashion – that is, only in a one-sided way? This question cannot be dismissed by appealing to the shared roots in the Axial Age. But these roots offer both parties a common starting point for dialogue even if they arrive at different interpretations of their relation to each other. However, we must pay close attention to the difference between the stances we adopt when we ascribe something to another person from the observer perspective of a third person and when we communicate with a second person as a participating first person. As for the complicated relationship between postmetaphysical thinking and religious interlocutors from whom we may be able to learn something, even though we reject their theocentric view of the world, the discussion of the next two contributions may take us a step further.

V Methodological Atheism and Agnosticism

Whereas Jay Bernstein[44] is a forceful advocate of a laicist self-understanding of philosophy, Matthias Frisch attempts to introduce a strong religious motif into philosophical discourse. With my combination of methodological atheism and agnosticism, I am somewhere between these two positions. Bernstein defines methodological atheism as follows: 'The secularist can be asked to see if there is a wholly immanent rational kernel to religious beliefs, but cannot be required to give up the determining authority of secular reason over cognitive worth.'[45] I agree with this, but Bernstein rejects agnosticism when he continues: 'This is not to deny that there is an existential excess to religious belief that defies the translation procedure; *but for us that excess is not simply unavailable to philosophical reflection, it is what is permanently lost in the transition to modernity.*'[46] What 'is permanently lost' here? The agnostic asserts only that these semantic contents are *inaccessible* and refrains from judging the truth claim that believers associate with them. When an agnostic leaves a truth claim *undecided*, she expresses her failure to understand a certain kind of discourse. From her perspective, religious 'truths' are formulated in concepts that are prior to the usual differentiation into descriptive, evaluative and normative statements.[47]

I share Bernstein's methodological atheism and argue (against John Rawls, for example) that the practical reason of political philosophy, rather than the truths proclaimed by religious communities, must have the final say when it comes to justifying secular constitutional principles. But that does not prevent me from adopting an agnostic stance on the dogmatic foundations of the validity claims of an enlightened religious interlocutor. As a (in Bernstein's correct description of us both) 'young Hegelian' – that is, as a student of Hegel who thinks in postmetaphysical terms – I am aware of the long process of mutual assimilation of concepts of Greek and Judeo-Christian origin, though I cannot know whether this process can also be continued. And as a social scientist I respect the conspicuous fact that shapes the current asymmetry between the two sides: while the philosophical side draws on an exclusively knowledge-based tradition of attempts to clarify our understanding of ourselves and the world, the other side relies on the theological explication of the teachings of a *religious community founded on ritual practices.* Both sides seek to elaborate an explicit understanding of oneself and of the world. But, in religious dogma, the cognitive dimension is combined with the social dimension of membership in a worldwide association that (from the secular perspective) remains connected with archaic sources of solidarity (which are buried beyond the reach of the secular side).

On the other hand, I share with Matthias Fritsch the agnosticism that allows for a receptive dialogue with theology and thus keeps open access to potentially unexhausted semantic contents of the religious tradition. Yet I am not sure whether his specific proposal can be justified from the anthropocentric perspective of methodological atheism.

(1) The equanimity of the agnostic stance has inspired resentment. At one time, there were good reasons for the militancy of the Enlightenment. It testified to struggles for emancipation against the secular clerical power of a religious authority that for long enough lent its seal of approval to outrageous political repression and social exploitation. We could *also* recall that, in more recent times, the clergy sided with both repressive and emancipatory causes. But it would seem that some wounds are still fresh. J. M. Bernstein makes the surprising claim that the Old Testament story of Abraham and Isaac is central to Western religious spirituality.[48] Appealing to Kierkegaard, he develops a reading of this episode according to which Abraham's blind obedience to God's command to offer up his beloved son as a sacrifice – a human sacrifice! – shows that the masochistic character of faith in God is a general trait of religion. The theological justification for this reading is somewhat more interesting: 'One can only be reborn in faith if one first dies to the world. In order to die to the world one must slaughter one's living attachments to the world, one must murder one's love of the world and offer it to God. One must sacrifice Isaac.'[49] Although Bible interpretation is not my specialty, this ahistorical and biased reading, which purges religious belief as such (!) of any cognitive or moral import, incites me to four brief observations.

(a) The sacrifice required of Abraham is untypical for Judaism, which abandons the pagan practice of sacrifice and condemns it as 'idolatry'. Sacrifices were performed for magical purposes in order to propitiate a deity or a divine power. But the Hebrew Bible is as hostile to sacrifice as it is to divination, which interprets observable happenings as signs of future events, and to magic, which flouts the natural causality governing events in the world. From the perspective of Judaism and Christianity, this 'superstition' fails to comprehend the transcendent sublimity of a God who is removed from the world while governing everything that takes place within it.[50]

(b) The Hebrew Bible incorporates traditions from different periods of Jewish history; thus the compilation of texts contains traces of earlier practices, pagan residues such as the practice of trial by ordeal or the ceremony of the scapegoat, the magical use of incense, etc. But, as in the case of Abraham's sacrifice, these remnants of popular belief are *reinterpreted* from the perspective of exile or post-exile Judaism. The story of the patriarch was among the most ancient traditions of Israel and its neighbouring peoples. The unembellished literary form in which the episode is related already stands in sharp contrast to, for example, the elaborate poetry of Job's lament, which approaches the problem of the devotion of a 'servant of God' from a different angle. The question of how God could issue such an immoral command could not have arisen in the same form for the members of the tribes of Israel of the pre-kingdom period as it must have under conditions of fully fledged monotheism. For an editor around the year 500 BCE reworking the ancient Israeli teachings from the monotheistic perspective of a Deutero-Isaiah, therefore, the cognitive dissonance may have been blunted by the fact that his readers could be expected to accept God's moral integrity as a matter of course. They would have assumed from the outset that the problematic command would be revoked, and they would have read the story only from the actually thematic perspective of an experimental testing of Abraham's devotion to God.

(c) The historical reception of Genesis 22 in Western art and literature exhibits a profound disquiet mingled with fascination over the biblical traces of the long since surmounted archaic power of human sacrifice. Given the current controversy with Islam, this revulsion even leads some Christian theologians to make a plea for 'taking leave of' Abraham.[51] In contrast, a late Romantic spirit such as Søren Kierkegaard immersed himself in Abraham's torn state of mind in an attempt to recover the dimension of the promise of salvation that was lost with the transition to a secular and purely rational morality. As in the doctrine of stages of *Either/Or*, in his interpretation of the story of Abraham in *Fear and Trembling* Kierkegaard is concerned with the pivotal difference between moral consciousness and religious faith. The moralization of the demonic forces of good and evil and the turn to a transcendent deity through which Judaism overcame myth and magic did not allow the proper core of religious experience, namely, the ambivalent dread inspired by the immediate presence of the sacred, to *disappear* into the binding power of mere morality. The complex idea of God's *redemptive* justice is a synthesis of which the impersonal justice of morality constitutes just *one of two* moments. *Law-abidingness* [*Gesetzestreue*] – obedience to the moral legislator – is founded on *devoutness* [*Glaubenstreue*] – trust in and loyalty to the omnipotent saviour – *but they are not identical*. Kierkegaard's point is that devoutness must not be subsumed entirely into law-abidingness, as it is in Kant: 'The story of Abraham contains . . . a teleological suspension of the ethical', because there is 'no absolute duty *to* God' if the latter, in his primary role as a *power of salvation*, calls on the patriarch to commit a *prima facie* immoral action.[52]

(d) Jay Bernstein argues too superficially when he reads into this episode the immoral call to 'hatred of the world' and confuses this with the *liberating* distancing from the capriciousness of the mythical gods and spirits. Monotheistic thought does in fact break with the fixation of mythical thought on natural processes in the world, just as the cosmo-ethical worldviews of the Axial Age – Buddhism in the first instance – do in a different way. The Bible passes judgement on a disenchanted world from which the many immortal but corruptible deities have withdrawn because all natural processes in the world are now entirely subject to the will and the laws of a power that is prior to and underlies this world as a whole, namely, the transcendent creator of the universe.[53] Through the existential relation to that God, the believer also achieves the cognitive distance from all natural processes in the world that enables him to judge his life and that of everyone else according to the same moral standards. Even the notorious saying in Luke 14:26 acquires a positive meaning in this context.[54] Moral universalism shatters the ethnocentric bonds of familial morality: Jesus preaches the repudiation of a life that is completely absorbed *in and by the world*.

(2) Recognition of the cognitive advance that took place during the Axial Age and openness to the possibility of continuing a process of translation of religious contents into a secular language must not

mislead philosophy into adopting a mystifying *imitation* of religious pretensions, as in the case of Heidegger's 'remembrance' [*Andenken*] of being. Methodological atheism implies a commitment to a rigorous form of discursively justified discourse that forbids the surreptitious rhetorical import of theologoumena. On the other hand, the translation of difficult texts, such as Celan's poetry, requires literary exertion. This is why the terrain bordering on religion is reserved mainly for the writers with literary ambition among the philosophers, such as Benjamin and Derrida. They develop innovative concepts and leave their contemporaries in the dark as to how suited these concepts are to discursive treatment. An interesting case in point is the figure of the 'other' with which Levinas introduces an asymmetry into the relationship of obligation between ego and alter.

Matthias Fritsch[55] examines whether this figure of thought is suitable for recovering a neglected aspect beyond the egalitarian-universalistic obligations of rational morality, as expressed in the second part of the following statement: 'God's gaze addresses all equally, but at the same time each one with infinite care for the individual soul.'[56] An intersubjectivist version of Kantian ethics which includes everything that one person owes to another person and is based on symmetrical and reciprocal relations of recognition does not fully capture the theological import of such a conception. It does not take into account the demand that ego should show *overriding* concern for the well-being of alter *in her singularity*. For this devotion presupposes a kind and degree of empathy that cannot be made into a duty that can be justified in universalistic terms. From a secular perspective, what I encounter in the morally grounded expectation of others is the authority of a universal norm that can be violated and that others who are affected can require me to obey. This authority is based solely on the correct application of a reasonable norm – that is, one which deserves universal recognition, including my well-considered assent. The binding force of these norms is not yet limited (as in contractualism) by the narrow constraints of rational egoism imposed by the *quid pro quo* rationality of parties to a contract; however, the strict deontological nature of duties reflects the structure of a process of justification steered by the *reciprocal* perspective-taking and the autonomous 'yes' or 'no' of participants who enjoy equal rights in deliberation.

Matthias Fritsch quite rightly agrees with Levinas that the justification of a solidarity that *goes beyond this* 'must' or 'ought' must appeal to a different authority. Here, my encounter with the concrete other is embedded in the asymmetrical relation to something *entirely* other hiding behind the second person before my eyes. But does this Other, with a capital 'O', derive his or her appellative force from an experience that can justifiably be universalized to all human beings? I must leave it with this question. A detailed response to Matthias Fritsch's arguments would take me beyond the limits of the present discussion.

VI The Role of Religion in the Public Sphere

How philosophy should interpret its relation to religion is one question; it is another question what the role of religious communities in the public sphere of secular constitutional states looks like from the postmetaphysical perspective of political theory. The credit for high-lighting this issue goes to John Rawls, with his Kantian concept of the citizens' 'public use of reason'. The starting point of the discussion is the assumption that citizens in a democracy should offer each other reasons for their political stances. The problem is that liberal constitutions exude an air of paradox in this regard. Although they are designed to guarantee all religious communities equal freedom to participate in civil society, at the same time they shield the public bodies that make collectively binding decisions from religious influences. The same people who are expressly authorized to practise their religion and to lead a pious life are supposed, in their role as citizens, to take part in a democratic process whose results must remain free from any religious 'contamination'.

The laicist answer to this problem is to banish religion from the public arena altogether. But as long as religious communities play a vital role in civil society, censoring the voices of religious citizens already at the source of the democratic process is inconsistent with the spirit of a liberal constitution. What restrictions do religious citizens have to accept? My proposal is that the polyphonic babble of voices cannot and must not be subject to regulation already at the bottom level of public political discourse. Religious contributions have to be translated into a generally accessible language, however, before their content can find its way into the deliberations of political institutions that make legally binding decisions. Contrary to John Rawls's proposal, this institutional filter has the meaning of a translation proviso that is not imposed on each religious citizen individually but, when necessary and possible, should be satisfied in a cooperative manner. For some this proposal goes too far, for others not far enough. Cristina Lafont's insightful objections, on the one hand, and Maeve Cooke's friendly doubts, on the other, provide an opportunity to respond to both sides. These problems of religious and metaphysical pluralism arise not only at the national level, however, but have precise counterparts at the supranational level. This is the focus of Jim Bohman's remarks, which I can address only briefly.

(1) Cristina Lafont's[57] central objection is directed against one of the two obligations that follow, according to my conception, for the secular as well as for the religious side from the ethics of citizenship implicitly recognized by all loyal citizens. Whereas religious citizens might experience the translation proviso as a burden, secular citizens, *in their role as citizens*, feel the burden of another obligation, namely, not to deny *a priori* that public utterances, even ones formulated in religious language, could have a cognitive content capable of being translated. Obviously, opening the democratic process up to religious utterances would be pointless unless every citizen acknowledged that all of her fellow citizens can in principle make potentially meaningful contributions to the political debate. For a *public practice* of pure secularism would mean that secular citizens could treat certain groups of their fellow citizens at best as species in need of protection because of their religious outlook. But in doing so they would fail to take religious citizens seriously as modern contemporaries and thus discriminate against them in their role as citizens. This attitude is as incompatible with the requirement of reciprocal recognition as it is with the willingness to adopt the perspectives of others in the give and take of arguments and positions. Cristina Lafont rejects the *ethical* expectation that secular citizens should exhibit such a post-secular self-understanding in exchanges with religious citizens as unacceptable on normative grounds. She thinks that this would amount to denying secular citizens the very right that religious citizens are granted when religious utterances are admitted into the public arena, namely, the right 'to adopt their own cognitive stance'.[58] I believe, on the contrary, that this expectation follows directly from the ethical (not legal) requirement that citizens endowed with equal rights should mutually recognize one another as *participants in the joint venture of co-legislation*. However, this controversy touches only on the content of an *ethics* of democratic citizenship *which cannot be legally imposed*. Both the secular and the religious side can only hope that a complementary learning process will give rise to those cognitive attitudes that are required to satisfy the demanding obligations on either side. These attitudes cannot just be prescribed by political theory. That was my point in the relevant essay.[59]

Cristina Lafont's own proposal – 'it is the obligation of democratic citizens to provide one another with justifications based on reasons that everyone can reasonably accept'[60] – has no bite. On the one hand, it is trivial, because it boils down to the obvious requirement that every citizen, when making contributions to public political debates, should respect the limits laid down by the principles of the constitution, whose recognition is not up for discussion but is instead presupposed. On the other hand, the proposal is empty because it does not speak to the two controversial questions, namely, whether religious fellow citizens must be taken seriously in the democratic process of opinion-formation *as such* and whether their religious utterances *can* possess a cognitive potential that the secular state must not ignore.

(2) Maeve Cooke's[61] objections are precisely the converse of those of Cristina Lafont. In Maeve Cooke's opinion, the controversy over how best to exercise political authority in a religiously and metaphysically neutral way is pointless because it is impossible from the start to make a clear distinction between secular and religious contributions to political will-formation. If I understand her correctly, the argument goes as follows: *all* substantive normative contributions to political discourse are embedded in some religious or metaphysical context; therefore, secular utterances in the public sphere pose the same interpretative problems as those with which we are familiar from communication between believers of one faith, believers of a different faith and non-believers. Thus secular contributions may not presume to have the advantage of being generally accessible. If religion loses its supposed exceptionality in this regard, however, then the secular character of the state enshrined in the constitution cannot be protected by channelling flows of public communication into a secularized space of supposedly neutral reasons for decisions. At the same time, in contrast to the kind of strong contextualism defended by Nicholas Wolterstorff, Maeve Cooke argues for the moderate position that, in the public sphere, *all* background premises must be exposed to *unrestricted* discussion, so that mere bargaining between incommensurable religious universes does not have the final say. Even when Wittgenstein's 'spade is turned', she argues, it must be possible for a discourse to continue: 'Both philosophers and self-reflective believers are likely to engage in processes of creative reimagining and rearticulating of even their core – dogmatic – convictions.'[62]

Since deductive arguments merely make explicit the relevant implications of propositions, substantial controversies always rest on reasons that are embedded in widely ramified contexts. But normally such non-thematic background assumptions, if they *can* be thematized, do not represent a barrier to the continuation of discourses. The 'spade turns' only when it reaches paradigm-constituting networks of concepts that found a view of the world *as a whole*. But the spade does not *break* when dialogue continues even then, having reached the bottom. For then it can transpire which assertions have an evaluative character or are so closely bound up with a metaphysical cluster of validity claims that they can meet with agreement only within the framework of particular cultures or religious communities. Maeve Cooke is correct when she attributes a world-disclosing character to religious languages in particular. This world-disclosive function can be beneficial when positions expressed in a rich religious language call attention to forgotten or repressed aspects in public debates over morally sensitive issues and, for instance, cast new light on previously inadequately described conflicts. This is why I am also against overhastily reducing the complex polyphonic diversity of voices within the political arena. Otherwise, democratic states are at risk of cutting off the democratic process from meaning- and identity-generating resources on which it can draw in the search for imaginative solutions to problems.

However, these correct observations do not support the problematic blurring of the boundary between secular and religious utterances. Let us recall the point of departure. Historically speaking, the at times bloody consequences of the clashes between militant 'powers of belief' necessitated the secularization of political authority. Until then, the conflicting parties had not been able to find a shared basis within their political community for resolving the pressing problems in ways convincing to all. It was only with the translation of the universalistic core of each religious community's fundamental convictions into the principles of human rights and democracy justified in terms of social contract theory that they discovered a shared language that bridged irreconcilable religious differences. It was only under the assumption of a 'natural' human reason shared by all that the parties to the dispute were able to adopt a common standpoint in political controversies that transcended the social boundaries of their respective religious communities. This *transgression of limits* marked a shift in perspective that later generations – ourselves included – can no longer ignore. Religious claims to validity are tied to the horizon of experience of membership in a religious community and, even in the case of proselytizing creeds that aspire to worldwide inclusion, remain particularistic. In this respect, the presumptively universal claim to validity of the major world religions resembles the *centred* universalism of the ancient empires; they sought to extend their political and cultural claims to domination outwards from the capital city to fluid frontiers that seemed to fuse with the horizon.

Whereas rational morality and rational law sketch the formal standpoint of an inclusive 'we' which obliges all parties to engage *equally* in *mutual* perspective-taking without prejudicing the outcome, a dogmatically fixed religious standpoint only allows others who are assimilated to be *incorporated* into the perspective of one's own religious community. The key issue in discursive will-formation processes, however, as in all processes of reaching an understanding, is the willingness to decentre one's own perspective. It is a matter not of conversion but of engaging in a process of reciprocal learning in which each participant's particular view becomes fused with that of everyone else in an enlarged and shared horizon (in Gadamer's sense). Secular citizens must also learn, of course, to distinguish their conceptions of the 'good life' (Rawls), hence their personal existential life projects and value orientations, from *generalizable* interests and *universal* standards of justice. But religious citizens bear a specific burden in addition to this. For what is of vital importance for religious citizens are not 'values' but 'truths'; whereas values are ordered transitively, truths observe a binary code. Religious citizens therefore face the twofold task of justifying the constitutional principles grounded in secular terms once again within the context of their faith and, what is more onerous, of recognizing the difference between fallible public reasons (that is, those which can be accepted by everyone in principle) and infallible truths of faith.

The boundary that Maeve Cooke, like Charles Taylor, wants to efface turns on this difference. It is a question not of the phenomenological difference between the respective ways of taking-to-be-true but of the difference between the incorporating and decentring meanings of 'universality': we claim universal validity for propositional truths in a different sense than we do for certainties of faith. Granted, 'truths of faith' are not *sui generis* truths from the point of view of the believer. Nevertheless, as a citizen of a democratic polity, there is an institutional expectation that the believer must recognize the political relevance of the distinction between these two kinds of truth claims. The epistemic contexts of public discourses are sufficient to bring the persuasive power of the usual kinds of empirical, pragmatic, legal, ethical and moral validity claims to bear. By contrast, as long as a religion retains its specificity – namely, its anchoring in the sacred complex which combines a specific interpretation of man in the world with the practice of communal worship – membership in a religious congregation remains relevant for faith itself: the cognitive and social dimensions are interdependent. This is because all of the world religions associate their own epistemic paths to the sacred with ritual practices – be it revelation, meditation and ascetic practice, or prayer. These particularistic ties explain why, when it comes to political will-formation in a pluralistic society, the generalizability of religious assertions must be tested independently of their epistemic context of origin. This is the point of the translation proviso.

Maeve Cooke argues that this requirement rests on a one-sided cognitivist conception of legitimation. Her objection touches on the important question of whether a political community of free and equal persons can be content with a *modus vivendi*. On this issue I agree with Rawls that democratic constitutional political systems are founded on principles whose legitimacy must be recognized by the citizens *for good reasons*. Aside from the fact that a form of rule that is only accepted *de facto* or that rests on a mere compromise is unstable, in such cases it would not be possible to speak of a political community of *autonomous* citizens. Regardless of how the background consensus on constitutional principles comes about, in pluralistic societies it has to be renewed in every subsequent generation on grounds that are acceptable to all. Therefore, its stability cannot depend on religious reasons that owe their persuasive power to the epistemic context of particular communities.

(3) With the emergence of a multicultural world society, religious pluralism is also increasingly playing a role at the international level. As the 2008 financial crisis brought home, at least temporarily, to the overtaxed nation-states, the scattered international organizations, despite the dramatic increase in their numbers, are not able to meet the growing need for coordination of the globalized markets (and of social subsystems in general). This led me to reflect on a constitutionalization of international law and on the design of a global multi-level system.[63] The long-term goal for the world society rocked by crises should be a political constitution without a world government. But how could the international community acquire the capacity to act politically without assuming the character of the state? What is required, among other things, is the satisfaction of a political-cultural condition that philosophy can help to clarify: whatever shape a global system assumes in future, if it is to be stable it must rest on a worldwide normative consensus on standards of justice. The fact that 192 states have signed the UN Charter represents a beginning, but nothing more. If we reflect that the cultures of the major world civilizations – in the first instance, those of the West, China, India and the Arab world – are deeply shaped by the religions that originated in the Axial Age, then it becomes clear that the problems we are discussing at the national level reappear in an exacerbated form at the international level.

However, the disagreement between Jim Bohman[64] and me turns less on the role of religions in the global public sphere than on the fundamental problem of how our notions of democratic legitimation could even find a foothold in the domains of transnational politics. My reflections on a *politically constituted* world society seem to be unnerving for a *civic republican* like Jim Bohman. How, he asks, is it possible to extend the channels of legitimation of democratic processes of opinion- and will-formation beyond the boundaries of nation-states? It may be more difficult for a citizen of the world's oldest democracy – of a self-sufficient republic of continental scale – to embrace such an idea. Be that as it may, Jim Bohman sets all institutional proposals aside and focuses on the global communicative network of an internationally enlarged civil society. Taking the historical example of the Women's International League for Peace and Freedom, he advocates the 'soft' communicative power that civil society actors can also exercise beyond national boundaries. Far be it from me to downplay the global influence exercised by the World Social Forum, for example, which mobilizes moral and political opposition to the capitalist World Economic Forum in Davos. The activists congregate in Brazil while the heads of government and economics ministers rush to meet with the managerial class of global capitalism in Switzerland. Yes, this example already indicates what the dispersed forces of civil society in the global public sphere lack, namely, an institutional counterpart on which they could exercise pressure. Jim Bohman rightly asks: 'Where does the legitimacy of "global domestic politics" come from?'[65] But if we content ourselves with the thoroughly asymmetrical global economic regime that developed in a haphazard, quasi-natural way and do not even attempt to *institutionalize* decision-making procedures at the supranational level, there will never be a global domestic politics that would then have to withstand the pressures exerted by a many-voiced globalized public. The transition from the debating society of the G7 to the summit of the twenty economically most powerful nations, which met for the first time in London in May 2008, took place under the pressure of the international financial crisis. In the meantime, the solemn declarations of intention to regulate the financial markets are no longer worth the paper they were printed on. If we continue to entrust the destiny of the global political system to the cunning of economic reason, we must docilely passively await the disastrous consequences of the next crisis.

VII Political Background Consensus under Conditions of Social Complexity

Over the decades I have learned almost as much from my friend Tom McCarthy[66] as from my philosophical mentor Karl-Otto Apel, albeit in opposite directions. Whereas for Apel I have gone too far in following, as he sees it, the fashionable trend towards detranscendentalizing the Kantian concept of reason, McCarthy allies himself increasingly emphatically with the pragmatist exhortations of Richard F. Bernstein and Richard Rorty that I should go further down the path of contextualizing reason. Faced with this quandary, I try to keep a clear head. The philosophical convictions that I have shared with Tom McCarthy from the beginning, through *Ideals and Illusions* up to his magnificent work *Race, Empire and the Idea of Human Development*, may have distracted me from clearly perceiving the differences now under discussion.

With customary aplomb, Tom McCarthy presents an accurate synopsis of the arguments I have offered to date for a postmetaphysical conception of philosophy which is open to an exchange with religious traditions.[67] In the process, he may have overlooked that these prolegomena serve to clarify only the self-understanding of the philosophical side. In order to begin a dialogue, it is neither necessary nor probable that the theological interlocutor should share the self-interpretation of his philosophical partner. Already here I would like to point out the differences, not just between the roles, but also between the cognitive attitudes that a philosopher must adopt when he takes part in religious conversations or, more generally, in intercultural discourses, as opposed to those he must adopt when he defends his understanding of postmetaphysical thinking against the objections of professional colleagues. In the one case, he is *engaging* in a difficult dialogue, regardless of the unclarified or controversial boundary between faith and knowledge; in the other, he is taking part in a normal expert discussion. Why should a dialogue that has to overcome deep differences between the respective background texts function better without such an internal clarification of preliminary philosophical questions?

This complex of issues continues to pose a series of questions which, whatever their intended effects, can be dealt with by social science or philosophy. For the moment I do not need to worry whether academic controversies over concepts of political justice, the ethics of citizenship, cultural and social modernization, faith and knowledge, secularization, the hermeneutic presuppositions of intercultural discourses, the metaphysical and religious pluralism of potential participants, etc., could one day influence the mindset of the political actors. As regards my general line of thought, however, I start from the *political* assumption that the era of nation-states is coming to a close and that the creation of institutions of global domestic politics must be opened up for discussion. These institutions cannot achieve stability without a transnational background

consensus on principles and procedures which make legitimate decision-making possible. Philosophers, too, can agonize over this issue.
Sceptical objections can have only the positive meaning of guarding
against underestimating the disagreements that must be reasonably
expected to accumulate *at the object level.*

The thrust of Tom McCarthy's objections is not altogether clear
to me. Thus I understand the tenor of his objections more as a methodological warning against overhastily breaking off the required
reflection on conceptual distinctions that fail to deliver in practice
what they promise on the conceptual level. Tom McCarthy is dissatisfied with analytical distinctions that I will review in what follows,
because they forfeit their supposed clear-cut character in contexts of
application.[68] Notwithstanding these problems, I will first address
the two theoretical objections. In the process, I will recapitulate
arguments at the risk, in Tom McCarthy's case, of revisiting old
debates (a)–(b). In conclusion, the three specific objections provide
an opportunity to return to the question of the location from which
each of us speaks (c).

(a) Philosophers certainly disagree over whether it is possible to
adopt an impartial point of view in moral-political questions (as
all Kantians, including John Rawls, affirm). When examining the
hermeneutic presuppositions of intercultural discourses, I start from
the assumption that universalistic questions of justice can be distinguished from particularistic questions of the good. Whereas the
former are geared to answers that can command universal agreement, the latter can be answered only relative to the values of the
reference persons or reference groups in question. Tom McCarthy
doubts whether these analytical distinctions can be upheld in practice. He summarizes a series of arguments developed elsewhere in
the assertion '"good" cannot be an inherently contestable concept
without "equally good for all" being so as well.'[69] I understand the
point of his argument to be that the participants in practical discourses, even with the best will in the world, cannot agree on what is
supposedly *equally good for all*, because the concept 'good for X' can
be used *only* with reference to interests which must be interpreted
and evaluated relative to the cultural background and lifeworld
horizon of the person or group in question which is affected.

This objection seems to me to miss the feature that distinguishes
questions of justice from ethical questions. Questions of justice can
also arise for the members of a collectivity which is embedded in
specific social and historical contexts; but even then, as moral questions, they differ from questions of the good life not in virtue of the
social and historical reference to something particular as such but in

according *equal* consideration to the interests of *all* those affected. This kind of equal and complete inclusion calls for a shift in perspective: all those involved must abandon the perspective from which they judge what is good for me or for us and adopt instead a uniformly inclusive 'we' perspective. This impartial point of view is not that of an ideal observer; it is a first-person plural perspective that includes all members of a collective or, as ultimately in the case of moral judgements presumed to be unconditionally valid, the ideally extended universe of all responsible persons. The *key point is the social-cognitive shift in attitude.* When we make the transition from the self-centred ethical perspective to the impartial perspective of justice, we leave behind the egocentric or ethnocentric viewpoint and thereby *break* the continuum of questions of the good life asserted by Tom McCarthy.

Every participant in practical discourse must seek to *enlarge* his understanding of himself and his situation through reciprocal perspective-taking to include the relevant aspect of all others' understandings of themselves and their situations. This must go so far that, within the area of overlap of this enlarged, and hence decentred, horizon of interpretation on which all positions converge from different sides, one proposal, or one family of proposals, is acceptable for all. The orientation to the 'single right' answer is already stipulated for practical reason by the context in which it operates: in the end, it should be conducive to social cooperation founded on intersubjectively recognized behavioural expectations. The pragmatic pressure to coordinate action bars the route to scepticism – that is, the luxury of idle reflection. The empirical extent of the differences of opinion does not constitute an objection against the orientation to a justified consensus. Contradiction and the orientation to consensus go hand in hand even in everyday communication. The coordination of practical goals in simple interactions must pass the risky thresholds of implicit 'yes' or 'no' positions on criticizable validity claims, while the ever-present risk of disagreement is absorbed by the shared lifeworld background. This is also the case in more complex social domains where establishing discursive procedures, on the one hand, involves mobilizing objections and multiplying religious and metaphysical differences, though, on the other, it fosters learning processes and the recognition of procedurally correct results. When systemic mechanisms are lacking or break down in domains susceptible to conflict, the need for coordination is met by institutionalized consultation and decision-making procedures.

(b) Tom McCarthy also doubts whether truth claims raised in the human sciences for interpretations of cultural and social modernity can be assumed to be more reliable than claims raised for religiously grounded alternatives. In his opinion, the one is as good as the others. But does the relatively weak status of the genealogies and theories of development of social science really justify erasing the boundary between philosophy, social science and the humanities, on the one side, and competing religious views, on the other? Before I address the sobering and disciplining character of organized academic research – which comes, of course, in many versions – I would like to recall the place from which each of us argues. The interdisciplinary controversy over the correct dialectical understanding of the 'achievements' of modernity is conducted in accordance with the usual academic rules and without any regard to whether it will ever affect the cultural background understanding of political actors. The strong or weak status of social theories which may be able to clarify implicit presumptions concerning the context of application of principles of distributive justice is of little concern to participants in G20 negotiations over a global regime for financial markets. Of course, this does not apply either to social scientists who compare theories or to philosophers who follow this controversy. At this level, I would like to defend the controversial distinction between religious interpretations 'of the present age' and corresponding secular interpretations which process the expert knowledge of various academic scientific disciplines.

To be sure, the humanities and social science differ from paradigmatic natural sciences in their hermeneutic mode of access to their object domain of symbolically embodied meanings. They gain this access not from the perspective of an *observer* who collects and processes the physically measured data but, instead, from that of an interpreter who must *participate* at least virtually in the relevant practices and language games, as it were, before he can objectify them – that is, convert them into data, describe them, and process them analytically. I agree with Tom McCarthy that the performative attitude of the interpreter ties the findings of historians and sociologists in a different and more intimate way to the time and place of the hermeneutic situation than even the findings of quantum physicists are tied to the context of the physical measurements. Historical representations regularly become 'obsolete' in ways that can be dated, whereas physical theories are 'superseded' by explanatorily more powerful theories. Representations in the humanities and social sciences always also express the inevitably unreflected features of a pre-understanding that is constitutive for cognitive access. Nevertheless, these practices also merit the title of a scientific discipline. They observe methodological standards of objectivity in the light of which all results are exposed to critical examination. Otherwise, we would not be able to distinguish between the academic enterprise of historical research and the pedagogical or political use of history: '*Geschichtspolitik*' is not the same thing as '*Geschichtswissenschaft*'.

On closer inspection, even the question of which side merits the title of greater objectivity is not as easy to answer as it may appear at first sight. The hermeneutically refracted claim to objectivity of the human sciences is at least less naïve than the 'view from nowhere' to which the natural sciences lay claim. For them, eliminating any reflection on what the knowing subject contributes to the construction of the data found is certainly necessary; but the hidden purpose of processing only data that fit physical measurements – for example, technical mastery of natural processes – could at the same time involve a functional restriction of the cognitive perspective. Be that as it may, philosophical theories are even more subject to the verdict of being dependent on context than are the human sciences. Here all that remains is the 'infinite conversation'. Today philosophy still sees itself as a scientific activity; however, when we attach the predicate 'scientific' to philosophical argumentation, we no longer mean that philosophy can be reduced to science or that it is one of the 'normal' academic disciplines. If an academic discipline is judged to be normal by the fact that it has *settled* on a method and an object domain defined in terms of a fixed conceptual frame, then the difference between philosophy and science consists in the fact that philosophy is 'non-settled thinking'. By distancing itself in a further stage of reflection from every form of knowledge acquired *intentione recta*, philosophy makes as it were an 'uninhibited' use of a basic feature of human cognition. Philosophy promises to provide us with a very abstract kind of enlightenment about ourselves. At any rate, the reference point that rescues the choice of philosophical problems from arbitrariness is the '*self*' of a process of reaching a *self-understanding*. While all scientific disciplines focus their attention exclusively on a single domain of objects, philosophy remains focused in addition on the self-referential aspect of the corresponding learning processes – that is, on what the knowledge we have acquired of a segment of the world means 'for us'. It operates in a dimension in which growth in knowledge about the world and changes in our self-understanding go hand in hand. In contrast to the sciences, however, philosophy has no need to be ashamed of this self-referential function. It ensures the objectivity of its scientific reflection not by obscuring but by *generalizing* the self-reference to an *inclusive* '*we*'. The 'self' of the self-understanding to be clarified through philosophical reflection is not a particular nation, a particular era, a particular generation, or even an individual, unless it be this person qua person. The philosophical meaning that something has 'for us' must be understood in the abstract sense of what is meaningful 'for us in our human existence as such'.

This perspective also throws interesting light on the origins of critical social theory in the critique of reason from Kant to Hegel. At the end of the eighteenth century, philosophical thought faced the challenge of a new, radicalized time consciousness, which was accompanied by the emergence of the social and human sciences. This experience forced a completely new topic on the attention of a by now postmetaphysically deflated philosophy, namely, modernity's self-understanding as apparently decoupled from tradition. Philosophy became even more acutely aware of the growing need for orientation the more clearly it rejected the search for metaphysical answers. With the intensification of the desire for orientation in each practical situation, philosophy, in addition to the tasks of its classical disciplines, was assigned the new topic of 'comprehending its time in thought'. Philosophy pursued this task of arriving at a self-understanding of modernity in collaboration with other disciplines, initially with political economy. After Hegel's death this role devolved to sociology;[70] thus social theory is the result of a relatively contingent constellation. This explains the hybrid character of the peculiar symbiosis between social science, which was emerging at the time, and the philosophical legacy of a self-referential discourse of modernity. Moreover, it throws light on the controversial status of the 'universal interpretations' that Tom McCarthy ascribes to analyses of contemporary developments derived from social theory.

With this sketch of the relation between human and natural science in general, and between philosophy and social theory in particular, I would like to suggest a perspective from which the various scientific claims to objectivity converge on one feature on which they all depend, namely, the discipline of research governed by methods and rules of argumentation. In each of those disciplines, we can achieve as much objective knowledge as the corresponding questions permit. The different degrees of objectivity that *can be achieved* do not prevent us from *correcting* each other *in the search* for a single right answer. What sets the scientific character of the projects of *social theory* apart from approaches to the same issues in *theology* is the *unconditional* and *unreserved* character of this search dictated by fallibilist consciousness. It is the unreserved openness and rationality of the approach that grounds the claim to scientific status, however weak the status claimed by the results may be. No interpretation by theologians, however liberal, can ultimately meet this procedural requirement. No theology can embrace the unconditional openness to critical self-revision as long as it has to administer

the means of salvation and is nourished by the lived faith of a prac-
tising community and does not shrink into just another academic
discipline.

(c) Tom McCarthy concludes by addressing the issue of the role
of religion in national public spheres. He supplements his sceptical
assessment of the possibility of reaching a cross-cultural understanding of the meaning of 'justice among nations' with arguments
against specific analytical distinctions which supposedly lose their
force in practice, so that reasonable disagreements become perpetual. When exercising their right of freedom of speech, secular citizens
are, of course, allowed to criticize not only religious utterances, but
also religion as such, in the sharpest terms. Tom McCarthy asks
how this *cultural* public sphere, in which colleagues such as Daniel
Dennett and Richard Dawkins present their books for discussion,
can be demarcated from the *political* public sphere in which the
ethics of democratic citizenship require these *same* citizens to exhibit
a certain restraint towards the persons and utterances of their religious fellow citizens. There is a simple answer to this question: all
parties can and should be aware of the consequences when, in their
role as citizens or potential voters, they engage in political opinion-
and will-formation on matters in need of legal regulation; *political*
utterances are simply contributions to discussions that in one way or
another issue in the *legally binding*, and hence *officially sanctioned*,
decisions of the authorized institutions.

Tom McCarthy sees a further difficulty in demarcating, on the
one hand, the normative contents of a rich religious metaphorical
language or allegorical discourse, which under certain circumstances
can remind agnostic fellow citizens of forgotten or suppressed
aspects of their own moral intuitions, from, on the other hand,
those descriptive religious statements or existential presuppositions
(on God, the creation of the world, etc.) which potentially clash with
mundane factual knowledge. I would suggest, however, that this
analytical distinction is less relevant for the *process* of translating
religious contents than for its *result*: after all, it is only the normative contents which can acquire importance for evaluating existing
regulations or constructing new alternatives to them.

Finally, there is a confusion concerning the requirements of the
'universal acceptability' and the 'universal accessibility' of proposed norms. The secularization of political authority is supposed
to ensure that the means of legitimate force held in reserve with
which collectively binding decisions are sanctioned and enforced do
not fall into the hands of any particular religious community (or of
any other ideologically based group). Establishing democratic and

constitutional procedures serves this purpose. Democratic procedures can generate legitimacy through a combination of deliberation
and inclusion because they justify the presumption that the results
are in the equal interest of all, and hence are *universally acceptable*.
However, the inclusion condition – that is, the requirement that
all those potentially affected should be assured appropriate access
to the procedure – would be violated if the collectively binding
decisions were not formulated *and justified* in a *universally accessible language*. Religious languages, in particular, would violate this
condition because they involve a category of reasons (for example,
revealed truths) that *prima facie* cannot claim to be generally acceptable outside of the corresponding religious community.

VIII Difficult Discourses

The difficulties posed by the discourses I now go on to address seem
to suggest that Tom McCarthy is right after all. I am not able to
accept the generous offer of two theologians who confront me with
philosophical arguments, or that of a philosopher who keeps open
the frontier to religious thought, and take advantage of the opportunity they present for a productive exchange. Insofar as this inability
is due to a lack of hermeneutical sensitivity on my part, I apologize
in advance to these three colleagues.

(1) Some academic discourses prove to be difficult because a
simple hermeneutic condition is not met, namely, familiarity with
a background of argumentation that guards against trivial misunderstandings. The unfortunate distortions that afflict the situation
of discussion between Nicholas Wolterstorff[71] and me cannot be
repaired through retrospective clarifications of differences between
our respective uses of expressions such as 'postmetaphysical'[72] or
'reasonable',[73] for that would simply be to reject the premises on
which the objections rest. However, I would like to address at least
one contentious issue and one confusion.

Nicholas Wolterstorff declares that the controversy over the distinction between religious and non-religious utterances is empty
because he does not think that the appeal to dogmatic sources, such
as revealed truths, is relevant. But without an appeal to revelation or
to some form of contact of the believer with the divine, be it through
prayer, ascetic practice or meditation, 'faith' would lose its specific
character, namely, its rootedness in religious modes of dealing with
'*Heil*' and '*Unheil*'.[74] The cultural Protestantism that shaped the
environment in which I myself grew up is aware of the danger of the

disintegration of religion into a mere worldview, which portends the end of religion as such.

In several places Nicholas Wolterstorff confuses the levels of discussion: the cognitive attitudes that citizens adopt as a matter of fact in the public sphere are a subject for empirical studies; the political ethos that a liberal constitution demands of its citizens is a subject for normative political theory; the cognitive presuppositions that are required to satisfy such a demanding ethics of citizenship, and the learning processes that would be needed to fulfil these cognitive presuppositions, are subjects for epistemology. The arguments with which a 'soft' version of naturalism can be defended against reductionist or 'hard' naturalism are in turn situated on a different philosophical level. Only the latter topic has direct relevance for the attempt to clarify the status of postmetaphysical thinking.

(2) John Milbank[75] presents the unusual conception of a revived Humean version of Platonism as a refreshing alternative to the anaemic 'postmetaphysical thinking' indebted to Kant. He claims that the latter fallback position is squeezed out by the clash between the only two vital intellectual forces of the present day, namely, Christian religion, on the one side, and hard naturalism, on the other: 'We live now in the era of Dawkins versus Ratzinger.'[76] This diagnosis leads Milbank to the conclusion that an agnostic conception of philosophy and a formalistic conception of democratic politics and a liberal constitution open up a void into which the fundamentalist movements stream. As historical evidence for his thesis, he cites the political destiny of the Weimar Republic. Against all empirical evidence, he puts forward the bold proposition that 'Weimar was thoroughly "Kantian" and Habermas repeats the Error of Weimar.'[77] In fact, the reason for the failure of the Weimar Republic was surely the failure of the bourgeois elites to appreciate how constitutional and democratic *procedures* safeguard liberty. If only the Kantian conception of the staunch constitutionalist Hans Kelsen had prevailed over the substantialist conception of the clerical fascist Carl Schmitt! As the case of Heidegger demonstrates, the 'deep' philosophical thought of the academic elite, which Milbank invokes against the dangers of the jejune Enlightenment, played a disastrous political role. However, the political argument merely serves John Milbank as rhetorical support for the daring thesis in the history of philosophy that Hume's theory of the emotions, with the central role it reserves for sympathy, opens the door for reappropriating a Platonizing version of Christianity. This original thesis – and here I must confess that I am not sufficiently acquainted with Milbank's philosophy – is puzzling for the conventional reader of

Hume; but the clever strategy of exploiting Humean scepticism for the purposes of a metaphysical renewal of Christian faith has its appeal. I assume that Hume experts have long since tested whether the alleged Stoic and Platonic connotations of Humean 'sympathy' can in fact establish a stable bridge to the ingenious hybrid of emotivism and speculation on the 'world soul'. As it happens, in a quite different way Friedrich Schleiermacher introduced feeling as the systematic connecting link between faith and knowledge in the architectonic of Kant's transcendental philosophy.

The few places where John Milbank refers to my own positions call for a reply. First and foremost, I fail to understand why a secular concept of communicative rationality, hence one introduced independently of 'faith', implies that there is no internal relation between rationality and feelings.[78] The rich vocabulary of evaluative expressions that we find in every natural language is an expression of the emotional life of the language community. And every evaluative statement expresses an emotional stance. Since Strawson's famous essay on 'Freedom and Resentment', it is a commonplace in analytic philosophy, too, that moral judgements express a certain kind of emotional attitude.[79] The propositional content of feelings is at issue not only in moral discourse but also in aesthetic discussion and in therapeutic conversations about repressed emotions which are excluded from communication. I am a bit baffled by Milbank's assertion that a procedural understanding of practical reason purged of substantive content provides the free will with no orientation except one to self-assertion.[80] No less perplexing is the construction of a regression of deontology into utilitarianism and the thesis that transcendental philosophy is somehow intellectually complicit with physicalism.

(3) The position of Hent de Vries[81] presents a different kind of challenge. It oversteps the boundary between postmetaphysical thinking and religion and seeks to replace the philosophy of religion with a 'religious philosophy'.[82] Hent de Vries expresses this intention in the question 'How does one adopt a reflexive, even critical, stance . . . while at the same time keeping the total archive of religion and metaphysics . . . at least in circulation, indeed, in play?'[83] This can be accomplished, according to de Vries, through aporetic figures of thought and paradoxes which extend the concept of rationality beyond merely 'giving and asking for reasons'. Without a doubt, the rich literature extending from Kierkegaard to Benjamin, Levinas and Derrida exhibits exemplary achievements when it comes to translating religious contents. In contrast, Heidegger's 'remembrance of being' is a veiled borrowing, not a translation. This example high-

lights the dangers involved in merely gesturing towards transcending the limits of '*Verstandesdenken*'. The pathos of 'depth' which claims that great thinkers have privileged access to truth has no place in a sober philosophical approach to religion. Philosophy may not be a scientific discipline in the conventional sense, but it nevertheless sees itself as a scientific activity.

Hent de Vries offers some thought-provoking sociological observations on the relation between the globalization of markets and electronic communication, on the one hand, and the virtual realization of the long-standing claim to worldwide inclusion in the shape of religious communities which are now globally networked via these media, on the other. With these empirical processes, he associates the philosophical interpretation of a supposedly new form, not of religion, but of religiosity. The latter is supposed to be purged of metaphysical contents, being on the one hand 'weak', in the sense of having minimal influence on everyday secular life, yet on the other hand 'strong' enough in virtue of its maximal proliferation and vague omnipresence. It may be that these rather vague descriptions of contemporary developments are consistent with the 'post-secular' transformations in the consciousness of societies which are largely secularized.

IX What We Owe to the Murdered Innocents

It is all too easy to lose one's footing on the slippery terrain of religious philosophy. Perhaps my suspicion of a mode of philosophizing that degenerates into religious kitsch has prevented me from being sufficiently adventurous. Max Pensky,[84] at any rate, ventures onto black ice without losing his foothold. He does not shy away from *spelling out* theologoumena in postmetaphysical terms. His impressive essay also presents my own reflections on coming to terms with our National Socialist past much more clearly than I managed to do myself. This holds especially for my complex relation to the theology of Johann Baptist Metz, who champions anamnestic solidarity as a means of answering the question of theodicy radicalized in the light of Auschwitz. In the context of the present volume, I find it gratifying that Max Pensky *performatively* silences the abstract debate over the possibility or impossibility of translating contents from religious traditions. He uses an example to show how this can be done: 'Translation is a process of analogical thinking. It searches for imperfect equivalents.'[85]

The essence of a political culture of remembrance, which has in the meantime spread to many countries, is the question of how later generations should cope with the legacy of the atrocities committed in the past by a regime that enjoyed the support of the domestic population and on what such a public practice of commemoration can draw. That members of a political community are also *liable* for one another *across generations* because they belong to the same traditions and are connected by threads of socialization is a pretty awkward idea, one that Karl Jaspers developed after 1945 in his famous text 'On the Question of German Guilt'. According to present-day moral standards, which are completely shaped by notions of individual personal responsibility, it makes no sense to speak of collective *guilt*. A duty towards the victims of past political crimes in the *strict moral* sense can be justified only in the case of those who participated in these crimes *in propria persona*. Nevertheless, the anguish over the mass crimes committed in one's own country gives rise to a persistent gnawing feeling that the descendants of the perpetrators also owe something to the murdered innocents. This indeterminate, in the broadest sense moral obligation can be interpreted as *collective liability*. The legal connotation of the concept points to compensation payments, insofar as material reparation (which necessarily remains incongruous) is even possible. But what kind of liability exists beyond that? Can the legacy of 'poisoned' social conditions establish a special responsibility – and, if so, for whom?[86]

That question concerns the level at which citizens who have to clarify their attitude towards the criminal past of their own nation form their ethical and political self-understanding. However, this commemorative practice does not seem to be able to break out of the circle of concern over one's own political identity and future. The practices of the politics of memory have something narcissistic about them even when they are not exhausted in prophylactic invocations of 'never again'. Max Pensky is not satisfied either with the more far-reaching interpretation of Pablo de Greiff. On the latter reading, the descendants of the generation of perpetrators owe those who were tormented and murdered the public gesture of recognition of past injustice, because otherwise the descendants of the generation of victims would not be able to breathe freely in the land of the perpetrators. Even this plausible reference to the reconciliation of the descendants of the one and the other side does not eradicate the reference of the nation of citizens to itself. Drawing on the famous correspondence between Max Horkheimer and Walter Benjamin, Max Pensky wants to read more than that into the practice of commemoration, namely, an expression of solidarity with the victims *themselves*. This runs up against Horkheimer's objection: 'the slain are really slain'. In contrast to God's judgement on the Last Day, the weak anamnestic force of collective remembrance cannot have any retrospective effects. It cannot atone for the injustices inflicted on the dead. The justice that is possible on earth is not *redemptive* justice. Nevertheless, a vague moral sense tells us that closing the file on such a process would be wrong *for the sake of the victims themselves.*

In the case of Auschwitz, Max Pensky proposes a non-deflationary interpretation: 'While any society generates ample opportunities for its diverse members to express remorse and regret, it is only in extreme cases, where the unjust destruction of a class of persons opens up a wound or a gap in the social fabric that continues to be perceived in the present day, that we speak of a solidarity with the dead.'[87] The commemorative political practice in the country of the perpetrators should call to mind *the gap* in the social fabric of the polity opened up by the crime. Recognizing the wound that refuses to heal[88] prevents the presentism involved in subsuming the past entirely into the present. Commemoration should preserve what happened in the past in the imperfect tense – that is, in the mode of *a past that continues to have a normative impact on the present.* The public act of remembrance should reaffirm the mourning for those who are missing by making present the void they have left in the cultural fabric of the political community.

However, this *perspective of grieving over those who are missing*, which is natural for mourning relatives, is more appropriate for the survivors and for the descendants of the victims than for the descendants of the perpetrator generation. The starting point for the latter is different, namely, the anguish over the violent exclusion of part of the population of one's own country who were stigmatized as a whole, and the consternation over the incomprehensible fact that extreme brutality could coexist with continuing normality in everyday life. On this side, the path to empathy with the victims leads over this threshold of consternation at the perpetrators and through a hermeneutics of suspicion concerning the cultural ties that connect 'them' with 'us'. The gulf separating the perpetrators from the victims continues in the invisible, but ultimately *unbridgeable* distance between the descendants of the one side and those of the other. The spontaneous grief over those who are missing contrasts with the distraught conscience that first provokes an awareness of what is missing. The gap between these perspectives cannot be closed, as is shown by the failure of obscene psychological, or even social, attempts to switch sides. Furthermore, how future generations will behave is an empirical matter. If things are to go well, it is a matter for the grandchildren and great-grandchildren to decide for themselves. But, for the time being, they should not be permitted to avoid the decision.

6

A SYMPOSIUM ON FAITH
AND KNOWLEDGE

Reply to Objections, Response to Suggestions[1]

When I reflect upon the interests that may have led the participants in this meeting to the topic of religion, I feel like something of an odd man out. Most in this group base their arguments on religious experiences also in their academic work and, unlike me, have the benefit of continuing familiarity with the practice of a religious community. To be sure, even those of a secular disposition among my generation were raised in a way that enables them to draw on memories of being socialized into a religious tradition. Moreover, in my case, growing up in a liberal Protestant household may have fostered a certain irenic relation to the church and theology. Today, at any rate, in the ideologically relaxed milieu of contemporary Western European societies there is no longer any place for militant forms of rejection of religion.

Furthermore, I have not forgotten that, during my student days, it was mainly academic teachers such as the theologians Gollwitzer and Iwand who had preserved their integrity during the Nazi period, and therefore had the courage during the early years of the Federal Republic to raise their voices against the stifling conformism and unreconstructed mindsets. But since we were more likely to learn a morally upright gait from theologians like them than from others, we were not able to brush aside in a polemical way the tradition from which they lived. That may explain why my interest in issues in the philosophy of religion is not strictly speaking a matter of *philosophy of religion*. I am not concerned with the appropriate philosophical conceptualization of religious speech and experience. Nor am I guided by the apologetic intention of establishing a justificatory relationship between the fundamental tenets of Christian teaching and contemporary philosophical discourses. On the other hand, I welcome the support of such arguments when I encounter them. In this way, there is a meeting of minds in the shared interest in the controversial question of the relations of inheritance between faith and knowledge.

Both faith and knowledge belong to the genealogy of post-metaphysical thinking – and that means: to the history of reason. Therefore, secular reason will learn to understand itself only when it clarifies its status vis-à-vis the reflexive religious consciousness of modernity and comprehends the shared origin of these two complementary intellectual formations in the cognitive advance of the Axial Age. In this way, starting from Kant, one can advance to a Hegelian line of thought without renouncing the Kantian way of thinking.

I On Kant's Philosophy of Religion

(1) I am in agreement both with Christian Danz's[2] interpretation of Kant's philosophy of religion and with his interpretation of my reconstruction of its main intentions.[3] Morality can be justified on the basis of practical reason *alone*. The transition to the philosophy of religion, as Danz argues following Kant, is a result of the 'self-interpretation of the practical self-consciousness' of moral actors: 'In religion, finite consciousness does not thematize the constitution of freedom but its realization.' With the idea that God reconciles natural necessity and morality, Kant's philosophy of religion responds to the unease of rational worldly beings who cannot remain indifferent to the consequences of their moral conduct – neither with regard to the subjective final end, their own happiness, nor to the objective final end, the highest possible good in the world, the happiness of *all* virtuous people.

Not only the layperson but also the philosopher, who is at once a Kantian and a morally acting subject, reflects on how things stand with the intended consequences of moral actions *as a whole* in the world – that is, in the domain of appearances subject to natural laws. The *Critique of Judgement* provides an answer to this question in terms of reflections on the final end of nature regarded *as if* it were a system of ends. This perspective suggests, in turn, the assumption of an 'intelligent cause of the world' which we conceive not merely as an intelligence which stipulates laws for nature but, at the same time, 'as a legislative sovereign in a moral realm of ends'.[4]

My main criticism of this theory is that Kant draws the boundaries of 'mere' reason too widely when he suggests that he could justify the assumption of the existence of God or of an intelligent author of the world, who ensures that justice can be brought into harmony with happiness, *in one fell swoop with* morality. My concern is with *the limits of postmetaphysical thinking*, which must also be clarified under Kant's own premises. Heuristically speaking, Kant's philosophy of religion is, as Christian Danz also stresses, closer to the philosophy of nature and history than to moral philosophy. Specifically, it tries to satisfy the understandable need of thoughtful actors who pause to reflect upon the ends and possible results of their moral action in the context of a rational history of the world or – as in natural philosophy – of the universe regarded in teleological terms. These heuristic as-if reflections of reflective judgement – as if history and nature were teleologically constituted – are *substitutive metaphysical* considerations: they should not be confused with theoretical knowledge nor, indeed, with moral insights of practical reason.

Christian Danz seems to be less troubled by this critique than Rudolf Langthaler or Herta Nagl-Docekal. What bothers him is instead the conclusion I draw from the critique of a presumptuous concept of rational religion. If, as I believe, Kant appropriates topoi from religious traditions such as the 'kingdom of God on earth' for philosophical purposes without acknowledging the methodological debt to inspiring historical sources, then the project of demarcating reason from religion in a self-critical way must assume a different, hermeneutically more cautious form. Danz takes issue with the thesis that the unexhausted semantic surplus of religious traditions represents at once an imposition and a challenge for secular reason. The heterogeneity of faith that I stress, he argues, betrays a 'substantialist' misunderstanding of religion and the 'ambiguity' of the 'appropriation' of its semantic potentials that I call for. I would like to offer three remarks on this criticism.

(a) If we scrutinize the building blocks of the civilization of the ancient empires, then the world religions are the only element that has preserved its vitality and relevance up to the present day. Religion has not only survived as a relic of the Axial Age but has remained an effective historical force. However, this holds only for the 'strong' traditions that offer a route to salvation and offer a credible promise of redemption, but not for Greek metaphysics, which, in a division of labour with Christianity in the course of the Middle Ages, withdrew from its own contemplative path of salvation and became specialized in cognitive tasks. Therefore, a form of religion that preserves its vitality even under the changed cognitive constellation of modernity represents the intrusion of an archaic element into the present. That religion which has remained vital and maintains a dissonant presence in the contemporary world is not just a sociological observation. Because religious certainties have preserved their credibility and remain connected with impressive testimonies of authentic life histories, I take the constellation of faith and knowledge seriously not merely as an empirical finding but also as a fact within the history of reason.

Postmetaphysical thinking cannot form an adequate understanding of itself as long as it fails to clarify its relationship to religion *as an external element* in terms of a genealogy of reason. The Enlightenment concept of 'rational religion', or *Vernunftreligion*, is as much an example of the premature appropriation of an alien element as is today, in a much cruder way, the reduction of religious meditation to the brainwaves of praying monks by neurology. If we want to guard against this false mode of familiarization, it is advisable to make a demarcation that does not have to be misunderstood in a substantialist way and as a reflection of a conception of religion hostile to reason. I speak only as a philosopher about the boundary between faith and knowledge; 'fideism' is the wrong word for this for the simple reason that it expresses a specific theological self-understanding of religion. And it is not a matter for secular reason to stipulate how religion should understand *itself* under conditions of modernity. Theologians make concessions to philosophy when they reaffirm the claim to demonstrate Christian faith as *fides quaerens intellectum*: 'This position must be maintained unreservedly even after the dissolution of the symbiosis of Christianity and philosophical metaphysics, if Christianity is not to sink to the level of esotericism.'[5] I am in complete agreement with theologians such as Markus Knapp who try 'to fulfil their duty to justify even under the premises of a form of thought which understands itself as postmetaphysical'.

(b) Christian Danz criticizes me for instrumentalizing religion as the reverse side of the substantialist misunderstanding. However, this criticism does not fit well with the intrinsic importance that I ascribe to religion as a *contemporary* intellectual formation. Now that the energies of social utopias have been exhausted and fantasies directed to the future have withdrawn into video worlds, science fiction and Californian visions of the 'new man', it is uncertain whether a modernity that has shrunk to technological improvements and accelerated capital flows can still regenerate its normative self-understanding from its own resources. This fear may also have sharpened the sensibilities of secular citizens for the unspent force of religious traditions. Although, from a postmetaphysical point of view, religious teachings are on the same level as other identity-assuring conceptions of the good life, they differ from non-religious ethical value orientations in their internal connection with 'truth' claims (of a distinctive kind): religions are worldviews, not values systems. As a result, they possess a cognitive content and a motivational force that secular outlooks on life lack.

This provokes the question of whether, after all, this view regards religion merely as a 'stopgap' for the deficient moral motivation of an exhausted modernity. A morality of justice grounded in practical reason alone cannot provide a rational answer to the question 'Why should one be moral at all?' Although in my view there is no longer any *reasonable* alternative to egalitarian-individualist universalism of Kantian provenance, the alternative which is *threatening* to take shape today is the demise of any kind of normative consciousness – of the consciousness of the normative structure of mind as such. I see the contemporary relevance of Kant's philosophy of religion as consisting in the intention to seek arguments for the 'self-maintenance of reason' through a critical appropriation of the religious heritage. The hermeneutically sharpened consciousness with which we pursue this intention today can preserve us from a pejorative understanding of 'ecclesiastical faith' as a mere 'vehicle' for promoting 'rational belief'. Nevertheless, from an agnostic perspective, the fate of religion itself remains open. This is because the interest of reason is directed at itself when it releases semantic potentials from religious traditions which play a role for *the species-ethical embedding* of our moral self-understanding as morally responsible persons. The question of whether something like moral commands, or norms in general, can still count as binding will be decided on this deeper anthropological level – namely, that of our understanding of ourselves as species beings.

(c) The diagnosis that my conception of religion is a false substantialist one prompts me to pose a question in return. In order to do so I must make a brief detour. I have the impression that Christian Danz does not agree with my proposed postmetaphysical demarcation between faith and knowledge because he wants to recover Fichte's speculations for general theological use. The concern seems to be that philosophy must not end up on the wrong – that is, postmetaphysical – side if theology has to rely on its help to meet the challenge of religious pluralism. Specifically, Danz wants to pass on the theological question 'about a constructive way of dealing with the different forms of religious life' – similar to Schleiermacher – to the *anthropology of religion*. With the formula 'religion as self-consciousness of finite freedom', theology, which understands itself 'as a theory of the realization of finite freedom', offers a *philosophi-*

cal concept of religious consciousness which makes possible 'the transparency of individual finite freedom for itself'.[6]

The fact of religious pluralism is, of course, also a concern of philosophy and jurisprudence. But the answers that these disciplines provide in the form of a 'morality of equal respect' and the 'ideological neutrality of state power' refer to demands that secular society makes on religious communities, not to the religious *self-reflection* of these communities. Religious consciousness cannot bring about a 'modernization of faith' through sheer adaptation to secular demands, but (as John Rawls illustrates with the image of modules) only *from the inside*, through a hermeneutic connection with its *own* premises. If theology – as was the case in the Western world – wants to play the role of a credible pacemaker, then it must perform the work of dogmatic reconstruction of articles of faith from the perspective of the religious practice of the community. But, because this perspective is not accessible to philosophy, Danz has to accept the conclusion that theologians, who could bring their own community to recognize the fact of religious pluralism *only with philosophical arguments*, would have to distance themselves from lived religion.

I understand the assertion that theological dogmatics can gain an awareness of its own contingency only through 'self-differentiation from lived religion'[7] in line with that path of argumentation. One must then recognize that the reflexive description of one's own religious tradition represents *one among several* possible descriptions of religiosity as such. If I understand Danz correctly, the Christian theologian would reconcile himself with the fact of religious pluralism through the philosophical insight that the different religions represent as many equally valid variations on the same mode of the 'self-givenness of finite freedom'. Doesn't this provoke the counter-question as to whether a form of theology that switches sides in this way and relativizes its own claim to truth in terms of the anthropology of religion has not lost its specificity? Or, in posing this question, do I once again betray a substantialist misunderstanding of religion?

(2) As a Kant philologist, Rudolf Langthaler[8] is so well equipped that he can effortlessly parry an interpreter of Kant who disagrees with him with an elegant thrust of the rapier. I know what I'm letting myself in for if I nevertheless disagree with him. Even in the conflict of interpreters we are, of course, only presumptively on solid ground. Someone who understands a text with as much hermeneutic passion, argumentative acumen and speculative flair as Rudolf Langthaler wants to assimilate the material in a critical way and make systematic use of the heritage.[9] We both share this goal, and in pursuing it our intentions proceed in parallel up to a certain

point. However, our paths diverge with the disagreement over the precise limits of postmetaphysical thinking. Langthaler thinks that more can be obtained from Kant than just weak reasons against defeatism based on a Kantian philosophy of history. According to Langthaler, Kant's interest in the 'self-maintenance of reason' cannot be reduced to the justified orientation to the highest *political* good. Kant, he argues, distinguished between the religious dimension of hope and the historical perspective of hope. Therefore, Langthaler wants to decipher Kant's speculations which revolve around the final end of creation and the supreme good as a 'meta-practical meaning potential' which points to an 'external offer' to practical reason. Langthaler speaks in this connection of 'practical limit knowledge', 'transmoral meaning postulate' or 'surplus of meaning', of a 'morally justified meaning perspective', hence of a dimension of meaning which is 'mediated' and 'laid open' by claims of practical reason.

I have no problem with this reading understood *as an interpretation of Kant*. However, I do have a problem with it if it is presented today as a still viable route to justifying rational belief at the postmetaphysical level in terms of a 'promise of the moral law'. We disagree over the cogency of the argument which Kant developed to justify the prospect of a happy life (and afterlife) in proportion to a virtuous observance of the moral law. The dialectic of pure practical reason is the place where Kant fills a systematic gap with the doctrine of the highest good. After all, his strict deontological morality *as such* does not provide an answer to the question which the ancient teachings treated as the key ethical question of the good or happy life. The controversial issue is how 'reasonable' such an ethics which derives its contents from the Christian tradition can be (and in what sense) if it 'proceeds' from a rationally grounded morality but nevertheless 'exceeds the concept of duty that morality contains', and 'hence cannot be analytically evolved out of morality'.[10]

Should we understand the assertion that 'morality . . . inevitably leads to religion'[11] in such a way that rational belief can be *justified* based solely on *insight into the moral principle* (which I accept as justified on the discourse-ethical reading of the formula of law)? (a) I reject this interpretation. (b) Rudolf Langthaler responds in turn to this criticism – but (c) in a way that leaves me unsure of what this metacritique is ultimately supposed to accomplish.

(a) The justificatory role of Kant's moral principle is exhausted by the examination of the generalizability of norms (where I understand the pragmatic meaning of 'generalizability' as the 'worthiness of recognition' of norms from the perspective of those possibly affected). Within the framework of this deontological conception, purposes or desirable goods can be judged morally only indirectly – that is, by asking whether they can be justified as an implication of the observance of valid norms. It makes no sense in light of this moral principle to ask for a *further* purpose for following morally binding norms: 'So morality really has no need of an end for right conduct; on the contrary, the law that contains the formal condition of the use of freedom in general suffices to it.'[12] The moral law must suffice as the 'sole determining factor' of the pure will because a higher-level end that morality itself is supposed to serve is incompatible with a deontological understanding, and hence with the unconditional validity of moral precepts.

Kant is scrupulous in pointing out that a good beyond morality for the sake of which morality would be observed 'would always produce heteronomy and supplant the moral principle [as a determining ground of the will].'[13] When he introduces happiness in combination with virtue as the highest good, Kant, as a realist about human nature, does take into account the dual nature of human beings as 'rational finite beings'; however, he also knows that he must justify the idea of the highest good 'in the judgment of an impartial reason'.[14] This idea, as a *supplement to* the moral law, is supposed to originate in practical reason, 'for it cannot possibly be a matter of indifference to reason how to answer the question *What is then the result of this right conduct of ours?*'[15] It is this 'natural need' to think for all of our moral actions taken as a whole 'some sort of ultimate end which reason can justify'[16] that the idea of the highest good addresses. Without such a remedy, the need would 'be a hindrance to moral resolve'.[17]

But how is the final end justified 'before' reason? It is certainly not justified by 'the characteristic, natural to the human being, of having to consider in every action, besides the law, also an end'.[18] Every additional motivation that the free will might acquire from such a 'need' would come into conflict with the moral law as the sole determining ground of moral action. Rather, the idea of the highest good must 'proceed' from morality itself. Rudolf Langthaler and I disagree over what is meant here by the ominous verb 'proceed'. The idea of the highest good and the religious substance of the rational belief woven around this idea acquire a more or less extensive justification depending on whether the question of what is involved in 'proceeding from morality' is settled in the court of the 'critique of judgement' or in the court of the 'critique of practical reason'.

If a person who acts morally reflects on her position in the world as a whole and on the condition under which the interaction between all moral actors could promote the highest good, then she will be pointed

to the need for an intelligent author of the world who arranges everything in such a way that the moral law harmonizes with the blind
process of natural causality. *This* idea of God is, of course, subject
to the heuristic proviso of teleological judgement which assumes
as a *hypothetical* matter that the world is arranged in a purposive
way. Such a form of rational belief serves the formation of the self-
understanding of moral actors and takes its place, as we would say
today, among the plurality of equally justified 'self-interpretations
of practical self-consciousness' (Danz). It could claim an entirely
different status if it could be shown in the context of the 'critique of
practical reason' that it is *a component* of moral *knowledge*.

This alternative rests on an assumed duty to promote the highest
good grounded in the moral law: '[W]e *ought* to strive to promote
the highest good.'[19] In his theory of religion Kant even extends this
duty to the command to operate in good faith 'in union with others'
towards realizing a whole 'of which we cannot know whether as a
whole it is also in our power'.[20] The *postulate* of the existence of
God is based on this duty. Because an individual cannot be required
to do more, morally speaking, then she can also accomplish by her
own power – *nemo ultra posse obligatur* – a 'duty' to promote the
highest good would be reasonable only if we postulate an intelligent
author of the world; for the fulfilment of the moral precept cannot
be thought of as possible without such an author's activity.

The objection to this line of argument is obvious: the problem
of how the realization of the highest good can be conceived as possible speaks less *for* the postulate of God than *against* the prior and
unjustified move to assume a problematic duty that first creates the
problem by positing an extravagant objective. Kant was quite clear
about the problematic status of this duty in his reply to Garve. The
duty 'to work to the best of one's ability toward the *highest good
possible in the world*' is addressed to 'a *special kind* of determination
of the will' – because in the process 'the human being [must think]
of himself by analogy with the Deity'.[21] Since this extravagant duty
goes beyond 'observance of the formal law' and cannot be justified
from this law alone, moral 'knowledge' does not provide a *sufficient* basis from which the idea of the highest good (and hence to
postulate the existence of God) could 'proceed' step by step in an
argumentatively compelling way.

(b) Rudolf Langthaler defends Kant against this objection by
arguing that the doctrine of the highest good belongs in the tradition
of ancient wisdom teachings and thus leads beyond moral theory,
'without, however, thereby tacitly revoking the well-founded misgivings concerning a metaphysically loaded "pre-critical" claim of the

"correct" and "good" life'.[22] This is correct, but it is not the full truth: the doctrine of the postulates blurs the boundary between the jurisdictions of practical reason and teleological judgement. Langthaler wants to avoid this difficulty by extending the justificatory accomplishments of practical reason *from the outset* beyond the domain of the morality of justice to 'the whole purpose of practical reason'. In doing so, however, he becomes entangled in ambiguous formulations, for example when he says that, in the idea of the highest good, 'a dimension of meaning which, although morally justified [!] – because inspired by justice – is ultimately transmoral [!], comes to the fore.'[23] The contentious issue is the 'justification' of this idea on the basis of a 'duty' to promote the supreme good in ourselves and others. On the one hand, Langthaler accords this injunction the status of a moral duty, so that it expresses a 'strong obligation'; on the other hand, the final end of practical reason should be associated only with 'claims to meaning opened up by critical "limit concepts"' which cannot be reduced to questions of justification.[24] The reason for this ambiguity seems to be that Langthaler stretches the moral-practical question 'What should I do?' so far that it *includes* the question 'What may I hope for?' dealt within the philosophy of religion.[25] In this way, he can draw upon the cognitive authority of rationally grounded morality to provide the questions *and answers* of a *docta spes* with a rational backing that extends beyond the validity claim of a merely ethical process of forming a self-understanding.

(c) However, a restriction to these controversial statements does not do justice to the substance of Langthaler's remarks. I admire the Benjaminian treasures that such a fervent reading of Kant brings to light from the depths of the transmoral dimension. I share his interest in Kant as the incomparable model for philosophical attempts at the rational appropriation of religious contents. Langthaler has convinced me that Kant himself was well aware of this role. On the occasion of a commentary on the translation of the Christian understanding of *fides* into morally motivated *rational faith*, Kant observes: 'But that is not the only case where this wonderful religion in the great simplicity of its expression has enriched morality with far more determinate and pure concepts than morality itself could previously supply, but which, once they exist, are freely approved by reason' – but then he goes on to add that these contents are 'assumed as ones that it could have arrived at and which it could and should have introduced by itself'.[26] This addendum prompts doubts: is it not the case that philosophy can reach the counterfactual conviction that it could also have invented them itself only retrospectively, after it has retrieved the concepts from a foreign shore?[27]

(3) In this question, Herta Nagl-Docekal[28] proves to be not only a
confident interpreter of Kant but also a passionate Kantian. She
defends the Enlightenment concept of rational religion[29] according
to which philosophy does not have to rely on the world-disclosing
articulatory power of religious languages to reassure itself about
the rational content of religion. Thus, it could have developed the
concept of an 'ethical community', for example, without drawing
upon the semantic potentials provided by the Christian tradition.
Philosophy, Nagl-Docekal argues, does not need the imaginative
power of religious images and narratives in which the laments, longings and hopes of the humiliated and downtrodden find moving
expression in order to be reminded of the fragility of social solidarity. As she conceives it, practical reason can confidently *go beyond*
the justification of a morality of justice and develop the idea of
a successful life uniting morality with happiness out of its own
resources. In the metaphors of 'divine rule' and the 'kingdom of
God', the philosophy of religion can uncover the rational core of an
ethical community because it has *a priori* access to this concept of an
exemplary form of life.

This conception is based on a reading of the dialectic of pure
practical reason which I have already addressed in the context of
the preceding section. Herta Nagl-Docekal is no more hesitant than
Rudolf Langthaler to justify the conception of the 'kingdom of
virtue' on the basis of the 'need of practical reason for a totality
of meaning' occasioned by the 'unforeseeability of the consequences
of our actions'. I do not want to reopen the dispute about the
cogency of this argument. I still do not see how, based on Kant's
individualistic conception of morality, one could justify an obligation to realize goals which can be achieved only through cooperation.
On my conception, only the historical self-understanding of the congregation as the anticipation of the people of God can prompt the
moral philosopher to look for a rational equivalent for the establishment of the kingdom of God.

This alone enables us to explain the following assertion of Kant's,
which is so amazing because it is by no means covered by the moral
legislation of practical reason: 'In addition to prescribing laws to
each individual human being, morally legislative reason also unfurls
a banner of virtue as a rallying point for all those who love the
good, that they may congregate under it.'[30] However, this duty is
anomalous not only because its addressee is a collective subject
but also because of the end to be pursued, the establishment of an
ethical community. The point is that this 'ethical-civil condition'
does not cohere with the alternative mapped out by the 'architectonic of reason' of being either located in the noumenal world – like

the kingdom of ends – or a republic in this world – like a political community.[31]

Let us concede for the sake of argument that rational belief is 'implicit' in moral-practical reason itself. This premise implies that ecclesiastical faith must be interpreted *in accordance with* rational belief; and then we must ask what role philosophy should actually play today in the politically intensified conflicts between the world religions. With regard to this question, Herta Nagl-Docekal does not, for example, defend the primacy of reason over religious pluralism in the form of a judgement that intervenes doctrinally from the outside. Nor does she think that philosophy should serve merely as an interpreter in interreligious dialogue. Rather, she expects philosophy to point all religious communities the way to an *internal* elucidation of the rational content of their respective traditions. For the concept of rational religion, she argues, grounds the expectation that through such a process of self-enlightenment the *same* core content will be shown to be reasonable by philosophy.

Is this conception really adequate to the present-day situation? To be sure, philosophy can and should adopt the role of advocate and interpreter of the requirement that all religious communities should not merely resign themselves to a *modus vivendi* with the self-understanding of modern societies but should, instead, try to forge a connection with the normative foundations of their secular environment from the internal perspective of their own religious convictions.[32] However, this demand should not be made from the paternalistic perspective of a philosophy which claims to know in advance what constitutes the essential core of all religious traditions. A 'modernizing' self-enlightenment of religious consciousness, as it were, has a genuine chance of success only when it is undertaken by each religious tradition from the inside, because in the end the community of believers must decide for itself whether the 'reformed' faith that has become reflexive is still the 'true' faith. The philosophical conception of the relationship between faith and knowledge rooted in the Enlightenment cannot do justice to the prophetic origin and positivity of traditional teachings, hence to what is proper to lived faith, because it overdraws the account of postmetaphysical thinking and claims to know more about religion than it is entitled to.[33]

From a postmetaphysical perspective, philosophy leaves the question of the reasonableness of religious traditions open. The general accessibility of the language and the public acceptability of the recognized reasons suffice as criteria for demarcating knowledge from belief. Only a form of philosophy that does not prejudge religious belief is sufficiently impartial to provide a basis for *mutual* tolerance between believers of one faith, believers of a different faith and non-believers. On the one hand, it remains open to learning from religious traditions by translating certain contents of religious belief from the confessional discourse of religion into public discourses. On the other hand, in concepts of political theory, it expects religious communities to recognize religious pluralism, the law and morality of the constitutional state and secular society, and the authority of science when it comes to empirical knowledge.

Postscript: I draw the boundaries of postmetaphysical thinking more narrowly than my two philosophical colleagues from Vienna because I relate the fact of pluralism, which does not allow a rational decision to be made between competing worldviews, also to ethical issues. But perhaps there is in fact a hidden ethical motive for rational morality, a need which explains why Kant did not want to restrict practical reason completely to the faculty of moral legislation. In the narrow beam of light cast by the moral point of view, it is only questions of justice, and no longer questions of the good or not misspent life, that still count as rationally decidable. This privileging of the right over the good is a result of transferring the true/false binary code of assertoric propositions (about what is the case) to the domain of value judgements. For only this sharp separation between statements which are and are not capable of truth singles out a subset from the set of all evaluative statements – the subset of categorical 'ought' statements that can be 'right' or 'wrong'. However, modern rational morality seems to have repressed this far from trivial step from its deontological consciousness. The continuing controversy between Aristotelians and empiricists, on the one hand, and Kantians, on the other, over the apparently not quite so compelling *step to cognitivism* reminds us of this threshold.[34]

The fact that this controversy persists can be explained somewhat loosely in terms of a genealogy that can be conceived as a thought experiment. Moral statements owe the fact that they can be true or false in the first instance to the historical circumstance that they had previously been embedded in religious-metaphysical worldviews. The fact of pluralism then led to the need to separate moral propositions from this 'truth-endowing' cosmological or eschatological embedding of propositions about essences. Many philosophers concluded from this convulsion of the foundations of validity that the meaning of the validity of moral judgements must be defined in conventionalist terms and must be adjusted to cultural values or to feelings and subjective preferences. The Kantians were the only ones to reconfigure post-religious morality based on procedural rationality, so that they could retain the binary coding of moral judgements as 'right' and 'wrong'. Now to my interpolation: perhaps it was less a compelling insight than an insightful motive that led them to adopt this path. They did not want to forgo the mode of social life familiar from homogeneous religious societies, which is regulated by moral insights and steered by moral feelings that are open to justification. Least of all did they want a life in a moral vacuum. But this 'wanting' is not an obligatory matter. Aware of the normatively shaped relations in cultures influenced by religion, Kantians had good 'ethical' reasons – not 'moral' reasons, mind you, but a 'need' – neither to withdraw to ethnocentric relativism concerning values nor to fall back on compassion or egocentric calculations of utility in the face of the epistemic problems posed by religious pluralism. If we start from such a genealogy, then modern societies would have switched over the practices of the lifeworld and of the political community to premises of rational morality and of human rights capable of being true or false because they had an *'ethical' objective* in mind – namely, to save and secure, through a secular morality of equal respect for everyone, the shared basis for an existence fit for human beings *notwithstanding radical differences in worldviews.*

II Objections and Suggestions from the Philosophy of Religion

(4) Wilhelm Lütterfelds's[35] perspective on Kant and religion is fundamentally shaped by a contextualist reading of Wittgenstein's late notes *On Certainty*.[36] In these notes, Wittgenstein argued more or less along the following lines. All attempts to justify statements of a philosophical, scientific or trivial everyday kind alert us to the insurmountable context of language games, practices and worldviews in which we find ourselves from the outset. At some point in the chain of our explanations we encounter bedrock where 'our spade turns'. We come to a halt at irrefutable certainties that no longer require justification – at propositions such as: 'I know that this is my hand', '2 times 2 is 4', 'I've never been on the moon', 'the earth already existed yesterday', etc. It is the overwhelming coherence with all other propositions held to be true, hence the fact that they are embedded in the context of a picture of the world taken to be true as a whole, that lends such premises *certainty* – and not, for example, their questionable truth value. In our lifeworld, we always inherently operate on the foundation of belief provided by a semantically closed universe in which all standards of rationality, all standards for what counts for us as true and false, good and evil, beautiful and ugly, are defined in self-referential ways.

Now, if there were a certain number or many of these holistically constituted and supposedly semantically closed universes, and if all cultural life unfolded in one or other of these universes, there would not be any third or neutral place of intercultural communication – no 'divine standpoint' – from which an interpreter could compare utterances (propositions and actions) in universe A with those in universe B. This is the controversial thesis of the 'incommensurability' of worldviews, which at the time – this controversy had its heyday in the 1970s – was read out of Wittgenstein's text (although, as Davidson and Gadamer showed, the thesis rests on a problematic reification of conceptual schemes or languages): a translation from or into foreign languages which makes mutual understanding possible was assumed to be impossible. According to this premise, interpreters do not encounter each other like interlocutors as first and second person but, instead, observe each other like messengers from alien planets. With this counter-intuitive assumption, the hermeneutic model of translation is thrust aside.

I have sketched this background because it throws light on Wilhelm Lütterfelds's interpretation of Kant.[37] If we understand Kant's 'rational belief' in contextualist terms as a 'worldview' and at the same time as a plausible interpretation of religion in general (for adherents of this worldview), however, then this has unwelcome consequences both (a) for the interpretation of Kant's philosophy of religion and (b) for the interpretation of the phenomenon of religion in general.

(a) If we model rational faith in terms of the late Wittgenstein's conception of a language game, then the religious articles of faith lose the status of assumptions that are capable of being true (which they retain even on Kant's own understanding of them as postulates of reason that do not admit of theoretical justification). In the same pragmatic way as, for example, the businessman's practice first gives rise to the belief in the reality of a possible profit, so too the religious practice of rational worldly beings is also supposed to 'justify' the ideas of God's existence and the immortal soul. This pragmatist perspective introduces a certain functionalism by the back door. The postulates are defined in terms of the use made of concepts such as God, the soul and freedom in the language game of ethical self-understanding. At any rate, the question of the existence of God loses its ontological significance when the meaning of the *pragmatically assumed* existence of God *is reduced to the role* that this assumption plays in the moral promotion of one's own happiness and that of others. I have the impression that this amounts to assimilating pure religious belief to an identity-founding life plan that does not admit of questions of truth because it can 'prove' its worth only in accordance with pragmatist criteria à la William James.

Other consequences follow from the holistic character of rational faith. In such a conception, the moral law (contrary to what Kant clearly and repeatedly asserts also in the philosophy of religion) cannot claim validity any longer independently of the background of the doctrine of postulates: 'In this respect, what underlies all truth, but also all falsity of moral knowledge, is the praxeological truth and falsehood of a practical belief of reason.'[38] Because the moral language game can operate only in the context and on the foundation of pure religious faith, the deontological meaning of the validity of rationally binding moral precepts falls by the wayside. In assuming that 'all knowledge is grounded by pragmatic faith',[39] Wilhelm Lütterfelds relates the categorical ought of binding norms to the final end of bringing morality into harmony with happiness. The *summum bonum*, *pace* Kant, becomes *the content of morality itself*.

(b) Understanding the phenomenon of faith in Wittgensteinian terms leads to an astounding levelling of the distinctive character-istics of religious faith. If religion is just one language game among others, and if everything becomes a dogma, then the difference between faith and knowledge is also levelled. The semantic closure of incommensurable language games accords esoteric doctrines equal status with religions and natural scientific theories. With this move, 'reformed epistemology' can indeed begin its game; but in the night in which all cats are grey the philosophy of religion loses sight of its actual object of interest. If the modes of validity of science and philosophy, of law and morality, of art and criticism, superstition and religion, become assimilated to one another on the everyday ground of pragmatically established certainties, then the mode of belief which is anchored in a practice of prayer also becomes trivial.

At first sight, the incommensurability of worldviews at least seems to offer a solution to the theological problem of how to understand one's own claim to truth in the face of religious pluralism. But this appearance is deceptive because the price to be paid for making reason internal to incommensurable worldviews is that the claim to truth of religion must be withdrawn to the level of the 'confirmation' of an identity-securing ethos.

The philosophical implications are equally unpalatable. Either one becomes entangled in a form of relativism that one cannot defend without contradicting oneself, because a relativist cannot specify the place from which he himself is speaking when he moves to a meta-level that he has just denied; or one meets this objection with Rorty's methodical ethnocentrism, according to which we have to assimilate alien meanings to our own standards of rationality if we want to understand different worldviews. One could also follow McIntyre in conceiving of a mutual ethnocentric struggle to recruit proselytes with the possibility of converting to the superior standards of rationality of the other side. Wilhelm Lütterfelds wants to do justice to the intuition that one's own claims to truth are compatible with the requirement of mutual tolerance. He mitigates the restrictions placed on the understanding by the semantically closed nature of worldviews by following Peter Winch in allowing common pragmatic points of contact at the cross-cultural level of elementary modes of conduct, ranging from eating practices to funeral rites. However, I then no longer see what could block a transfer of further meanings in the communication between the semantic and pragmatic levels.

I continue to defend the hermeneutic model of understanding, according to which the pragmatic universals of the speech situation (with reciprocal perspectives of speaker and hearer, participant and observer, with mutual assumptions of rationality and shared systems of reference) provide a sufficiently secured starting point for *mutual* understanding. Philosophy can play a moderating role in the conflict between religious worldviews and cultural forms of life precisely because, within the limits of postmetaphysical thinking, it restricts itself to the universalism of law and morality, while refraining from privileging one's *own* conceptions of the good.

(5) Hans Julius Schneider[40] makes a rather different use of Wittgenstein's theory of language. He does not heighten the pluralism of language games into a thesis of incommensurability. Rather, a concept of language that differentiates between the content and the mode of linguistic utterances leads him to a special interpretation of religious forms of expression which is inspired by Wittgenstein's mystical leanings.[41] The Wittgensteinian reading of William James's *The Varieties of Religious Experience* ultimately leads to a definition of the religious as something which finds different expressions in the major world religions.[42] The appeal to Wittgenstein prompts the question of the status of the language game that the analyst himself makes use of here: Does the philosophical characterization of a certain understanding of religiosity (of the consciousness of finitude, powerlessness and redemption, but without the hope for salvation) remain itself within the boundaries of the very same language game? Does this reconstruction involve rendering transparent the grammar of a particular language game – a Zen Buddhist one, for example – from its own perspective?

Wittgenstein studied philosophical language games as a philosopher and therefore could understand his phenomenological investigations of language as a therapeutic self-enlightenment of philosophy. Hans Julius Schneider, by contrast, must either perform his explication as a believer from within a particular religious tradition or, as a philosopher, he must step out of the circle of religious speech – which is presumably his intention. Otherwise he could not neutralize the dogmatic competition between the truth claims of different religious traditions in the Jamesian manner he takes for granted. However, in the role of a philosophical observer of religion, Schneider would have to translate religious language games into the generalizing language game of philosophy in a way that is incompatible with Wittgenstein's notion of a reflecting self-explication.

Hans Julius Schneider, if I am not mistaken, is guided by the intention of the philosophy of religion to provide a philosophical commentary on religious experience in general (and, in addition, perhaps even to justify one particular religious tradition as reasonable). In doing so, he faces a series of questions: 'Is it possible to argue philosophically about a "view on the whole"?'; 'Do the articulations of such a view have a content that is accessible through argument?'; 'Is it necessary (and possible) to abandon the religious forms of speech for philosophical purposes, and do we have to translate the statements of religion in such a way that they acquire a propositional form in more than a superficial way?'[43] Schneider answers these questions in the affirmative because he understands the task of philosophical translation in the apologetic sense of offering a rational explanation for the perspective of religious worldviews. This attempt by the *philosophy of religion* to make philosophical sense of religious language games leaves the self-understanding of religion less intact than my idea of a translation of religious meaning potentials into a public language, which Hans Julius Schneider criticizes as a futile attempt to 'separate valuable materials for recycling'.[44] My intention in translating is aimed not at the meaning of the religious mode of belief but at critically appropriating certain articles of faith. This need not affect religious speech itself.

Partial translations of religious doctrines anchored in the liturgical practice of a community into a publicly accessible language are relatively trivial procedures. For example, we encounter quite inconspicuous infiltrations of everyday language when we trace the semantic connections between the German words *beten* and *bitten* (pray/request), *Zeugnis ablegen* and *bezeugen* (bear witness/testify), and *heilig* and *heil* (sacred/unhurt) or when we reflect on the sacral origin of such terms as 'adore' and 'curse', 'praise' and 'revile', 'revere' and 'condemn'. The vocabularies of guilt and atonement, of liberation, human dignity and humiliation, the talk of solidarity and betrayal, the language of moral feelings, of fears and yearnings, often have a religious background and preserve connotations on which we can draw rhetorically to revitalize faded meanings.

However, it is not just a matter of renewing the vocabulary of evaluation but of opening secular languages and concepts for sensitive semantics of non-everyday origin. Such semantics become differentiated in ever more subtle ways in the dogmatic elaboration of a religious teaching the more often and the longer the process of securing the tradition is exposed to the pressure to confirm its worth in the light of changing historical conditions and of new experiences which challenge the articulatory power and the hermeneutic efforts of the interpreters. A Hegelian perspective on the history of philosophy reveals the countless borrowings and translations from the Judeo-Christian tradition. In recent times, it was interesting to observe that a wealth of philosophical books about 'evil' appeared in the wake of the attacks of 11 September 2001. Here, too, it is a matter of the vexing semantic differences between 'evil' and 'bad' and between 'sin' and 'guilt', hence of revitalized semantic nuances that we have yet to capture in secular speech.[45]

For the target language into which religious terms are to be translated, the simple criterion of publicity is sufficient: all statements are permitted that can be defended not only towards members of a particular language community but, in principle, towards an unlimited circle of addressees. In secular spheres of life such as the everyday life of modern societies or the professional context of science, statements are not acceptable if revealed truths, hence propositions with a historical index, which appeal to the personal authority of a particular founder, have to be cited in support of their validity. Think of Kierkegaard's impressive comparison between the 'truths' that can be traced back to Jesus and Socrates respectively.

This very distinction between the epistemic modalities of faith and knowledge becomes blurred if we follow the later Wittgenstein in levelling the differentiation between the validity claims we raise for assertoric, normative, evaluative or expressive propositions. Hans Julius Schneider does not discuss the pragmatic theory of language that I developed through a critique of Grice, Searle and Dummett.[46] Therefore, I will leave aside the discussions in the philosophy of language with the exception of one difference that is relevant in the present context: I agree with Michael Dummett's criticism of the use theory of meaning that revokes Frege's distinction between content and mode.[47] Together with the relation between propositionally differentiated speech acts and 'the world', the late Wittgenstein neglected the cognitive dimension of propositional content. Along with the illocutionary-propositional double structure of speech acts, the special status of rational discourse gets lost. In this game of argumentation, the validity claims which are generally raised and confirmed in a naïve way are thematized as such and exposed to the crucible of criticism with reasons pro and contra.

The difference in levels of reflection between communicative action and rational discourse is also what distinguishes the devotional practice of the religious community from theological discourse. But theology remains dependent on articles of faith such that, in contrast to philosophy, it cannot expose all validity claims to criticism without reservation. A theory which denies that propositional contents can vary independently of their modes remains insensitive to this procedural difference between *open* and *bound argumentation*. The difference between theology as guardian of the faith and philosophy is by no means that theology specializes in articulating a 'perspective on life', whereas philosophy focuses on propositional knowledge. Without doubt, prophetic teachings are sustained in a special way by their innovative world-disclosive power; but, as the idiosyncratic terminology of the great philosophers demonstrates, philosophical languages can open our eyes to radical new worlds as well. The difference between faith and knowledge does not reside in this dimension. Conceptions of language that accord the creative articulation of worldviews *independent force* vis-à-vis the stubborn corrective function of true propositions about something in the world fail to appreciate this fact. In this respect, the late Wittgenstein is in the same boat as the late Heidegger.

(6) I applaud Ludwig Nagl's[48] attempt to direct the attention of philosophers to the Christian experiences and motivations underlying American pragmatism.[49] The rootedness in early nineteenth-century transcendentalism can still be discerned in the thought of pragmatists such as John Dewey and Richard Rorty who are tone deaf when it comes to religion. If we disregard Rorty's early physicalistic phase, then the recollection of Emerson's fraternal relationship to nature dissuaded all pragmatists from a crude form of naturalism based on naïve faith in science – despite their at times pronounced leaning towards a functionalist understanding of reason and an instrumentalist conception of knowledge.

Among the religiously tinged basic concepts of pragmatism, Ludwig Nagl rightly highlights 'community' as the motif which shapes the intellectual movement as a whole. The Christian connotations of the community are still explicit in Josiah Royce; but *all* of the pragmatists, from Charles Sanders Peirce through William James and George Herbert Mead to John Dewey, share the Hegelian intuition of the concrete universal as a form of socialization. The same

intuition is expressed by the statement inscribed above the entrance
to James Hall on the Harvard University campus:

The community stagnates without the impulse of the individual.
The impulse dies away without the sympathy of the community.

The 'community' embeds the individualism of Kant's egalitarian-
universalistic morality of respect in a form of life which guarantees
the closeness and concern of solidary relations without threatening the distance between and the distinctiveness and otherness of
individual members. This concept of *individuating socialization* is
associated with the idea of the orientation to an 'ever wider community'. The community is imbued with a logos that simultaneously
points beyond the limits of any particular community.

This idea shaped contemporary *conceptions of practice* in both
everyday life and research and led the way to intersubjectivistic
approaches in moral philosophy and the philosophy of language,
in epistemology and the philosophy of science. Through the theories of Mead and Dewey, the community conception also acquired
social and political importance. In Europe, there had been an early
parallel among the Young Hegelians, ranging from Feuerbach's
communism of love to the naturalistic humanism of the young
Marx. However, these intersubjectivist approaches in the theory of
communication and society were not able to develop any tradition-
forming power here in Germany. This is shown, for example, by
Michael Theunissen's 1962 postdoctoral dissertation *Der Andere*.[50]
In this, the author had to look for support in Karl Löwith's postdoctoral dissertation inspired by Young Hegelianism and in Martin
Buber's conception of the I–You relationship in order, painstak-
ingly, to expose the buried roots of a 'dialogical philosophy' against
the Husserlian and Heideggerian conceptions grounded in the philosophy of the subject. Notwithstanding Scheler and Gehlen, a
serious reception of pragmatism in Germany began only in my generation, prompted mainly by Karl-Otto Apel's pioneering work.[51]

While I agree with Ludwig Nagl's suggestive interpretation, in
some places I would choose a slightly different emphasis.

- In contrast to Hegel's harsh criticism of his socially more successful
  competitors, I have a higher opinion of the late Schleiermacher's
  arguments (in the introductory paragraphs of his 'Dogmatics' of
  1830).[52] One must acknowledge the ingenious separation between
  the *philosophical* justification of religious feeling – as a general
  anthropological phenomenon – and *theological* dogmatics as the
  interpretation of one particular religious tradition among others

from the internal perspective of an ecclesiastically organized religious community which wants to find its place in a pluralistic modern society.

- Of all of the pragmatists, Charles Sanders Peirce is the most fruitful figure when it comes to looking for traces in the philosophy of religion – if one disregards Royce, in whom the connections are even more obvious. Specifically, the model of the infinite community of interpretation, which is subject only to the logic of imaginative learning, inspired this most powerful pragmatist thinker continuously from his earliest writings up to his late, semiotically grounded metaphysics of firstness, secondness and thirdness.

- Finally, Richard Rorty, who otherwise feels closest to William James, agrees with Dewey when it comes to religion. He shares the latter's humanist hope in the collective promotion of a 'better' world. On the other hand, for Rorty, religious orientations are nothing other than ethical lifestyles which are essentially private in nature and hence can unproblematically disappear from the political public sphere. In this regard, Rorty not only underestimates the cognitive meaning of religious validity claims, which forbids their peaceful privatization, but also contradicts his own later concessions to Gianni Vattimo's watered-down postmodern version of Christianity. This kind of 'lukewarm' religion, which is reduced to the psychological impulses of compassion and loses any cognitive thrust, is too powerless to change anything in the world. Such a form of religion is, I think, irrelevant for the reproduction of that 'unjustifiable hope' which aims to change public conditions – even though, for Rorty, this goal is the only reason for tolerating religion.

(7) On the whole, I find myself in agreement with the account of Klaus Müller.[53] My early Hegelian view of religion as a formation destined to be dialectically superseded in the modern world has indeed changed. The empirical evidence of the survival of religion under modern social conditions has accumulated in recent decades. One can, of course, read a cognitive challenge for philosophy out of the indicators of the renewed vitality of religious energies (especially in other global regions) only if one interprets the empirical evidence as a symptom of the continued existence of an *intellectual formation*. Only under this description does 'persistence' mean survival for internal or rational reasons. This new emphasis has less to do with a change in my personal assessment of religion (especially because political expressions of religious fundamentalism in the West and in the East are deterrent enough) and more to do with a more sceptical assessment of modernity. Are the intellectual potentials and social

dynamics that the globalized modern world can muster *from its own resources* strong enough to check its self-destructive tendencies, in the first place the destruction of its own normative content? However, this doubt is not a new motif in my thought, as is shown by my 1972 essay on Benjamin's 'redemptive criticism'; but it has become stronger (and is perhaps merely a reflection of the pessimism of old age). Benjamin entrusted art criticism with the task of converting beauty into the medium of truth. He understood truth in this context, as he notes in a rather Heideggerian vein in *Ursprung des deutschen Trauerspiels*, 'not [as] a process of exposure which destroys the secret, but [as] revelation which does justice to it'.[54] Since I first encountered Benjamin's texts in 1956, I have been fascinated by the idea of a secular liberation of semantic potentials which would otherwise be 'lost to the messianic condition': 'Benjamin's critique of empty progress is directed at a joyless reformism, whose faculties have been blunted to the difference between the improved reproduction of life and a fulfilled life, or perhaps we should say, a life that is not a failure.'[55]

With the theme 'Athens and/or Jerusalem', therefore, Klaus Müller touches a nerve with me.[56] Reason – in the contemporary guise of postmetaphysical thinking – misunderstands itself as long as it has not fully reconstructed its 'genealogy'. It must clarify the status of Greek philosophy from the participant perspective – as it were, 'from the inside' – in the context of emergence of the other world religions during the Axial Age and review its own learning processes, which it underwent in a division of labour with Christianity, while renouncing its own path of salvation (i.e., the contemplation of the good). Reviewing the reciprocal learning processes, reason must try to comprehend the *relationship* to untransparent religious validity claims. This attempt does not have to follow Kant or Hegel in seeking to *eradicate* the lack of transparency and to render the religious form of experience as such *obsolete*. Confirming one's own standards by contrast with the uncomprehended other through a critique of religion is a different matter from trying to comprehend religion in a self-critical way.

As regards the congenial discussion that I have conducted on occasion with the revered Johann Baptist Metz, I can recognize my intentions in Klaus Müller's presentation. However, I am reluctant to be pressed into the role of the philosopher who takes a stance against Metz in a *theological* controversy and provides *philosophical* support to the conception of 'reason twinned with faith' which Metz attacks. In such a terrain littered with misunderstandings one needs to be clear about where one is speaking from. I cannot say anything from a non-theological perspective about the statement over which

Metz and Ratzinger disagree, namely: that the Christian faith is a synthesis of the faith of Israel and the Greek spirit mediated through Christ. From a philosophical perspective, however, I would question one presupposition of the controversy: I do not think that philosophy 'after Kant' could still satisfy the theological expectation to provide a justification of what is supposed to be universally valid in the Christian discourse about God. Joseph Ratzinger also thinks that 'the philosophical basis of Christianity has become problematic through the "end of metaphysics".'[57] Insofar as the goal of *fides quaerens intellectum* is metaphysical talk of the absolute, postmetaphysical thinking must throw in the towel. The fact that Jewish faith and Greek philosophy formed a symbiosis is uncontroversial as far as it goes. The Christian message of redemption was first worked out and articulated in dogmatic terms, and hence 'rationalized' in Max Weber's sense, with the conceptual means of metaphysics. At the same time, however, the heterogeneous contents of a monotheistic history of creation and salvation (which, like the Trinitarian structure of God or the idea of creation out of nothing, are foreign to Greek cosmological thought)[58] also exercised a subversive and transformative effect on the conceptual framework of metaphysics in the course of a long process of philosophical elaboration and assimilation of religious contents.[59] The dispute within theology turns on whether the Hellenization of Christianity led to a Platonizing *alienation* of the existential motifs of the early Christian expectation of salvation, the coming kingdom of God, the problem of theodicy, and the Last Judgement, or whether this symbiosis instead represented an enrichment – that is, whether it first rendered the rational character of faith explicit and created a legitimate place for the mystical experience of God (which is more at home in the Asian religions).

Whether one accepts the evaluation of Metz or that of Ratzinger is less interesting from a philosophical perspective than another question: What position does modern philosophy, as thinking after metaphysics, take on Athens and Jerusalem? I'm not sure whether Klaus Müller attaches sufficient importance to the difference between these two questions. With the modern separation of knowledge from faith, philosophy renounced sacred knowledge once and for all. It cannot provide comfort, but at best encouragement. Not the least merit of Kant's philosophy of religion is to have shown that, although postmetaphysical thinking cannot provide any assurance, it can protect practical reason against defeatism.

When I emphasize against Metz the Christian motifs that philosophy in turn has appropriated and incorporated into the universe of rational discourse, I am concerned with the controversial question

to which Dieter Henrich and Michael Theunissen provide conflicting answers:[60] whether what has been exhausted in the modern
world is the content of metaphysical-cosmological thinking or that
of the monotheistic tradition.[61] Klaus Müller provides an accurate
outline of the direction my answer takes, while he himself seems
to be more concerned to defuse the conflict between cosmotheism
and monotheism. He wishes to secure a future for metaphysics,
albeit in the guise of the philosophy of consciousness of German
idealism. My objection will come as no surprise to him. If the
absolute, as in Henrich, is supposed to be revealed through the
meditative dissolution of the problem of self-consciousness in an
original awareness-of-oneself [*Mit-sich-vertraut-Sein*], this message
betrays the original affinity between Platonism and the Far Eastern
world religions. Anyone who tries to build a bridge leading from
this position to the Christian tradition will reach at best the mystical
undercurrents of this tradition.

III Conversation with Contemporary Theology

The theme 'Athens and Jerusalem' already brings me to the conversation with the theologians. It is more than merely a *façon de parler*
when I express my gratitude for the intellectual impulses from the
discussions that Catholic theologians in particular have engaged
in with me since the 1970s.[62] The debate with philosophers of religion, however stimulating and instructive, remains within the space
of familiar arguments and refers to a shared literature, whereas in
the encounter with theologians one is no longer on home ground.
While one absorbs objections and appeals, one must at the same
time reflect on a difference between language games that tends to
remain blurred in the more familiar academic environment. In
addition, there is the resonance that biblical images and theological figures of thought can still evoke in secularized minds which
were trained in a culture shaped by Christianity. This resonance, of
course, also provides a hermeneutic bridge for the desired transfer
of meaning in both directions. Both sides could have an interest in
these 'translations' – if only for the sake of political communication
in pluralistic public spheres.

(8) I am in sympathy with Walter Raberger's[63] proposal to apply the
Trinitarian formula of the Council of Chalcedon to the specific case
of reason and revelation in the modern age. The relationship between
postmetaphysical thinking and a form of revealed religion which
has turned its back on affirmative metaphysics can be construed

as 'unmixed' but 'unseparated'.[64] This same formula, of course, may have a different meaning from a non-theological perspective than from a theological one. In my view, the predicate 'unseparated' refers retrospectively to the shared origin in the revolution of worldviews during the Axial Age and to a genealogy of reason which has intertwined philosophy with monotheism. With reference to our present situation, however, the predicate 'unseparated' is a problematic designation for unclarified relations of inheritance: postmetaphysical thinking must not allow the breaking off of the connecting threads to the still vital semantic potentials of religion which nevertheless *remains* external to it. Therefore, to speak with Raberger's Kant, it is not in the interest of reason 'to rashly declare war on religion'.[65]

Like Kant, Adorno regarded the critical appropriation of these still unutilized potentials from the perspective of the social dynamic of 'approaching the kingdom of God on earth'. But agreement with his statement that 'nothing of theological content will persist without being transformed; every content will have to put itself to the test of migrating into the realm of the secular'[66] should not conceal the disagreement over what undergoes the more radical transformation in this process of assimilation, the profane or the sacred. Even greater is the difference among the philosophers themselves. If, after metaphysics, we also renounce the philosophical imitation of the figures of thought of negative theology, then we must do even without the support of the history of philosophy for what was left of Messianic hope in Adorno (and perhaps also in Derrida).

The disenchantment goes so far that the fallible reason embodied in linguistic practices can draw, if not assurance, then at least encouragement against the defeatism implicit in itself only by having recourse to the idealizing surplus of unavoidable pragmatic presuppositions of communicative action and discourse. The encouragement is rooted in the fact that even pathologically distorted forms of communication still contain the sting of truth claims, so that no delusion can reproduce itself without this sting, and, hence, neither can it shield itself against it once and for all. A form of transcendence from within operates in the communicative constitution of our form of life. This is only a faint echo of that transcendence whose self-revelation Walter Raberger understands as 'intervention' [*Einsage*] – as intervening from above against the 'fact of the history of human self-delusion and the resulting destruction of victims'.[67] At any rate, transcendence from within sufficed for Kant to construct a 'scales of understanding' [*Verstandeswaage*].

The postmetaphysical reduction of eschatological hope could not be better exemplified than by the heart-warming image that Walter

Raberger quotes from Kant's *Dreams of a Spirit-Seer*. The quotation is too good not to deserve repetition:

The scales of understanding are not quite impartial after all, and one of their arms which bears the inscription 'Hope of the Future' has a mechanical advantage, causing even those light reasons that fall into its pan to pull the speculations of greater weight on the other side upwards. This is the sole inaccuracy which I cannot set aside, and which in fact I never want to.[68]

If one is willing to enter into a dialogue across clearly defined boundaries in accordance with the Chalcedonian formula, however, a certain balance must be preserved which guards against mutual paternalism. Like other colleagues, Walter Raberger discovers 'moments of appropriation' in the way I propose to define the relationship between postmetaphysical thinking and revealed religion. I would say instead that all these attempts betray an unavoidable asymmetry insofar as this dialogue takes place under conditions of *restricted* perspective-taking. While the Catholic theologian can pull out all the philosophical stops in order to justify his faith before reason, the philosopher must not accept revealed truths. Therefore, I cannot engage in criticism of religion 'in the mode of *genitivus subjectivus*', as Radberger claims, either. Equally unfounded is the suspicion that secular thought wants to be 'represented' by theology when it comes to the function of comforting, 'which can be envisaged only on the assumption of transcendence in the here and now.'[69] As I understand it, the 'translation' from a religious into a generally accessible language does not aim at the kind of secular self-understanding that 'transfers' 'a basic religious option' into its own horizon.

But doesn't the asymmetrical relationship between philosophy and revealed knowledge lead to the very paternalism that Raberger suspects? Here we must distinguish between the two perspectives that we adopt when we either speak *about* devout members of a religious community or speak *with* them. When talking about religion, a political philosopher making normative judgements adopts the objectifying attitude of an outsider in a similar way to the descriptive historian or sociologist. The one describes, for example, the adaptation of religious consciousness to modern living conditions as a kind of 'modernization', while the other justifies unavoidable normative expectations addressed to all citizens of a constitutional democracy, religious and non-religious alike. In both cases, the practices and beliefs of religious communities are the objects of and not partners in an investigation; the seriousness of objections, including those from the religious side, is measured by the rules of the respective discipline alone. This has nothing to do with paternalism. By contrast, a tendency towards usurpation may very well be detectable in the dialogical relation to second persons. This is always the case when the secular person in the conversation with the believer simultaneously talks about him in a diagnostic way – for example, tells him about the expiration date of his religious convictions. Then the first person, the speaker, assigns the second person, the addressee – about whom the speaker knows something and in relation to whom she can reveal something that the addressee himself (supposedly) cannot know – *simultaneously* the inferior position of a third person.

The temporal index of the expression 'still' that I used in certain contexts when I claimed that postmetaphysical thinking *still* coexists with religion seems to confirm the suspicion that here a philosopher presumes to know about the end of that – 'for the time being' incomplete – process of translation of unexhausted semantic potentials. I concede that the statements cited by Raberger do not exclude this interpretation. However, they were meant in an agnostic sense. If one no longer believes that it is possible to make claims about the telos of history, one cannot know whether the interpretive power of religious semantics will be exhausted under future conditions and the knowledge then available, and whether people will then speak of the 'death of religion' in the way we already speak today about the 'end of metaphysics'. Religious practice and mundane knowledge could just as well continue to coexist as different intellectual formations – or as different language games. This alternative is quite independent of the question of whether and to what extent religious semantic potentials can be freed up for the moral consciousness of the political public sphere and for the benefit of the – on the whole – secular political community. A zero-sum game between philosophy and religion is ruled out for the simple reason that it is absurd to assume in an 'intellectualist' way that religious experiences rooted in the practice of worship and prayer of a community could be converted *without remainder* into a public practice of discourse and justification.

(9) I'm not quite sure why I agree so fully with the theological remarks of Magnus Striet[70] in spite of my agnosticism.[71] Perhaps this is just the smug response to a generous offer to lend some of my rhapsodic remarks a dimension of depth derived from the theology of creation, which can only put me to shame given my ignorance of theology. We agree, first, in our interpretations of the religious content of Hegel's system: 'The experiences of exodus, revelation, and promise resist Gnostic attenuation.' The circular movement

of Spirit in Hegel's *Encyclopaedia*, which is ultimately impervious to the openness and contingency of the history of salvation, stands in a peculiar contrast to the author's self-understanding as a (professing?) Lutheran. Striet's intersubjectivist approach, which relates creation in the light of the covenant theology to God's intention to recognize himself in an alter ego, coheres with my view of Schelling's philosophy of the 'world ages'. If God wants to establish a relationship of *reciprocal recognition* – hence a humanly understandable interpersonal relationship, notwithstanding the anticipatory character of God's love – the being singled out in this way must, according to Striet, be endowed with 'freedom' in a radical sense: 'The creature released into freedom should correspond to God in its own autonomy.' I also find Striet's theological definition of faith and knowledge convincing when he asserts that Christian faith strives for 'understanding even if faith remains heterogeneous vis-à-vis reason insofar as it presupposes the fact of the logos made flesh which is accessible only through faith.' The conceptual orientation of this theology of freedom coheres well with postmetaphysical thinking. These complementary positions share the premise that 'the sociocultural processes of forming a self-understanding should be in conformity with the principle *etsi deus non daretur.*'[72]

In the most exciting part of his text, Magnus Striet goes on to develop the question of the implications of a possible self-instrumentalization of human beings for their self-understanding. Until now, the quasi-natural structure of our form of life ensured that our own organism is not at our disposal, a fact which, as it now turns out, provided the basis for modes of interaction informed by individualistic-egalitarian universalism. Today we are approaching the technical ability to intervene in the genetic make-up of emerging human life which previously had been the result of a random combination of the parental sets of chromosomes. This threatens to violate the communicative constitution of our form of life right down into its deepest moral layers. Striet situates the question of God in this context. If the question is no longer what is morally required but why we should still even act morally (especially as, according to the latest pronouncements of neuroscience, it no longer seems to be guaranteed that we *can* act responsibly), then must we not 'fill the empty space left by God in a new way . . . if an ethical vacuum is not to prevail'? I do not find the answer implied by this rhetorical question compelling, because, in the concrete case of the permissibility of human embryo research or of liberal eugenics, the answers inspired by Kant are not very different from the theologically motivated answers.

Faced with the new challenges of bioethics, alliances are emerging which do not fall into religious and secular 'camps' but are, instead, forming along the fronts within philosophy between Hume and Kant. A situation that leaves it up to human beings whether they want to experiment with the basic constituents of their own organic nature, even at the cost of the principle of equal respect for everyone, can be interpreted in religious terms as a challenge posed by God, even as an ultimate implication of God's intention in creation: *human beings must decide.* Do we want to understand our own cultural life in Nietzschean terms as an 'experiment of unbridled life forces' and, as libertarians, surrender responsibility for the consequences of our actions to anonymous market forces or, as naturalists, renounce it entirely? Or should we not instead continue to subject the development and use of the new range of options possibly expanded by genetic engineering, neuroscience and artificial intelligence to political and legal regulations informed by moral considerations? The choice between these two alternatives can just as well be justified whether we make explicit reference to God or not. The actual decision will in any case be one made at the meta-level between conscious political decision and a practice of non-decision that follows the quasi-natural forces of a capitalist economy.

Magnus Striet is right to stress the new scale of the inevitable bioethical questions that will arise in the wake of legally permitted and perhaps even morally required scientific and technical progress, which is at any rate politically desired and supported and *de facto* unavoidable. As prognostic knowledge increases in scope and technological interventions increase in depth, the moral weight of the 'lesser' evil imposed on responsible individuals and citizens is growing – whether they understand this responsibility in religious terms or not. The reflexive decision whether we still even 'want' to see ourselves as persons who act responsibly may weigh more heavily on Kantian than on religious fellow citizens, because it is no longer a moral question that can be clearly answered in accordance with standards of moral obligation. The answer depends instead on the context of henceforth plural understandings of self informed by an ethics of the species.[73] In the meantime, the set of different versions of a species ethics includes naturalistic self-descriptions that are no longer compatible with a normative self-understanding of morally responsible persons (as understood until now). According to Striet, if scientific naturalism proved victorious, the self-evident assumption 'that egalitarian freedom is a moral imperative' would be shaken, and, as a result, 'the last bastion of Western intellectual history rooted in Judeo-Christian faith would be razed to the ground.'[74]

In a universe of discourse in which such positions compete with an equal right to be heard, we cannot operate with moral reasons and must be content with the weaker force of ethical arguments, unless we want to fall back on deceptive metaphysical or religious certainties. This is what underlies the concern that we must reasonably expect continuing disagreement, specifically when it comes to the existential question of how we should understand ourselves as species beings. From a theological perspective, this concern may at first be absent, because religious belief raises a truth claim for its own teaching also in the discourse with other 'comprehensive doctrines'. But even religious citizens will be gripped by this concern once they recall that religious claims to truth cannot be enforced by political means. Renouncing political enforcement of religious claims to truth is the price that all religious communities in the constitutional state have to pay for legal guarantees of religious toleration. Religious and non-religious citizens are in the same precarious boat when they add their voices to public debates.

No one will dispute this. What remains is a difference in the perspectives from which the question of the existence or non-existence of God is posed for believers and unbelievers respectively. Magnus Striet sets himself the task of justifying faith, not 'from', but 'before' reason. He argues that theology should be able to justify the possibility of the existence 'of a God who reveals himself' at least *a contrario* by discrediting the philosophical reasons put forward for the hypothesis of his non-existence. I wonder whether in this case theologians and philosophers are talking about the same thing. Here Wittgenstein's warning to heed the differences between language games seems appropriate to me. The ontological interpretation of the existential quantifier differs according to the domain of application. Numbers and semantic contents do not 'exist' in the same sense as symbolic expressions or physical objects.

If the existence of God was attested by the kind of 'trust' that his obliging love awakens in the hearts of receptive persons concerned about their well-being, and if this trust is directed to the pledge of assistance that transcends all worldly affairs, wouldn't it be understandable that statements about the 'existence' of such an interlocutor who is present only in the dimension of care and promise should give rise to 'a certain perplexity'?[75] Although that is not my problem, this perplexity could serve as a healthy warning against false or overhasty analogies for all participants in the controversy over the 'existence of God'. In this respect, I can understand the caution of negative theology which, instead of adopting a consistent avoidance strategy, prefers to accept the paradoxical structure of thought.

(10) Johann Reikerstorfer[76] builds me inviting bridges. I encounter my own words as interspersed quotations in the different context of an imploring speech about God. The appeal to the 'remembrance of unatoned suffering' also touches on the basic theme of Walter Benjamin. The intention, tone and choice of words testify not only to a certain proximity to the theology of Johann Baptist Metz but are also reminiscent of the characteristic style of thought of teachers familiar to me from Frankfurt.[77] But I must confess that I also find these suggestive interpretations a bit oppressive. On the one hand, specifically this practical theology, which laments what is missing in the normality of social modernity, its mistakes and failures, confirms my intention not to 'write off' religious traditions overhastily as a palliative against the blunting of all normative sensibilities. On the other hand, the *theological* reconstruction of this buried 'knowledge of what is missing' from the Passion narrative of Jesus Christ cannot provide any reason *for a secular philosopher* to 'bind communicative reason with its "language *a priori*" . . . back to a "suffering *a priori*"'.[78]

Under 'language *a priori*' I understand a concept of communicative reason that can be developed on the basis of the normative content of unavoidable idealizing presuppositions of communicative action and argumentation. This concept makes explicit the ideal content of the pragmatic presuppositions of rational discourse – i.e., of conditions governing the redemption of criticizable validity claims. Johann Reikerstorfer, by contrast, discusses very special validity claims whose capacity for truth he maintains can be demonstrated only within the horizon of the human history of suffering. The idea of atonement for past injustices and of making amends for past suffering is bound up with such loaded intuitions that no strong 'moral' claims to validity, but only weak 'ethical' ones (to use my terminology), can be derived from it.[79] In arguing thus, I do not altogether mean to deny that I feel a certain 'sympathy' for the theology of Metz – but only in the half-hearted, ambivalent manner of an outsider who is aware that in our latitudes we live off the biblical heritage and that we must not lose the moral sensibilities which were once exercised in religious terms with the secularization of this heritage.

Johann Baptist Metz takes the question of theodicy in the wake of Auschwitz seriously and thus accords central importance to the Old Testament question of social injustice. His negative theology takes as its starting point phenomena of what is missing. It keeps alive the sensibility for the possibility of a radically different condition, whereby the prohibition of images forbids a relapse into the false positivity of self-centred longings and utopias. But the incorporation of communicative reason into a history of salvation updated in terms of negative theology remains an imposition for a form of philosophy that continues to be aware of its 'temporal core'. Helmut Peukert contacted me in the early 1970s when he was preparing his impressive epistemological study.[80] This lucky circumstance marked the beginning of a fruitful dialogue with many students of Johann Baptist Metz – though it did not alleviate the latter's sceptical reservations. Metz consistently invokes anamnestic reason against communicative reason's insensitivity to time. But, on a non-theological interpretation, communicative reason can certainly make the idea its own that, without the belief in a 'God in history', the radical historicization of reason leads to the abandonment of reason itself – to the paralysis of the reflexive power to distance oneself temporarily from everything and on occasion to transcend every context. I am, of course, sensitive to the accusation – also from another side[81] – that, despite all of my political efforts, I do not take the breakdown in civilization of the twentieth century seriously *at the philosophical level*, hence that, unlike Adorno and Levinas, I do not make 'Auschwitz' the crystallization point of *all* reflection. Since I felt strangely helpless in the face of such accusations, it came as a relief when one day Jan Philipp Reemtsma offered me an answer:

Although thinking can engage seriously with the breakdown in civilization only if, in full awareness of the horror, it renounces the illusion that it can somehow 'master' it intellectually, if it does not want to regress to the level of ritual, it must take account intellectually and emotionally of the fact 'that life goes on' and that, although this keeps the disaster alive, it does not do so, notwithstanding Benjamin, only *as* disaster.[82]

What can become of the false rituals of philosophy can be seen from the pseudo-religious jargon of the late Heidegger.

Already at our first meeting, Helmut Peukert confronted me with the question that also motivates the doubts of Johann Reikerstorfer: Can a discourse theory of morality provide an exhaustive account of the universalism of responsibility inherent in the negativity of the *memoria passionis*? Certainly not 'exhaustively' in the biblical sense, because postmetaphysical thinking lacks the confidence in the restitutive and restorative power of a redemptive God. Merely from the desirability of such an authority one cannot infer that it exists and has such effects. These are old patterns of argumentation and constellations, from which I cannot free myself. I don't understand the source of the dissatisfaction: a clear boundary between faith and knowledge is also conducive to mutual understanding.

IV The Status of Religion in Post-Secular Society

The final three conference papers deal primarily with arguments that I developed on the ethics of the interactions between religious and secular citizens in the political public sphere.[83] This is also a matter of the functions that religious communities perform for the dynamics of the democratic process. However, I examine this role in the first instance from the normative point of view of political theory. Of course, the normative expectations that the ethics of democratic citizenship should fulfil already presuppose certain cognitive attitudes. Thus, political theory runs up against mentalities and learning processes which must be examined from a different theoretical perspective. Whereas naturalism raises epistemological questions, the self-enlightenment of religious consciousness under conditions of modern life brings theological questions into play. This explains my interest in Schleiermacher, Kierkegaard and twentieth-century theology, even though I still understand far too little about it. Finally, the theme of the relationship between faith and knowledge in post-secular society leads me via these questions of political ethics and epistemology back to the oft-mentioned problem surrounding the genealogy of reason. From the perspective of forming a self-understanding, I am interested in the position philosophy adopts on the contemporaneity of a theologically enlightened consciousness which also seems to be viable under modern conditions. This is why I conduct an academic conversation with theologians and philosophers of religion without any hidden strategic agenda.

(11) This preliminary remark is apposite because Reinhold Esterbauer[84] blithely ignores the differences between the theoretical perspectives from which I make particular assertions about religious teachings (or their theological interpretations) in the relevant contexts. He stylizes me into a kind of Foucault who addresses religion in functionalist terms as a form of knowledge that exercises power.[85] Guided by a hermeneutics of suspicion, he attributes to me an absurd picture of religion, as though I was not aware that neither the political legislator nor any form of philosophy, not to mention theology, decides what counts as 'true' religion in each instance but only the practice of the religious community itself. Certainly it would never occur to me as an outsider to play off Christian revealed truths against religious truth claims from other traditions, and certainly not to single out one Christian confession as superior to the others.

In saying this, I do not mean to immunize myself against the objection that I employ a false concept of religion. I already addressed the objection that I misunderstand religion in a substantialist way in my reply to Christian Danz. There remains the general objection to a form of functionalism that reduces the content of religious teachings to their potential contribution to stabilizing society. As I have repeatedly stressed, my interest in the relationship between faith and knowledge is explained, to put it in Kantian terms, by the self-referential philosophical interest in the 'self-maintenance of reason'. But this constellation between intellectual formations can be illuminated only from the participant perspective, not from the observer perspective of a theorist of power who thinks in functionalist terms. And as long as we remain within the horizon of postmetaphysical thinking, fallible reason is subject to narrow limits especially when it comes to extrapolating future constellations. Quite apart from the uncertainty of all *empirical predictions*,[86] it must remain open which current of thought among the alternatives emerging today could prove to be right for *intrinsic reasons*.

Prima facie, all that occurs to me is a rather arid scenario of alternatives selected more or less at random which does not make any claim to exhaustiveness.

- There are good reasons to assume that the naturalistic self-objectification of persons will run up against conceptual limits. Nevertheless, in the course of the globalization of uncontrolled markets and unbridled productive forces, we can imagine overwhelmingly invasive self-manipulative practices that will reinforce a normatively hollowed-out human self-understanding under the sway of a naturalistic worldview.
- Instead of scientistic naturalism, the theory of modernization could also prove to be right. Once the flows of energy currently streaming through the denationalized capitalist and religious networks had been successfully politically tamed once again,[87] a largely pacified world society could foster different versions of rational religion or of post-religious humanism founded on human rights and, based on a thoroughly secularized world culture, condemn *all* religions to the fate of watered-down liberal church Protestantism.
- Given the global turmoil, the 'cold' European societies which are already largely secularized cannot be expected to generate any appreciable impulses and counter-movements, unless postmetaphysical thinking could tap into the semantic storehouse of religious traditions as a source of new energies and regenerate the normative substance of an enlightened, but *politically and socially committed* self-understanding – but without suppressing religion

and in such a way that both sides transform themselves through dialogue and shared social practice.

- It is just as likely that scientific culture could lose its power to shape worldviews, resulting in a further spread of esotericism and Californian gimcrackery or a widespread return to cosmotheist worldviews and worldviews founded on a theology of creation in the Far East and the West (so that the advance of intelligent design in school curricula would turn out to be a portent of future developments rather than an expression of a retrograde clash of cultures).

I have the impression that Reinhold Esterbauer misunderstands the questions I am addressing. The examination of such alternatives – which are undecidable because they depend on the *implementation of intrinsic validity claims* – informed by a speculative philosophy of history is intended only to indicate the perspective from which the relationship between faith and knowledge in post-secular societies interests me.

(12) One learns the most from former students with whom one has maintained contact well beyond the time of their dissertation. Thus it was Thomas Schmidt[88] who first drew my attention to the American discussion about the political status of religion in the constitutional state. My discussions with him led me to develop my reflections on the 'cognitive presuppositions for the "public use of reason" by religious and secular citizens'.[89] This explains why we have already addressed our most important differences. I can therefore limit myself here to two observations.[90]

(a) From an analysis of religious faith comprising a cognitive component of the taking-to-be-true of 'p . . .' and a volitional component of trust in the promise of 'h . . .', Thomas Schmidt develops a very insightful account of the concept of rationally justifiable hope in 'historical progress'. This he circumscribes in a cautious negatory way as the expectation that globalization 'will not exhaust itself in the multiplication of consumer goods and profit and in increasing domination of nature'. This rational hope can provide believers and unbelievers with a shared basis for processes of mutual learning and translation. However, the secular side must also find an equivalent for the component of the religious conviction connected with the knowledge component – 'philosophy can also have its chiliasm'. This is how Schmidt explains the search of postmetaphysical thinking for an equivalent for Kantian 'rational belief' – that is, for justified encouragement which serves to protect against defeatism without inspiring confidence.

Perhaps reason's exploration of its own genealogy offers itself as such a mode of rational self-confirmation. Schmidt leaves open how reason's confidence in itself (which according to this analysis would have to serve as the functional correlate of trust in God) can be justified. He is interested in the side of religious certainty of belief. He argues that it should also be possible to 'test this like a hypothesis, that is, to bring it into a reflexive and coherent relationship to fallible knowledge'.[91] He develops a picture of a 'secular believer' who exposes his religious convictions to the dissonant environment of a pluralistic society in a constant reflexive alternation between internal and external perspectives: 'In these processes of justification, the convictions do not lose the qualities of certainty and immediacy; however, they are placed in a wide reflexive equilibrium (Robert Audi) with other, secular convictions.'[92] I cannot comment on this self-characterization of the religious intellectual under conditions of scientifically enlightened modernity. However, one conclusion that Schmidt draws from this reflected understanding of faith is controversial.

(b) I was impressed by one of the revisionist arguments from the debate over the ethics of citizenship that the liberal state may expect from its religious citizens. According to this argument, the liberal state which grants freedom of religion must not require its religious citizens to divide their minds into private and public parts in a search for secular translations and justifications for the public use of religiously motivated stances. Thomas Schmidt defends the opposing position of Robert Audi, who thinks that this is reasonable, with the following argument: the secular state may require all religious citizens to abstain from religious utterances in the political public arena because, in a pluralistic society based on mundane knowledge, religious certainties are also integrated into a network of inferential justifications in such a way that they inherently communicate with beliefs of the secular environment.

This may hold for 'secular religious' citizens. But may the constitutional state, normatively speaking, subsume its religious citizens without exception under this description of 'secular believers'? Does the theory of the constitutional state not pitch the demands it makes on the ethics of citizenship too high when it denies *all* religious citizens, whether intellectuals or not, the right also to use the language in which they take counsel with themselves and those closest to them concerning difficult moral questions (for example, 'voluntary euthanasia') in the political public arena? I have in mind the case of a religious citizen who is unreservedly open to the political contributions of his secular fellow citizens, but who does not think that his own intuition, which is informed by strong moral feelings, is captured by the arguments presented in public discussions of a highly controversial issue. I believe that this citizen must have the right to express his intuition (which in his view is relevant but nevertheless is absent from the public debate) in religious language – if this is the only way that he can lend it a voice.

He must make use of this right, however, in the knowledge that he depends on the cooperation of the other (religious or non-religious) citizens, because his stances can 'count' in the political decision-making process of parliaments, courts and governments only when their relevant content has been translated into a publicly accessible language.

(13) Maeve Cooke's contribution to the volume takes issue with this claim.[93] Unlike Thomas Schmidt, she considers the translation proviso, which I affirm for all institutionalized consultative and decision-making processes, to be too restrictive. She joins American hardliners such as Nicholas Wolterstorff in calling for complete freedom for religious speech even within the institutions of the state. She accepts the price to be paid – namely, the abolition of secular state power – with the argument that the historical situation in the West has changed since the end of the early modern Wars of Religion: 'New religious communities arise, in part from other historical-cultural contexts, which have not undergone the specific historical learning processes of Western modernity. . . .'[94] But should the intensification and multiplication of religious pluralism not lead us to draw the opposite conclusion? The liberal state must confront all religious minorities with the uncompromising expectation that, if necessary, they must *learn* to come to terms with the justified principles of the constitutional state, to which they themselves owe their freedom, from the internal perspective of their own religious teachings.

There are good reasons for immigrants and minority cultures to meet this expectation. They would be the first victims of the abolition of religiously and metaphysically neutral state power, because the removal of restrictions on religious speech in combination with the procedure of democratic majority decision-making only paves the way for political domination by a sectarian majority culture. As soon as the political representatives of the majority culture make laws, deliver court verdicts and enact regulations in their own exclusive language, they are using the power of the state to implement rules and measures formulated in a language which is incomprehensible to believers of a different faith and to non-believers, and which cannot be justified to them in ways they can

understand either. This would amount to transforming constitutional majority rule into authoritarian government by a clerical
majority. This is not, of course, the picture of the 'post-secular state'
that Maeve Cooke has in mind. But I cannot find anything in her
text that would avert such a political danger. I am at a loss and must
have misunderstood something. After all, we cannot simply leave it
with the starry-eyed appeal that parliamentarians, judges, ministers
and officials (whose decisions are backed up by state power) should
please cultivate 'non-authoritarian thinking'.

Maeve Cooke cites three arguments for the reinterpretation of
secular state power that I do not find convincing.

- First, she argues that the condition that the language used for
  political purposes should be accessible to all citizens equally
  can also be satisfied by non-secular languages. I do not want to
  quibble over words. But in every modern society with a more or
  less large proportion of secular citizens, vocabularies and patterns
  of justification of traditions which can be traced back to one or
  another prophet are not generally accessible.
- Secondly, she argues that political discourse should not be forced
  into a linguistic corset which excludes the use of world-disclosing
  vocabularies. I also think that this speaks in favour of admitting
  religious speech into the political public arena, because in this
  arena it is a matter of mobilizing the widest possible range of
  fruitful themes and contributions. But what is good for the public
  sphere does not qualify these same languages for use in political
  institutions whose decisions affect all citizens equally.
- The third argument is that the civic autonomy of religious citizens
  who may make use of a religious language in the public sphere is
  restricted when these citizens have to submit to rules and measures which can be formulated and justified only in a secular
  language. But religious citizens, if they recognize a liberal order,
  also see themselves as members of a self-governing community
  of free and equal persons who expect the state to exercise power
  under conditions of religious pluralism in ways that are neutral
  towards religious and metaphysical worldviews.[95] They must also
  be able to want their public religious utterances to be subject to
  the translation proviso *for the sake of the equal political autonomy
  of all citizens*.

III

POLITICS AND
RELIGION

7

'THE POLITICAL'

*The Rational Meaning of a Questionable Inheritance
of Political Theology¹*

In the welfare state democracies of the latter half of the twentieth century, politics was still able to wield a steering influence on the diverging subsystems to counterbalance tendencies towards social disintegration. Thus, under the conditions of 'embedded capitalism', politics could successfully steer subsystems *within the framework of the nation-state.* Today, under conditions of globalized capitalism, the scope for exercising direct influence over social integration through policies is becoming dangerously restricted. As economic globalization progresses, the picture that systems theory projected of social modernization is acquiring increasingly sharper contours in reality.

According to this interpretation, politics as a means of democratic self-determination has become as impossible as it is superfluous. Autopoietic functional subsystems conform to logics of their own; they constitute environments for one another and have long since liberated themselves from the under-complex networks of the various lifeworlds of the population. Meanwhile, 'the political' has withdrawn so far into the code of administrative subsystems steered by power that all that seems to be left of democracy is the deceptive façade that the executive agencies present to their helpless clients on the input side. Systems integration responds to functional imperatives and is leaving *social* integration behind as a far too cumbersome mechanism. Because social integration must still proceed via the minds of actors, it can no longer operate through the normative structures of lifeworlds which have become more and more marginalized.

From this by no means unrealistic perspective, the picture of a 'well-ordered' society painted by normative political theories may appear to be sheer sentimentality. Be that as it may, the sociologists' deflationary description can at any rate serve as a reminder to high-flown normative philosophical theories that the lifeworld, which is the precarious location from which alone, today, politics can still influence the integration of society *as a whole*, has shifted to the periphery of society and is threatened by marginalization. Under the constraint of economic imperatives that hold sway over private spheres of life, individuals increasingly withdraw timidly into the bubble of rational egoism and insulate themselves from their environment. At the same time, the willingness to engage in collective action, and even the awareness that citizens can collectively shape their social destiny through solidaristic action, is fading under the perceived force of systemic imperatives.

The private and public networks of communication of the lifeworld and civil society have been squeezed to the margins of society under the pressure of the functional differentiation and the spread of systemic mechanisms. However, these networks continue to function as a sounding board for all of the external costs that the functional subsystems shift onto the individual existences of their clients. It is only here that the disruptions of social integration, which has to proceed via communicative actions, norms and values, find an echo. Here society's awareness of itself as a whole, however diffuse, remains alive; and this can express itself in turn only in the circuits of communication of public spheres. Against the centrifugal social trends which seem to be branding democracy as an 'obsolete model' (Lutz Wingert), the defensive forces of civil society are gathering, lending renewed relevance to the supposedly antiquated concept of 'the political'.

For some contemporary French and Italian philosophers in the tradition of Carl Schmitt, Leo Strauss, Martin Heidegger and Hannah Arendt (for example, Claude Lefort, Ernesto Laclau, Giorgio Agamben and Jean-Luc Nancy, to mention just a few), this concept serves as a critical probe.[2] These colleagues develop a concept of 'the political' that reaches into metaphysical and religious domains and transcends the familiar institutionalized forms of political competition and administrative power. Claude Lefort appeals to the difference between 'politics' (*la politique*) as we know it and 'the political' (*le politique*) in order to make us aware that 'any society which forgets its religious basis is labouring under the illusion of pure self-immanence and thus obliterates the locus of philosophy.'[3]

I share Lefort's intention, but believe that the days when philosophy could elevate itself above the sciences in an elitist way are gone, for good reasons. Today the social sciences lay claim to the political system as their subject matter; they deal with 'politics', the acquisition and exercise of power, and in this context also with 'policies' – that is, with the ideas and strategies pursued by political actors in different political fields. With the exception of normative political theory, philosophers have lost their special competence for the political system. Today 'the political' no longer seems to represent a serious scientific topic alongside 'politics' and 'policies'. On the other hand, the centrifugal forces being generated by a process of functional differentiation of society that is becoming global in scale are reviving memories of the old European talk of 'the political' which still seemed to encompass society from an imaginary centre to its periphery. Therefore, my question is whether we can lend a rational meaning to the highly ambivalent concept of 'the political'.

(1) This expression seems to retain a clear meaning only for historians. 'The political' designates the symbolic field with whose help the first societies organized as states formed an image of themselves. The traces of 'the political' lead us back to the origins of early civilizations such as Mesopotamia and Egypt in which, around the turn of the fourth to the third millennium BCE, social integration changed over from kinship structures to hierarchical royal bureaucracies. The evolution of a new complex of law and political power gave rise to a completely new need for legitimation. It is by no means obvious that one person, or a handful of persons, can make decisions that are collectively binding on all.[4] Only by establishing a convincing connection between political authority and religious beliefs and practices could the rulers enjoy authority and law-abidingness among the population. While the legal system was stabilized by the sanctioning power of the state, political rule had to draw on the legitimizing power of sacred law in order to be accepted as just. Law and the monarch's judicial power owed their sacred aura to the heritage of the mythical narratives which now fused the ruling dynasties with the divine. At the same time, traditional ritual practices became transformed into state rituals, that is, into forms of collective self-representation of bureaucratic political authority.

Society as a whole was represented in the figure of the ruler. It is in this symbolic dimension, therefore, that the legitimizing alloy of politics and religion emerged to which the term 'the political' can be properly applied. 'Religion' derived its legitimizing power from the fact that it had roots of its own *independent of politics* in notions of salvation and misfortune [*Heil und Unheil*] and in corresponding practices of dealing with redemptive and protective forces [*heilsstiftende und Unheil bannende Mächte*].[5]

Mythical narratives and rituals had always fulfilled the function of confirming a collective identity. But an additional moment of reflexivity arose with the transition from tribal to bureaucratically organized societies. In the ruler's self-representation, the collectivity sees itself mirrored as a political community which *intentionally*, hence deliberately and consciously, produces its social cohesion by exercising political power. Thus, 'the political' refers to the symbolic representation and collective self-confirmation of a community that differs from tribal societies through a reflexive turn to a *conscious*, as opposed to a spontaneous, form of social integration. In the self-understanding of this kind of polity, the locus of control shifts towards collective action.[6] However, 'the political' as such could not become a topic of discourse as long as mythical narratives remained the sole means of symbolic representation.

We owe the first discursively articulated *conceptions of 'the political'* to the nomos thinking [*Nomosdenken*] of Israel, China and Greece and, more generally, to the cognitive advance of the Axial Age – that is, to the articulatory power of the metaphysical and religious worldviews which emerged at that time. These worldviews constructed perspectives that enabled the emerging intellectual elites, comprising prophets, wise men, monks and itinerant preachers, to transcend events in the world, including political processes, and to adopt a detached stance towards them en bloc.[7] Henceforth, the political rulers were also subject to criticism. The reference to a divinity beyond the world or to the immanent vanishing point of a cosmic law liberated the human mind from the grip of the narratively ordered flood of events controlled by mythical powers and made possible an individual quest for salvation. Once this transformation had occurred, the political ruler could no longer be perceived as the manifest *embodiment* of the divine but could be seen only as its human *representative*. As a human person, he was henceforth also *subordinated* to the nomos against which all human actions had to be measured.

Because the axial worldviews made legitimation and criticism of political authority simultaneously possible, 'the political' in the ancient empires was marked by an ambivalent tension between religious and political powers. On the one hand, the state conducted religious policy in order to secure the consent of religious groups and institutions; on the other hand, religious convictions preserved a moment of intangibility because of their relevance for the salvation of the individual. Even though religiously backed belief in legitimacy can be manipulated, it is never *completely* at the disposition of the ruler. This precarious balance can be studied deep into the European Middle Ages in the relationship between the emperor and the pope.

The bold historical leap that I have to make into the early modern period hints at the broad span of time during which talk of 'the' political had a clear meaning. 'The political' refers to the symbolic order of the collective self-representation of political communities as reflected by their rulers whose authority was legitimized by the reference to some form of 'sacred power'. Under the completely transformed cultural and social conditions of the modern period, however, the conceptions of 'the political' spelled out in Greek philosophy and in Christian political theology have lost their 'setting in life'. For Carl Schmitt, the unifying and integrating power of 'the political', which had also survived in the Roman Empire of the German nation in the tension-fraught dualism between the pope and the emperor, could be maintained only in the shape of the sovereignty of the Christian monarchs. Schmitt even thought that he recognized a reformed version of the medieval pattern of legitimacy in the absolutism of the early modern state.

In what follows I will first examine the thesis that 'the political' assumed the shape of an absolutist regime à la Hobbes in the early modern period (2) and then discuss the infamous conception with which Schmitt, from his historical perspective of an 'era of statehood' drawing to a close, tried to renew the concept of 'the political' under conditions of an authoritarian mass democracy (3).[8] Following that, I will use John Rawls's political liberalism as a counter-example (4) before returning in conclusion to the systematic question of whether we can still lend the religiously connoted concept of 'the political' a rational meaning under current conditions of liberal democracy (5).

(2) In the ideal type of the sovereign state developed by Carl Schmitt, political authority remains the pinnacle and centre of society: it continues to derive its legitimacy from belief in the authority of an all-powerful God, and the rational features of the modern state apparatus intensify the conscious character of a form of social integration ensured by political means. But, from Schmitt's perspective, essential aspects of the traditional concept of 'the political' that had been tailored to the ancient empires now seem to be concentrated in the decision-making power of the sovereign. This suggestive picture of continuity is deceptive. Carl Schmitt ignores two main elements that from the very beginning betray a certain instability in the early modern form of political sovereignty. The formations of the early modern state can be understood in functional terms as an answer to the explosive potential inherent both in emerging capitalism and in the pluralism of worldviews. Simplifying drastically, the bureaucratized state is tailored, on the one hand, to the economic imperatives

of a system of economic exchange which is regulated by markets, and hence operates independently of political structures, and, on the other, to pacifying bloody religious wars.

Already at the beginning of the era, the emerging capitalist economic system proved to be the driving force of a process of functional differentiation that led to a heterarchical reordering of society, while at the same time restricting the bureaucratic administration more and more to the role of one social subsystem alongside others. But this marked the gradual dissolution of the mutual interpenetration of political and social structures typical of traditional societies. As a result, society, as Carl Schmitt asserts in agreement with Hegel and Marx, lost it 'politomorphic' traits. If we continue to understand 'the political' as the symbolic medium of self-representation of a society that consciously influences the mechanisms of social integration, then the expansion of markets within territorial states does in fact mean a certain degree of 'depoliticization' of society at large. But, contrary to Schmitt's diagnosis, this shift in emphasis of 'the political' from the state to society already began in *early* modernity within the framework of the sovereign state.

However, the citizens, who had achieved economic independence, though at the cost of being forced into private domains outside the state, could not be excluded indefinitely from civil rights and political participation. At the same time, the religious conflicts which, following the Reformation, could not be permanently suppressed through authoritarian toleration edicts generated pressure for recognition of freedom of expression and of religion. These two developments prefigured the 'neutralization' of 'the political' already in the early modern period, whereas Carl Schmitt wants to lay the blame for this depoliticization at the door of the liberal regimes of the nineteenth and early twentieth centuries. In fact, the functional differentiation of society robbed the early modern state of the power to permeate and structure society *as a whole* in the manner of the ancient empires. Schmitt is mistaken when he attributes the dissolution of the amalgamation of religion and politics that we associate with 'the political' in its traditional form to the constitutional revolutions of the late eighteenth century. These revolutions merely ratified the secularization of state authority.[9]

However, it was not only the Reformation which required a secular form of state authority that could guarantee the equal treatment of all religious communities. The self-empowerment of the liberal citizenry already called for a democratic procedure which strips the legitimation of the exercise of power of its metasocial character – that is, of its legitimizing reference to a transcendent authority beyond society. Thus, Schmitt believes that, in liberalism, he has identified the force which robs politics of its socially integral significance: 'the political' disappears, on the one hand, in the course of its displacement into civil society and, on the other, in the course of the privatization of religion decoupled from the state. He is troubled by the question of whether the secularization of state power closes off the dimension of 'the political' – and whether as a result the concept of 'the political' becomes historically redundant.[10]

Or could the locus of 'the political' shift from the level of the state to opinion- and will-formation among the united democratic citizenry without losing its integrative power in civil society? After all, it is not settled *a priori* that 'the political' cannot also find impersonal embodiment in the normative dimension of a democratic constitution. But Schmitt draws very different conclusions from his diagnosis. He wants to preserve the authoritarian kernel of sovereign power with its legitimizing relation to Christian sacred history even under conditions of modern secularized mass democracies. Therefore, he devises a concept of 'the political' adapted to modern conditions out of motifs of 'reluctant modernism'.

(3) Carl Schmitt attacks liberalism as the enemy which destroys 'the political' through neutralization. By 'neutralization' he means not only the withdrawal of politics into a functionally specified subsystem but also the loss of the religious aura of state authority and the dissolution of sovereign decision-making power in discursive will-formation. Liberalism, he argues, 'wants to dissolve metaphysical truth in a discussion'.[11] Schmitt cherished clear sympathies for the political philosophy of counter-revolutionary thinkers such as de Maistre and de Bonald, but most of all for the militant thinker Donoso Cortés. This Spanish Catholic recognized that the era of Christian monarchy was over and, in the mid-nineteenth century, called for a 'dictatorship of the sword' against the 'disputatious class' of liberal citizens. Here the permanence of repression already reveals the intrinsically polemical nature of 'the political'.

As a professor of constitutional and international law in the Weimar Republic, Carl Schmitt was well aware that the democratic idea of popular sovereignty was irrevocable. Yet, for him, two aspects of counter-revolutionary thought retained more than merely nostalgic significance: on the one hand, the theological background of the 'bloody decisive battle that has flared up today between Catholicism and atheist socialism';[12] and, on the other, the conviction that 'the metaphysical kernel of the political' is not the institutionalization of freedom and equality but, instead, the moment of 'pure decision not based on reason and discussion and not justifying itself, that is . . . [in] an absolute decision created out of nothingness.'[13] In

order to provide some kind of justification for such an existentialist
concept of 'the political', Schmitt constructs an identitarian conception of democracy based on a homogeneous population and led by
a charismatic leader.[14] The concept of 'the political' condensed to
a social movement preserves the authoritarian kernel of political
power; however, the constitution of the belligerent mass democracy
lacks the religious reference to legitimation by a higher power which
was decisive for Schmitt.

Carl Schmitt fills this gap with an idiosyncratic conception of
political theology – though not a normative one but one based on a
peculiar reading of sacred history. The charismatic leader legitimizes
his decisions ad hoc through rhetorically effective and superficially
convincing *interpretations of current crisis situations*, where the latter
are supposed to lose their arbitrariness within the coordinates of a
teleological history of salvation. For Schmitt, the struggle against the
power of the 'Antichrist' extends across the whole eon between 'the
appearance of our Lord at the time of the Roman Emperor Augustus
and the Second Coming of our Lord at the end of time'.[15] This
struggle assumes Manichaean traits with the figure of the Christian
Epimetheus, whom Schmitt contrasts with the Promethean figure
of rebellious mankind.[16] Within this gnostic framework,[17] Schmitt's
own diagnosis focuses on the fateful revolution of 1789. Since then,
according to Schmitt, partisanship for revelation and against enlightenment, for authority and against anarchism, for obedience to God
and against human self-empowerment, has led to an intellectual rift
in the struggle against evil.

Although this clerical fascist conception of 'the political' is certainly a thing of the past, it must nevertheless serve as a warning to
all those who want to revive political theology.[18] On the other hand,
the motivation for such attempts seems to persist to the present
day. A harmless impulse of this kind finds expression in attempts
to repair the revolutionary breach of 1789 and to play down the
differences between metasocial justifications of political authority
and justifications of liberal constitutional principles in exclusively
rational terms.[19] Even John Rawls's political liberalism has not
silenced the objections of a scaled-down, postmetaphysical version
of political theology. The diagnosis of a progressive 'negation of the
political' does not seem to have been *completely* refuted.

(4) In contrast to the classical works of the social contract tradition,
which had stripped the concept of 'the political' of any serious references to religion, John Rawls recognizes that the problem of the
political impact of religion in civil society has not been solved per
se by the secularization of political authority. The secularization of

the state is not the same thing as the secularization of society. This explains the air of paradox which to this day has fed a subliminal resentment within religious circles against the justification of constitutional principles 'from reason alone'.

Although liberal constitutions are designed to guarantee all religious communities equal scope for freedom in civil society, they simultaneously shield all public bodies with responsibility for making collectively binding decisions from religious influences. The same people who are expressly authorized to practise their religion and to lead a pious life are supposed, in their role as citizens, to take part in a democratic process whose results must remain free from any religious 'contamination'. The laicist answer to this paradox – namely, the complete privatization of religion – remains unsatisfactory. For, as long as religious communities continue to play a vital role in the public sphere, all citizens must be aware that deliberative politics is as much a product of the public use of reason on the part of *religious* citizens as on that of those who are *non-religious*.

Needless to say, the concept of 'the political' remains a dubious heritage as long as political theology attempts to trace the legitimacy of political authority to a metasocial source. In liberal democracies, the legal exercise of power has lost its religious aura. In view of the persistence of pluralism in modern societies, it is hard to see how the historical step towards secularization of state power could ever be reversed. This requires that the constitutional principles and all collectively binding decisions be justified in ways which are neutral towards the cognitive claims of competing worldviews, and there is no alternative to democracy as a procedure for generating legitimacy. The idea of replacing democratic legitimation by some presumably 'deeper', but nevertheless generally binding foundation amounts to obscurantism. But that does not mean that the contributions of religious communities and citizens to the democratic process may be ignored.

The collective self-understanding of a democratic community cannot remain unaffected by the religious element within the pluralism of worldviews either.[20] In this sense, 'the political', which has, as it were, migrated from the level of the state to civil society, does indeed retain a reference to religion, however indirect, in the secular state – at any rate, as long as religious and non-religious citizens respect one another *as such* and treat one another as post-secular contemporaries. With his idea of the public use of reason, Rawls points to a revised concept of 'the political' which takes account of the effective contributions of religious citizens to legitimation.

The only spontaneous element that transcends the boundaries of institutionalized power politics is the noisy, anarchic use of communicative freedoms in civil society which keeps alive the spring tide of informal flows of public communication from below. Through these channels alone, vital and non-fundamentalist religious communities can become a transformative force – all the more so when frictions between secular and religious voices provoke disputes over normative issues that stimulate and keep alive an awareness of their relevance.

(5) Rawls has sparked a lively discussion with his proposal for a rather restricted role of religion in the public sphere: 'Reasonable comprehensive doctrines, religious or non-religious, may be introduced in public political discussion at any time, provided that in due course proper political reasons ... are presented that are sufficient to support whatever the comprehensive doctrines introduced are said to support.'[21] This 'proviso' is primarily a response to two objections: on the one hand, the empirical objection that many citizens *cannot* or *are not willing to* make the required separation between contributions couched in religious terms and those expressed in secular language when they take political stances; on the other hand, the normative objection that a liberal constitution, which also exists to safeguard religious forms of life, *must not* inflict such an additional, and hence asymmetrical, burden on its religious citizens.[22] Both of these objections can be met through a suitable institutionalization of the transition proviso.[23]

According to this conception, all citizens should be free to decide whether they want to make use of a religious language in the public sphere; but then they have to accept that the contents of religious utterances will be translated into a generally accessible language before they can find their way onto the agendas and into the deliberations of public decision-making bodies. Instead of requiring individual citizens to cleanse their public comments and opinions of religious rhetoric, an institutional filter is introduced between informal communication in the public arena and the formal deliberations of public bodies that lead to collectively binding decisions. This proposal achieves the liberal goal of ensuring that all *publicly sanctioned* decisions can be formulated *and justified* in a universally accessible language without having to restrict the polyphonic diversity of public voices at its very source. However, the 'monolingual' contributions of religious citizens then rely upon the translational efforts of cooperative fellow citizens if they are not to fall on deaf ears.

Such a regulation imposes burdens on both sides. Religious citizens who regard themselves as loyal members of a constitutional democracy must accept the translation proviso as the price to be paid for the neutrality of political authority towards competing world-views. For secular citizens, this same ethics of citizenship entails the similarly onerous duty of reciprocal accountability towards all citizens. In the public sphere, they must not simply ignore religious utterances or even dismiss them from the outset as nonsense. When making public use of their reason, secular and religious citizens must be able to meet each other on an equal footing, because the contributions of the one side are in principle no less relevant for the democratic process than those of the other.

Each side is expected to exhibit a demanding epistemic mindset which is morally required but cannot be legally imposed.[24] Whether the expectations associated with the ethics of citizenship *can* actually be fulfilled depends, of course, on complementary learning processes. From the religious side, the public use of reason demands a reflexive consciousness that

- forges a rational relationship to the competing religions which have for their part become reflexive,
- leaves decisions concerning mundane knowledge to the institutionalized sciences; and
- makes the premises of the morality of human rights compatible with its own articles of faith.

On the other hand, the discursive confrontation with religious citizens endowed with equal rights demands that the secular side reflect in a similar way on the self-imposed limits of a postmetaphysical kind of reasoning. The insight that vibrant world religions may be bearers of 'truth contents', in the sense of suppressed or untapped moral intuitions, is by no means obvious for the secular portion of the population. A *genealogical awareness* of the religious origins of the morality of equal respect for everyone is helpful in this context. The occidental development has been deeply shaped by the fact that philosophy continually appropriated semantic contents from the Judeo-Christian tradition; and it is an open question whether this centuries-long learning process can be continued or even will remain unfinished.[25]

Admittedly, everything that Carl Schmitt feared has in fact occurred: the sovereign power of the king has been dissolved and has dispersed in the flows of communication of civil society. It has assumed procedural form in the process of political opinion- and will-formation. Claude Lefort is also right when he says that the disembodied and dispersed sovereignty of the state has left behind an 'empty place'. But the complementary relationship between secular and religious citizens in public discourse means that 'the political' retains at least an indirect reference to religion in the civil society of a secular state. Although religion can neither be reduced to its *moral* kernel nor be equated with *ethical* value orientations, it can nevertheless contribute to keeping an awareness of both elements alive. The public use of reason by secular and religious citizens has the potential to spur deliberative politics in pluralistic societies. The discursive encounter with religious traditions and, especially, the attempt to recover still vital semantic potentials in a reasonable form constitute buttresses against the hegemony of instrumental rationality committed to maximizing utility.

The eschatological impulse of a political theology which has been reviewed under democratic conditions[26] also serves to remind normative political thought of the temporal dimension in which we raise normative claims. In contrast to ideal theories of justice which present the outlines of a just society beyond time and space, Johann Baptist Metz makes the case for 'sensitivity to time' and for developing a sensibility for the suffering of the past, the risks of the present, and the potentials of the future.[27] Only a dynamic understanding of our established liberal constitutions can promote a more acute awareness of the fact that the democratic process is also a learning process, one often blocked by a deficient sense of what is lacking and what is still possible.[28] Any democratic constitution is and remains *a project*. Within the framework of the nation-state, it is geared to *exhausting* the normative substance of constitutional principles ever more thoroughly under changing historical conditions. Since the foundation of the United Nations, the universal claim to validity of its human rights principles also points to the global task of developing a political constitution for the emerging multicultural world society through the constitutionalization of international law.

8

THE 'GOOD LIFE' –
A 'DETESTABLE PHRASE'

*The Significance of the Young Rawls's Religious Ethics
for His Political Theory*

We owe the editor Thomas Nagel and the trustees of the Rawls estate, Margaret Rawls and Thomas Scanlon, a debt of gratitude for publishing this unusual work, which John Rawls submitted to the Princeton University philosophy department in 1942 as his BA thesis. The informative commentary by Joshua Cohen and Thomas Nagel which enhances the accessibility of the text, together with Robert M. Adams's situating of the text within the theological discussion of the time, leave little room for further commentary. Therefore, I will limit myself here to four observations.[1]

This confident work, which is strikingly mature for a 21-year-old, merits interest in the first instance as a surprising biographical testimony concerning the work and person of the most important political theorist of the twentieth century (1). A religious ethics developed in terms of a theory of communication forms the philosophical substance of Rawls's senior thesis. It already exhibits all of the essential features of an egalitarian and universalistic ethics of duty tailored to the absolute worth of the individual (2). At the same time, the posthumous insight into the biographical sources of the author's work offers an outstanding example of the philosophical translation of religious motifs. It is as if one were examining the religious roots of a deontological conception based on reason alone under a magnifying glass (3). The student's senior thesis also foreshadows his later recognition that the secularization of state power must not be confused with the secularization of civil society. Rawls owes his unique standing in the social contract tradition to the systematic attention he devotes to religious and metaphysical pluralism (4).

(1) A reader who comes unprepared to the first lecture in Rawls's 1993 book *Political Liberalism* will be amazed to find that strong normative basic concepts are introduced there without further commentary. The theoretical edifice rests on two pillars connected by an architrave. The ideas of the *well-ordered society* and the *political conception of the person* are linked by the idea of *justice as fairness*. Rawls stipulates that all citizens are endowed with a clear sense of justice and with the ability to develop and rationally pursue a plan of life of their own, for which the *basic structure of society* is supposed to guarantee *fair conditions of cooperation*. The concepts of the person and of society intermesh in that they refer symmetrically to the same conception of justice. The latter can in turn count on the agreement of all citizens if it distinguishes precisely those framework conditions which are equally good or advantageous for all those concerned.

In *A Theory of Justice*, Rawls had laid down these normative guidelines in a similarly dogmatic fashion. In that work he had already amalgamated the normatively charged concepts 'person' and 'society' into a conception of the just society. The model of the 'private society' of self-interested market participants developed by classical economics served as a contrasting foil:

> The social nature of mankind is best seen by contrast with the conception of private society. Thus human beings have in fact shared final ends and they value their common institutions and activities as good in themselves. We need one another as partners in ways of life that are engaged in for their own sake, and the successes and enjoyments of others are necessary for and complementary to our own good.[2]

What persons are and ought to be by their very nature follows from the imperatives of social cooperation in which all participants depend on each other.

The network of normative concepts stretching between 'person' and 'society', Rawls argues, is open to confirmation in terms of the everyday intuitions of any population which is accustomed to the rule of law and democracy.[3] In the *Lectures on the History of Moral Philosophy*, Kant serves as the model for this link with common sense. There Rawls also explicates the categorical imperative itself as a procedure for justifying moral judgements whose *form* reflects only the *substance* of sound common sense, as spelled out by Kant. We all have an intuition of a legally regulated social body of free and equal persons, where the latter are conceived both as 'reasonable' and as 'rational' beings.[4] Moreover, Rawls cites Hegel as the source of the idea that human beings develop into persons only in a social environment: 'The concepts of person and society fit together; each requires the other and neither stands alone.'[5]

The present recently discovered historical source reveals that Rawls did not first have to read Kant and Hegel in order to embrace these premises. As a student he had employed similar concepts to express his community experiences as a member of an Episcopalian congregation. The apparently dogmatic premises of the mature political theory continue to be informed by some of those convictions which first emerged in a purely Christian context. The young Rawls already objected to the misconceived individualism of the contract theories which derive the social condition from the enlightened self-interest of independent individuals:

> They fail to see that a person is not a person apart from community and also that true community does not absorb the individual but rather makes his personality possible ... Therefore the reconciliation between the *person* and *community*, between the individual and society, can be understood by analysing the concepts themselves. They are mutually interdependent. One cannot exist without the other. (*A Brief Inquiry*, p. 127, emphasis added)

Here, to be sure, Rawls still discusses political problems in the same breath with ethical problems (pp. 135, 156) and understands the normative structure of society in terms of the religious relation between sin and conversion. The religious congregation and its practical faith serves as a model from which he can read off the correct relation between 'individual person' and 'society'. From this perspective, only face-to-face relations count and all conflicts are intrinsically moral; hence the institutional dimension for resolving social conflicts and disagreements that must be reasonably expected is missing. But, for all the selectivity of this view, the religiously tinged concepts of 'person' and 'community' already bring with them the normative content which would later be integrated into the foundations of Rawls's mature political theory. Here we find the characteristic connection between an uncompromisingly individualist understanding of the responsible conduct of life and the unreserved egalitarian inclusion of all individuals in the social network of reciprocal relations of recognition.

Rawls even emphasizes an important dimension of the model of the religious community which he would later lose sight of. *Communicatively mediated* interactions are at the centre of the analysis: 'One person establishes contact with another person not directly, because the nature of the case makes that impossible, but by means of signs, such as words, facial expressions, gestures and so forth. Personal relations require this self-revelatory action, or else no personal contact can be established' (pp. 117f.). Granted, Rawls is interested only in the ethical implications of these relations and does not explain what this has to do with 'the nature' of communication as such; but, insofar as he differentiates 'personal' from 'natural' relations in terms of the pragmatic stances that speakers and addressees adopt towards one another, he implicitly introduces the moral-philosophical analysis from the point of view of a theory of communication. Amazingly enough, he overlooks the relevance of American pragmatism, even though within this tradition the work of Josiah Royce would also have offered him a theological point of reference.[6] The pragmatists had developed quite similar conceptions of the individuating power of socialization and of the internal relations between the concepts 'person', 'community' and 'communication'.

In interpersonal relations, Rawls regards the *orientation to reaching understanding* which a speaker adopts as a first person towards an addressee as a second person as morally obligatory. I–thou relations are 'personal' in the further sense of the perception of and concern for individual uniqueness which ego exhibits towards alter in his role as a first person vis-à-vis a second person. The *objectifying attitude* of an observer or a third person, by contrast, is appropriate when it comes to the cognitive understanding of states of affairs and to cognitively guided practical interventions in causally regulated, and hence impersonal, natural occurrences. Self-centred purposive action steered by individual preferences is also morally unobjectionable as long as the satisfaction of needs does not disrupt the personal character of I–thou relations: 'Man does possess appetitions by nature ... These desires are good and their objects are good' (p. 120).

However, this 'natural' egoism of individual drives turns into morally objectionable egoism once the agent adopts an objectifying attitude not just towards natural objects but also towards persons and in doing so manipulates the objectified other as a mere means to his own ends: 'The egoist treats other people as so many objects to be used as instruments for his own appetitional satisfaction, and thereby he destroys community' (p. 123). This prohibition of instrumentalization reads like a communitarian justification of the categorical imperative (in its second formulation).[7] From the 'egoistic' inversion of the I–thou relationship, Rawls distinguishes another, even more extreme form of immoral self-centredness, namely, 'egotism'. This does not impair the interpersonal relation as such but hollows it out from within, as it were, by refusing the reciprocity of recognition.

Egotism is the antithesis of 'fellowship' – i.e., social interaction founded on solidarity. A perverse form of self-worship which is concerned only with one's own mirror-image in the eyes of a degraded other ruptures the social bond which holds members of a community together. Egoism can also find expression in hatred and contempt. But, in the virtue catalogue of the young Rawls, arrogance and self-aggrandizement, the elitist desire for fame, honour and differential recognition of one's own merits represent the true antipodes of the obligatory love of your neighbour. For they reveal what lies at the heart of the destructive potential of self-love, namely, the humiliation and degradation of another person. Egoism, which *inverts* the nature of interpersonal relations and *replaces* it with an objectifying relation by instrumentalizing the other as a means for satisfying one's own desires, is a less serious matter than egotism. The latter can unfold its evil effects only *within* interpersonal relations, by taking advantage of the reciprocal dependence on one another in a one-sided fashion. Evil has its origin in the spiritual domain itself, whereas nature, 'the flesh', is inherently blameless.

(2) Ultimately, arrogance and self-aggrandizement are, of course, ciphers for the repudiation of God. They deny that human beings were created in God's image. The rejection of the community with God is synonymous with the destruction of community itself. This is because the latter exhibits a triadic structure comprising two complementary patterns of interpersonal relations. Overarching the centreless but inclusive network of the horizontal relations uniting all persons is the nexus formed by the relations of each individual person to God which converge concentrically on the latter as a unifying reference point: 'Ultimately all personal relations are so connected for the reason that we all exist before God, and by being related to Him we are all related to each other although we may never have met one another. That personal relations form such a nexus leads us to the conclusion that religion and ethics cannot be separated' (*A Brief Inquiry*, p. 116).

One's individual relation to God, together with the mutual knowledge that each person has an individual relationship to God, are constitutive for the inner forum of conscience no less than for belonging to 'God's people' (of which Kant speaks in his philosophy of religion). The members of this community are *united* by the moral awareness of their individual personal responsibility towards *the same* all-knowing God whose judgements are both impartial and merciful and who, at the Last Judgement, will call them, as irreplaceable

individuals, to account for their life conduct and for all of their imput-
able actions in the light of the Christian commandment to love one's
neighbour. 'We know that we are existing before someone and that
this someone is judging us' (p. 116). At the same time, the concept
of a community of believers living in the sight of God defines the
normative dimension of right and wrong. The moral failure to live in
accordance with the divine commandment means the egocentric segregation from God, hence not just guilt, but sin. Sin is a more serious
matter than a moral error. It signifies a misspent life which harms the
communicative context of the community as such. Only conversion to
the true faith redeems the sinner from his misspent life, and this marks
the return to the solidarity of the community.

This monotheistic conception of the triadic structure of the community is of major importance in the present context, for it specifies
the four aspects which are not only essential for the religious ethics
of the young Rawls but remain equally so for a Kantian ethics justified 'from reason alone', and hence also for Rawls's later political
theory. The description of the triadic structure of the religious community explains the deontological and individualistic meaning of
the egalitarian universalism which marked Rawls's unerring moral
sensibility throughout his life.

(a) The deontological meaning of 'unconditionally' valid moral
commands follows from God's transcendence as a being who stands
apart from the causal nexus of worldly entities and lends his commands the rational authority of 'truths' free from arbitrariness and
compulsion.[8] The categorical nature of binding validity is incompatible with a consequentialist understanding of moral commands.
Religious believers must not make obedience to moral commands
conditional on personal salvation – this remained a troubling
problem for modern theology. Kant solved the problem by stipulat-
ing that those who act morally do not achieve happiness but acquire
the 'worthiness to be happy'. Nor does the young Rawls want to
uncouple the moral conduct of life from the individual expectation of salvation at the cost of embracing the irrational Calvinist
doctrine of divine election. Instead he envisages the 'community
of creator and created' as the goal of creation which is achieved
only when all members persistently follow the moral commands.
With this eschaton in mind, individual salvation becomes for everybody synonymous with the construction of a community in the full
sense: 'and while it may be true that man's natural being is fulfilled
therein, such fulfilment is secondary to the community itself' (*A
Brief Inquiry*, pp. 219f.).

The deontological conception of morality necessitates a clear distinction between the binding validity of morality and the attrac- tiveness of desirable goods. This priority of duty over inclination (which is reflected in the political theory in the priority of the right over the good) follows in Rawls's senior thesis from the moral interpretation of the formal-pragmatic considerations mentioned. Morality is implicit in the proper mode of interpersonal relations insofar as these require communicative actors to take and treat their addressees as second persons. By contrast, a self-centred actor pur- suing his own preferences does not become involved in interpersonal relations in the proper sense. By assuming the objectifying attitude of a third person, he intervenes in the natural course of events in order to satisfy his needs, of which he is aware as a first person. In this dimension of I–it relations, the person himself remains absorbed in natural – i.e., morally indifferent – processes. As a 'natural' person, he does not raise himself into the domain of morally sensitive I–thou relations. On this view, classical ethical systems which are based on the teleological model of action and are geared to the prudent optimization of desirable goods do not even touch the moral dimen- sion:[9] 'We do not believe that the so-called "good life" (detestable phrase) consists in seeking any object, but that it is rather some- thing totally different, a matter of personal relations' (p. 161). As in Adorno, there can be no question of the 'good life' in Rawls, but at most a question of the 'not misspent' life.[10]

(b) The second aspect emphasized by the religious ethic is the incom- parable dignity of the individual. The addressee of the message of salvation is the individual. To be sure, the individual develops into a person only through socialization, hence only within a community; however, in his role as the subject of morally responsible actions, he cannot allow anybody to take his place when he must account for himself before God. The counterpart of the onus of the *irreplace- able* addressee is the inviolability and integrity of the individual, who differs from all others as an *unmistakably unique* person. This uniqueness protects the person from being treated as an exchange- able factor in a calculation which trades off the weal and woe of one individual against that of others. The objections against utilitarian- ism presented by Rawls in *A Theory of Justice*[11] are implicit in his religious ethics. Here the decisive characteristics of individuality follow in turn from the structure of a community of persons who relate in a performative attitude to a *non-exchangeable* other insofar as they recognize each other as both unique and irreplaceable:

Personal relations are unique in the case of each person in relation to another, whereas natural relations are readily *exchangeable*. If there are several apples on the table, one apple is as good as another provided they all will satisfy the taste. In personal relations not only ought we regard each relation as unique, but we often . . . realize the *uniqueness* of personal relations. (*A Brief Inquiry*, p. 117, emphasis added)[12]

(c) and (d) Morality in the deontological and individualistic sense is supplemented by two further aspects which Kant also emphasizes in his ethics, namely, the demands for equal treatment and for complete inclusion. A form of egalitarian universalism is implicit in the powerful image of the Last Judgement, when God will perform the paradoxical task of pronouncing a differentiated, at once just but merciful (and ultimately redemptive) judgement on the actions and omissions of each person in the light of his or her individual life history. The young Rawls's sensitivity to violations of egalitarianism is reflected in the elevated position that pride assumes in his catalogue of vices. 'Pride' counts as sin not only when it leads immediately to the hybrid separation from God. Rawls likewise repudiates social self-aggrandizement, the meritocratic 'pride' in one's own achievements.

Pride in this sense jeopardizes reciprocal recognition of the equal dignity of each individual when somebody insists on having praiseworthy achievements attributed to *himself* as qualifications for being regarded as a superior person. Even when success can be attributed to one's own accomplishments, these in turn required talents and abilities. Regardless of whether a creator God or the lottery of nature decides how such resources are distributed, the beneficiaries may not impute the fact that they can draw upon such a potential to themselves as their own merit. This very distinction has in the meantime been obliterated by triumphant market liberalism. The fact that certain individuals and not others can be classified as a functional 'elite' based on success and achievement does not justify any difference in the kind of respect and treatment we owe to the equal dignity of each person.[13] As it happens, Rawls embodied this ethos of equal treatment and personal modesty in an inconspicuous fashion. Anyone who had ever met him personally, however fleetingly, was struck by the naturalness of this impressive habitus.

The Christian belief in the existence of a unique God before whom *all* human beings are equal implies, in addition to the egalitarian notion of the absolute worth of each person, the all-inclusiveness of the covenant between God and his people. The young Rawls defends this universalism against what he denounces as the contemporary phenomena of an ethnocentric closing off from others. In the exclusion or oppression of incriminated races and classes, foreign

religions, peoples and cultures (*A Brief Inquiry*, pp. 195ff.), he recognizes a generalized 'egotism' raised to the collective level: 'The
development of the closed group has been a distinctive factor in
Western civilization. Closed groups are now tearing that civilization
to pieces' (p. 197). Just a few years after he wrote his senior thesis,
egalitarian universalism would find a historically new expression in
international law in the shape of the UN Universal Declaration of
Human Rights. In contrast to the Christian community of believers,
a legal community can no longer rely upon the ethics of brotherly
love but must be founded instead on the legal implementation of
rationally justified moral principles which are acceptable to secular
and religious citizens alike.

(3) The history of John Rawls's work exhibits a philosophical
reshaping of religious ideas comparable to the one first undertaken
by Kant. The essential features of the religious ethics of community
can be sublimated into an individualistic and egalitarian universalistic secular deontology, because the triadic pattern of relations we
find in monotheistic communities remains intact in the 'kingdom of
ends' – that is, in the universal community of rational moral persons
who submit to self-legislated moral laws in the light of practical
reason. In this community, members do not stand in a *direct* relation
to each other either. Instead all interpersonal relations are mediated by the relation of each to the authority of an impartial 'third',
namely, to the authority of the moral law. The place of the relation
of the individual to the single transcendent and unifying God is now
taken by the moral point of view from which all autonomous actors
deliberate equally on how they shall behave in cases of conflict.
  Because the moral law claims categorical validity, the transcendental tension is not *abolished* but is incorporated into practical
reason: 'The perspective of eternity is not a perspective from a
certain place beyond the world, nor the point of view of a transcendent being; rather it is a certain form of thought and feeling
that rational persons can adopt within the world.'[14] Transcendence
no longer breaks into the world from beyond but operates *in the
world* as an idealizing and norm-generating force which *transcends*
all natural processes in the world from within. The anthropocentric
inversion of the direction of movement in no way compromises the
objectivity of the spontaneous ideas of reason. They are supposed
to remain free from arbitrariness and contingency. Thus the triadic
structure of the community of morally responsible persons remains
unaffected by the transition from religious to rational morality.[15] In
A Theory of Justice, the transcendence sublimated into the moral
point of view is embodied in the 'original position'. This is Rawls's

term for the situation of deliberation concerning the correct conception of justice. This situation is determined by equal restrictions on information and equal roles and endowments of the parties involved and is thereby structured in such a way 'that the principles that would be chosen, whatever they turn out to be, are acceptable from a moral point of view.'[16] There are also methodological points of contact in the young Rawls's theological thought for the transformation of the divine standpoint into a structurally generated perspective that compels self-interested participants to make a moral use of their practical reason. For, just as the young Rawls had conceived the place and role of God from the performative perspective of a second person who *encounters* him in communication, later on he discloses the moral dimension from the performative attitude of a person who becomes embroiled in conflicts and in the process *learns* through communication what he owes other persons. The harsh polemic against the objectifying perspective of natural theology shows that, from his theological beginnings, Rawls was familiar with the procedure of reconstructing a kind of implicit knowledge that is accessible only from the participant perspective.[17]

Needless to say, Rawls also had personal motives for abandoning the theological depiction of the 'good life' within the Christian community of faith in favour of the sober secular justification of the institutions of a 'well-ordered society'. Rawls sought to explain his loss of faith in private notes written in 1997 ('On my Religion'). They relate that the religious convictions of the morally sensitive young man were shattered by his war experiences, in particular by a military chaplain's political reinterpretation of the universalistic message of salvation and by the disturbing experience of being inexplicably spared when a close comrade lost his life. After the war, when he learned of the Holocaust, Rawls also wrestled with the question of theodicy: 'Where was God in Auschwitz?' A further motive is indicative of his rigorous moral sensibility, namely, his doubt whether the reasons for moral action can be sufficiently separated from the self-centred motives of the quest for personal salvation: 'our own individual soul and its salvation are hardly important for the larger picture of civilized life' (*A Brief Inquiry*, p. 265).

A Theory of Justice incorporates into the image of a civilized society all of those features of the social division of labour, of political power and of coercive law which the morally regulated interpersonal relations of the religious community lacked. Cooperation in a complex society, and especially the regulation of distributional conflicts, calls for institutions of social cooperation which are recognized as legitimate. The young Rawls already found nothing morally objectionable in human needs from which preferences and inclinations spring; but this natural source of individual conceptions of the good acquires an unprecedented importance in the mature political theory. For henceforth the legal freedoms which ensure that each individual has equal scope to develop and realize a more or less rational plan of life of his or her own form the kernel of political liberalism. Yet 'justice' still enjoys priority over 'the good' insofar as the institutions must be constructed so that they lead to a fair distribution of the basic goods. For only the latter ensures that equal rights also have equal value for all citizens.

However, the *meaning* of justice as fairness is not revealed by the word of God, nor is it given in the form of an innate idea. In order to be able to convince all citizens, the conception of political justice must be developed constructively out of common human reason. The correct use of practical reason consists in regarding interpersonal relations in need of regulation from the moral point of view. All of those concerned must submit to this substitute for a transcendent authority, regardless of whether the moral point of view is modelled as an 'original position' or is explicated in some other way. The moral point of view ensures that the constructive deliberations of practical reason are guided by an equivalent for the idea of *objectivity* which theoretical reason claims in virtue of its reference to objects in an independently existing world.

But *A Theory of Justice* is silent on the topic of religion; one searches in vain for corresponding entries in the index. If this were the author's last word, the posthumous discovery of his senior thesis would have only limited biographical value. As I see it, its true significance lies elsewhere. It may be that the vacuum left behind by the suppression of religion in the social contract theories of the Enlightenment ultimately bothered Rawls only because of his youthful religious experiences. In the two decades following the publication of *A Theory of Justice*, Rawls devoted himself to the question of whether our common practical reason, which is sufficient for constructing a concept of political justice, has enough substance to rival a moral theory intrinsically linked to religion. In the end he came to the conclusion that the liberal conception of justice acquires flesh and blood in a political community only when it finds support in religious and metaphysical contexts.

The tangible evidence of contemporary American society, in which the religious communities have preserved their vitality and play an important role in the public domain, is undoubtedly a motive for developing *A Theory of Justice* further towards *Political Liberalism*. For the need for political regulation is not only a result of social conflicts of interest and problems concerning distribution; it can also originate in value-laden conflicts between different cultural

forms of life and in disagreements between worldviews that must
be reasonably expected. Nevertheless, the relevance of what Rawls
came to regard as the 'fact of pluralism' is not sufficient to explain
the further development of the theory, for this points beyond the
problem of toleration. Addressing the problem of toleration per
se does not compel practical reason to restrict itself to questions of
political justice.[18]

Although the conception of justice as fairness does not undergo a
major change in *Political Liberalism*, its status within the framework
of the *extended* theory does. Rawls henceforth accords the 'correct'
political conception of justice the status of a 'freestanding' theory
which is supposedly independent of moral beliefs, though it relies
upon the agreement of all groups who share one of the 'reasonable'
comprehensive doctrines. I conjecture that this step is rooted in the
religious memories of his youth from which he had in the meantime
distanced himself. In his senior thesis the student wrote: 'We all
exist before God, and by being related to Him we are all related to
each other . . . That personal relations form such a nexus leads us to
the conclusion *that religion and ethics cannot be separated*' (*A Brief
Inquiry*, p. 116, emphasis added). In view of the political challenge
posed at present by religious and metaphysical pluralism, a generalization of this statement may have acquired renewed relevance
for Rawls. If moral convictions are not to forfeit their existential
motivating force, they cannot be severed from the thick context of a
'comprehensive' religious or metaphysical doctrine.

(4) With this move, religion acquired new importance for the moral
foundations of a liberal social order. In contrast to the classical works of the social contract tradition which had stripped the
concept of the political of all references to religion, Rawls recognizes that the problem of the political impact of the role of religion
in civil society has not been solved by the secularization of political
authority. The secularization of the state does not entail the secularization of society. This explains the air of paradox which to this
day has nourished a subliminal resentment within religious circles
concerning the justification of constitutional principles 'from reason
alone'.[19] Although a liberal constitution is designed in such a way
as to guarantee all religious communities equal scope for freedom
in civil society, it is at the same time supposed to shield the public
bodies responsible for making collectively binding decisions from
all religious influences. The same people who are expressly authorized to practise their religion and to lead a pious life are supposed,
in their role as citizens, to take part in a democratic process whose
results must remain free from any religious 'contamination'.

Laicism resolves this paradox by completely privatizing religion. However, as long as religious communities play a vital role in civil society and the public sphere, deliberative politics is as much a product of the public use of reason by religious citizens as by those who are non-religious. Although Rawls defends a cautious position on the role of religion in the public sphere, in his view the *justification* of liberal *constitutional principles* depends on a cognitive contribution by religious communities. According to Rawls, practical reason, which is shared by all citizens, can master the problem of legitimation only through a division of labour with religious and metaphysical doctrines. This is because a 'reasonable' concept of justice will convince citizens only within the context of their *more comprehensive* understandings of themselves and the world; it must be able to fit into their respective worldviews like a module and win universal agreement in the manner of an 'overlapping consensus'. This idea is the core of *Political Liberalism*.

Rawls models the constitution-founding act as a sequence of three steps.[20] First, the philosophers present several political conceptions which have been justified on reasonable grounds as a basis for choice. Then, in a second step, each citizen examines whether one of these competing conceptions coheres with his or her more comprehensive personal worldview. Once the results of these individual private tests become public, finally, a process of mutual inspection reveals whether there is sufficient overlap among the values of the various religious and ideological groups within society that a consensus can be found on one of the liberal conceptions of justice. This cognitive division of labour between reasonable insight and faith-based certainty confers a kind of right of confirmation on the religious and metaphysical worldviews actually represented in the society in question. The idea is that the worldview contexts are first supposed to confer 'truth' on the 'reasonable' module.[21]

This problematic contrast between public reason and private truth[22] acquires at least a certain plausibility in the light of the conception of the young Rawls. At any rate, by stripping morality of its claim to universality and transferring this claim to the religious sphere, Rawls decisively weakens reason. However, he pays a high price for hollowing out practical reason in this counter-intuitive way.[23] It remains unclear whether the overlapping consensus of the communities of belief is necessary only for the factual recognition – that is, the *stability* – of a constitution that has been put into force, or whether it is also necessary for the worthiness of recognition, and hence the *validity*, of the constitutional principles themselves. Rawls stipulates that only the voices of the 'reasonable', hence non-fundamentalist, religious communities can 'count' in the production of the overlapping consensus. Just those people are 'rational', according to Rawls, who are aware of the fallibility of the human mind (that is, who accept the 'burdens of judgement') and who in their role as co-legislators are prepared to adopt the perspective of others when they make public use of their reason.[24] Thus it ultimately remains undecided which of the two authorities should have the *final* word when it comes to justifying the political concept of justice – faith or knowledge.

For Rawls, too, the secularization of the political authority is a foregone conclusion. Thus a liberal constitution needs to be justified in a way which is neutral towards worldviews. At the same time, it must not ignore the cognitive potential of the belief systems present within society, and it must not truncate their contribution to the formation of public opinion and political will already at the level of civil society. Regardless of what one thinks of Rawls's position, he was the first to make clear the relevance that religious communities continue to have in and for the secular constitutional state. Because Rawls did not repress his own religious socialization but instead *reworked* it, we now have a better understanding of why he was the first among the major political philosophers to take religious and metaphysical pluralism seriously and to launch a fruitful debate over the status of religion in the public sphere.[25]

9

RAWLS'S POLITICAL LIBERALISM

Reply to the Resumption of a Discussion

I was at first surprised to learn of Gordon Finlayson[1] and Fabian Freyenhagen's[2] initiative to revisit the debate with Rawls from 1995; now, having read their reasons in the lucid introduction to this volume and seen the result, I am grateful to the two editors for realizing this project.[3] Admittedly, my reply bears the blemish of an irremediable asymmetry that afflicts this undertaking: the blind chance that I have outlived John Rawls places me in a precarious position, since he can no longer continue the debate *in persona*. However, this accidental constellation pales into insignificance in view of the noble and generous spirit of this person whom we all revere, and even more so in the light of the enormous importance of his outstanding work. In any case, nobody can have the final word in the 'unending conversation'.

In their review of the debate at that time, the editors speak of a 'missed opportunity'. Perhaps the expectations were pitched too high because of misapprehensions concerning the circumstances surrounding the debate. In consultation with John Rawls, the *Journal of Philosophy* had invited me in autumn 1991 to comment on his new work, *Political Liberalism*, which was scheduled to be published by Columbia University Press. I regarded *A Theory of Justice* as an epoch-making turn in the development of practical philosophy, and the desire of its important author to debate with me left me feeling somewhat overrated. Moreover, the correspondence which followed between us consistently referred to the 'comments' that I would write. On 26 May 1992, Rawls sent me a copy of the manuscript which was now ready for press; in January 1993 he thanked me for my 'comments' and, finally, in April of the same year he sent me a copy of the book, which had just appeared, with the relieved dedication: 'It gives me great pleasure to be able to send you this, done at last!'

I mention this background in order to make clear that I saw my role at the time rather as that of a reviewer who could expect a response from the author; at any rate, in writing my commentary my intention was not to bring my recently published philosophy of law into play as a theoretical programme in its own right.[4] However, the fact that I had this discourse theory in my head may also have been an obstacle when reading Rawls's new book. I have grasped the true significance of the transition from the 'theory of justice' to 'political liberalism' – which at the time irritated me – only gradually. It is the systematic importance which Rawls attaches to the fact that, in spite of the secularization of the state, we must *reasonably* expect to continue to encounter religious and metaphysical pluralism in civil society itself that justifies his unique status within the pantheon of classics of social contract theory.[5]

I On the Scope of Practical Reason

Gordon Finlayson and Fabian Freyenhagen have the merit of rendering the contrasting architectonics of the two theories transparent and of bringing the decisive difference in the discussion into sharp focus. How far are morality, law and politics amenable to rational justification and how do they relate to the normative content of the ethical-existential life orientations and worldviews of individuals and communities?[6] For my part, I follow Kant in assuming that, with the concept of autonomy, the practical reason shared by all persons offers a reliable guide both for the moral justification of individual actions and for the rational construction of a legitimate political constitution for society. Kant understands 'autonomy' as the ability of persons to bind their will to universal norms which they *give themselves in the light of reason*.

Rawls takes this individualistic and egalitarian universalism into account only in his exposition of a concept of *political justice*, however, whereas he situates *moral* conceptions on the particularistic side of the plurality of 'comprehensive doctrines'. Nevertheless, the 'priority of the right over the good', as I understand it, sets the parameters in such a way that the concept of political justice, understood as fairness, is composed entirely of universalized contents that can also count as 'morally' justified in the Kantian sense and are not shaped by values of a particular political culture. Finlayson and Freyenhagen challenge this claim by appealing to the leeway that the 'reflective equilibrium' achieved in a liberal political culture allows for the operation of universalization undertaken in the 'original position'. For if the reflective self-understanding of a liberal political culture – with its characteristic concepts of the 'person' and 'social cooperation' – enters into the definition of the original position itself, this predetermines the generalization performed by the parties in that position: 'The political values and ideas taken from public political culture might include materials that Habermas would classify as ethical rather than moral.'[7]

I am not convinced that this contextualist reading (first proposed by Richard Rorty) does justice to the claim to universality that Rawls associates with justice as fairness. But it has the advantage that it solves a problem which, in my view, besets the construction of the 'overlapping consensus'. On the one hand, the correctness of the political conception of justice is supposed to be measured by whether it can be integrated into the different comprehensive doctrines as a module; on the other hand, only 'reasonable' doctrines which recognize the primacy of political values are supposed to be admitted to this test. It remains unclear which side trumps the other, the competing groups with a shared worldview, who can say 'no', or practical reason, which prescribes in advance which voices count. In my opinion, the practical reason expressed in the citizens' public use of their reason should have the final word here, too. This admittedly calls for a philosophical justification of the universal validity of a morality of equal respect for everyone. Rawls wants to sidestep this task by confining himself to a 'freestanding' theory of political justice. I will return to the difficult questions that this alternative poses for both sides in sections II to V.

Other problems arise in the context of my philosophy of law. Gordon Finlayson and Fabian Freyenhagen offer a beautifully clear outline of the architecture of the theory which does not deduce the principles of constitutional law from a higher-level moral principle but instead *constructs* them step by step via *the interpenetration of the 'principle of democracy' and the 'form of law'*. The distinction between law and morality underlying this construction not only refers to the positive and coercive character of law; it rests in the first place *on the legal form* of what in the continental tradition are called 'subjective rights'. Such rights define spheres of individual choice within which legal subjects may act or refrain from acting as they wish. This form of law presupposes the principle that whatever is not prohibited is allowed. Accordingly, legal *claims* enjoy a primacy over legal *duties* in modern legal systems, whereas morality always accords priority to the 'Thou shalt' and grounds moral rights on the basis of prior duties.[8] But if the *form of law*, in conjunction with the discourse principle, is supposed to be sufficient to justify legitimate law without an immediate appeal to morality, the question arises whence the system of rights derives its moral content. I will return to the complex relation between law and morality in section VI. Having discussed the foundational problems, in sections VII, VIII and IX I will turn to reflections on the role of religion in the public sphere, the constitutionalization of international law, and the status of human rights.

II Moral Impartiality

Christopher McMahon's[9] objections provide an opportunity to review the arguments for the universal validity of a morality of equal respect for everyone.[10] Our shared starting point is a constructivist understanding of moral judgements which do not represent facts or express merely subjective attitudes or feelings but give expression to obligations, namely, what one *should* do or refrain from doing. They state how practical conflicts should be resolved in accordance with rules. Valid norms are 'right' in the sense that they *deserve* the agreement of their addressees because they coordinate actions in the equal interest of all concerned. The binding validity of moral rules, understood in terms of worthiness of recognition, has the epistemic meaning that these rules are supported by good reasons; should the need arise, universal agreement can be reached *in discourse* on the basis of these reasons.[11] Once moral norms have lost their nimbus and can be exposed to unreserved criticism, the 'justice' of impera- tives converges with the 'impartiality' of a form of examination to which they can be subjected in practical discourses.[12]

However, discourse ethics is not content with explaining the validity of moral commands in terms of 'justified acceptability'. This interpretation first has to be operationalized in the form of a rule of argumentation that expresses the content of the Kantian principle of universalization; but then its claim to universality also has to be justified in the face of contextualist objections.[13]

The justification of the moral principle (U) is the decisive step which Christopher McMahon addresses.[14] The controversial thesis states that anyone who participates seriously in a process of argumentation *at all* unavoidably accepts certain pragmatic presup- positions and their strong idealizing contents. The validity of the principle of universalization can be deduced from these implicitly assumed contents in combination with the goal of argumentation – that is, with the knowledge of what it means to justify a moral norm. The idea underlying such a 'deduction' can be easily stated in an informal way: assuming that the practice of argumentation rests on four general pragmatic presuppositions, namely, (a) the inclusive participation and (b) equal status of all those affected, (c) the truthfulness of their utterances, and (d) the structurally guaranteed freedom from any kind of coercion, then, in virtue of (a), (b) and (c), all relevant contributions can gain a hearing, but only those reasons can expect to meet with universal agreement which give equal consideration to the interests and values of everyone; and, in virtue of (c) and (d), only reasons (and not other motives) can tip the scales when it comes to agreement on a controversial norm.

Christopher McMahon raises two objections against this justification strategy:

- the impartiality of a judgement arrived at in moral discourses cannot be completely explained in terms of concepts of a shared discursive practice because it depends on *factors external to discourse* such as the beliefs and cognitive operations of the individual participants; and
- the validity of moral judgements *does not have a purely cognitive meaning* because an agreement arrived at in discourse also depends on the empathy of the participants, their willingness to identify with the fates of the other participants.

The first objection rests on an intentionalist description of the agreement arrived at in discourse. The idea is that such a consensus should be described only as the result of the aggregation of all of the individual stances, but not as a collective stance. I cannot address the premises underlying this distinction here but can appeal only to an intuitive understanding. When participants in discourse accept an argument for the same reasons, a shared practice of argumentation has led to an agreement. Monological reflections conducted by an individual *in foro interno* when weighing up the pros and cons of reasons and objections can also be understood on the model of an internalized discourse. Therefore, a discourse analysis need follow individual trains of thought only when it is a matter of explaining a disagreement or when individuals reach an agreement for *different reasons* (as in the case of a compromise or an 'overlapping' consensus). Otherwise all that is needed is a description of the structural requirements which competent participants in practical discourses fulfil.[15]

But can this structural approach account for the motivational and emotional aspects of moral reasoning? Whether one enters into moral discourse and, in that case, whether one takes moral insights to heart as required, and hence acts accordingly, is certainly a question of motivation. But the theory of discourse need not concern itself with feelings and attitudes that may accompany the cognitive operations. Moral attitudes and feelings certainly have a propositional content and are important empirical indicators for the appropriate description of a conflict *at the level of content*. But, for the participants in argumentation themselves, all that counts in practical discourses is the cognitive task, as is generally the case when it comes to solving problems. However, they already have to have an intuitive understanding of the point of morality in order to know *what* it is that they are arguing *for*. Only creatures who are individuated through communicatively mediated socialization processes need morality and act in the light of intersubjectively binding norms. For persons can develop their unique ego-identities only along the precarious route of *externalizing themselves in social relations*, and they must rely on social networks to stabilize their identities. Moral norms are a response to this vulnerability and dependence on the recognition by others – in other words, to needs which emerge from the mode of socialization itself. They accomplish two things at once: on the one hand, they guarantee the integrity of the individual; on the other, they found the social space in which individuals recognize each other as mutually dependent beings.

It is an interesting fact that the practice of argumentation, analysed as a form of communication, is already tailored to this core of morality.[16] *With the freedom to take justified 'yes' and 'no' stances*, discourses enable *each individual* to express her interests; but at the same time, *through the required orientation to the goal of reaching understanding*, discourses prevent participants from dissolving the social bond of mutual recognition. An agreement arrived at in discourse depends simultaneously on the autonomous 'yes' and 'no' responses of the individual participants and on their willingness to transcend cognitively their egocentric points of view. This is due to the fact that in practical discourses anyone's self-understanding and the worldview can also become exposed to public debate. For the descriptions under which the parties bring their needs into play are not a private matter; these interpretations of needs must be open to criticism even if they remain subject to the epistemic authority of a first person *as the final court of appeal*. This type of invasive criticism leads in turn to a *dynamic of mutual perspective-taking* (G. H. Mead) that prompts a decentring of each individual's perspective and the reciprocal inclusion of the other in the horizon of one's understanding of self and the world.

This reciprocal perspective-taking may call for something like 'empathy'.[17] But then empathy must not be understood as an element introduced into discourses from the outside – an irrational 'source of impartiality' which leads to reciprocal 'concessions'. What is involved is rather a methodological attitude adopted *for cognitive reasons*, one which anyone who engages in moral discourse must adopt towards the utterances of other participants. Otherwise what is going on is not a discourse – at any rate not a moral discourse. I find Christopher McMahon's image of an incremental construction of our moral world convincing. But how can he account for the *rational direction* taken by the process of mutually correcting collective prejudices which Hannah Arendt once described as an 'enlargement of the mind'?[18] Since he seems to deny that process a cognitive character, he has to explain it in psychological terms with a mixture of Hume and Bentham.

III Postmetaphysical, Not Freestanding

It will not come as a surprise that I do not have much to add to Joseph Heath's[19] helpful comments.[20] At the time I did not defend myself more energetically against the charge of developing a 'comprehensive' theory in Rawls's sense because I regarded it as a misunderstanding. Rawls seemed to differentiate the political conception of justice from 'comprehensive doctrines' in terms of the principle of the priority of the right over the good which I also shared. Given the other connotations of 'freestanding', my assumption was perhaps somewhat overhasty. But Rawls's project is obviously also inspired by Kant's critique of metaphysics, even if he lent it a different emphasis. At any rate, this critique provides the decisive impulse for my own conception of 'postmetaphysical thinking'. This mode of thinking attempts to employ only those sets of arguments that *prima facie* still 'count' after the nominalistic devaluation of totalizing propositions and essentialist claims. To put it in a nutshell, we no longer think that we are in a position to make unqualified statements about the whole of nature and history, about the totality of being, at least not without referring to our reflexively analysed means of representation. On the other hand, we associate a discursively redeemable validity claim with *all* philosophical propositions that remain within this framework. I cannot think of any serious philosophical study, in whatever subdiscipline, that would and could not seriously make truth claims (and instead aim at effect – for example, the rhetorical effect of political utterances).[21] The pattern of arguments and the circle of addressees for which the corresponding propositions in each case claim validity vary according to the issue, the field and the type of discourse. Ethical statements about what is good 'for me' or 'for us', for instance, remain captive to the perspective of a particular understanding of oneself and the world; but we claim (with this relativizing qualification) validity for them, too. Otherwise ethical advice would be pointless. Of course, we claim universal validity only for descriptive statements and for statements concerning justice (where I understand 'justice' in the Kantian sense). On these premises, all theoretical approaches pursued in a postmetaphysical spirit are 'freestanding', even those which employ weak transcendental arguments. Joseph Heath underlines the innocuous status of these kinds of statements.[22]

Rawls, by contrast, employs the concept 'freestanding' in a more specific sense when he refers to the independence of philosophical subdisciplines from (or their dependence on) one another. It often comes down to personal styles of thought, and not just to professional specialization, whether a philosopher devotes himself exclusively to the problems thrown up by a well- but narrowly defined subject matter or develops an implicit idea into a comprehensive theory that is open to criticism on numerous fronts. Donald Davidson, for example, developed his theory of rationality and truth in an elegant manner within the framework of a theory of meaning and language, which he went on to integrate in turn into a unified theory of mind and action. Rawls's concern to insulate his theoretical programme from controversies in neighbouring disciplines has to do with the meaning of normative political theories. He hoped that this would enable the concept of justice as fairness to secure broad public acceptance.[23] I am sceptical in this regard because each of Rawls's basic conceptual distinctions – *moral vs. political, rational vs. full autonomy, the right vs. the good, true vs. reasonable, reasonable vs. rational, truth vs. objectivity*, and so forth – compels him to take positions in specialist discourses far beyond the boundaries of political theory. Fallibilism and continued controversies on all fronts are the inevitable price to be paid for metaphysical abstinence.

Joseph Heath's final remark on the more or less 'realistic' content of political theories leads me to reiterate that a reconstructive approach, such as I pursue, tries to steer a course between 'ideal' and 'non-ideal' theory (a distinction which makes good sense from the strictly normative perspective of social contract theory).[24]

IV Acceptability vs. Acceptance

Anthony Simon Laden[25] interprets the 'freestanding' character of the conception of justice in a neo-Aristotelian sense. He wants to tailor political theory from the outset to public acceptance within civil society because it belongs to the domain of rhetoric:[26] whereas argumentation in other philosophical and scientific disciplines is aimed at a specialist public, Laden thinks that political philosophy must be geared to a 'political' mode of justification because it strives for the agreement within the broad public arena. The price that this mode of justification must then pay for the agreement of a wider circle of addressees reaching beyond the profession is a marked indifference to the pivotal question: Are the reasons for such an agreement merely effective or also *good* reasons that would stand up to impartial assessment? In the rhetorical success of a political argument, the acceptance of a proposal is supposed to somehow coalesce with its acceptability.[27]

Obviously Anthony Simon Laden is not a non-cognitivist concerning practical questions. Political justification would be unnecessary if the agreement of the public did not have to be reached on the basis of reasons. But what is so special about the political context that renders the question moot as to whether the persuasiveness of reasons rests on their intrinsic features or on a fortuitous agreement with corresponding local background convictions? The practical pressure to reach prompt decisions may often curtail a deeper examination of the values prevailing in a particular context. But that in no way diminishes the *aspiration* of the justification of political principles to achieve an ever broader and, in this comparative sense, universal agreement, a fact which Anthony Simon Laden does not dispute either. In the final analysis, he grounds the problematic demarcation of 'political' from 'philosophical' justification in terms of the intersubjective character of public discourses: 'Unlike philosophical justification in most of its guises, political justification is a fundamentally intersubjective form of reasoning.'[28]

If we assume that all validity claims must be redeemed discursively, however, that criterion is not sufficiently selective. More to the point is the distinction between validity claims made for descriptive statements as opposed to those made for normative statements. The non-epistemic concept of 'truth' carries the ontological connotation of the reference of factual statements to independently existing objects 'in the world', whereas the 'objectivity' or 'rightness' of normative statements has the epistemic meaning of rational acceptability 'for us'. But, even in the case of the truth of contested descriptive propositions, there are no definitive or irresistible arguments impervious to doubt; this is the reason why we have to rely *in both cases* on fallible discourses which remain within the limits – however ideally extensible – of an intersubjective shared world. There are, of course, differences between the patterns of argumentation and the kinds of reasons that are appropriate for justifying, for example, statements of physics as opposed to moral statements;

but in both cases the mode of discursive justification must decide whether the statements are true or right.

What does this mean for the distinction between philosophical and scientific justification, on the one hand, and political justification, on the other? Depending on the issue and the state of knowledge in a society, it may be possible to justify a statement only in more or less specialized languages that require a certain level of professional expertise. The 'linguistic division of labor' (Putnam), and hence the *de facto* exclusion of all non-specialists from the respective expert discourses, increases with the level of complexity of a society. The statements which are asserted to be true or right must nevertheless be comprehensible in principle to anyone who has learned to follow the relevant arguments.[29] The discourse of political philosophy is no exception in this regard. Ultimately, we, too, debate among colleagues. One thing must be kept in mind, however: if political philosophy is to make a contribution to clarifying the grounds of legitimation of *a particular* political community, the bridge formed by translations that mediate between its specialized discourse and the general discourse of the citizens must remain intact. For the citizens of a constitutional state must be able to convince themselves – and repeatedly as the occasion arises – of the legitimacy of the system of rule of which they are a part.[30]

V On the Normative Substance of Moral and Legislative Procedures

More promising than a neo-Aristotelian interpretation is the attempt to understand Rawls's political theory from the perspective of Hegel's critique of Kant. In his *Lectures on the History of Moral Philosophy*, Rawls already demonstrates unmistakable sympathy for Hegel's philosophy of right because it respects the ethical rootedness of persons in the existing institutions of civil society and because it treats this embeddedness of morality in ethical life as the main focus of the theory of justice. James Gledhill[31] chooses this perspective as the point of departure for his highly instructive comparison. He reveals a new facet of Rawls to me, for until now I had not regarded him as the better Hegelian.[32] My reconstructive approach, which Gledhill understands quite well, originates, after all, in a Hegelian–Marxist appropriation of Kant's moral and legal philosophy; generally such an approach should be better suited than strictly normative approaches to grounding the political theory of justice in a social theory. That may be true. But from such a normative point of view, which is focused exclusively on explaining the legitimacy of the constitutional state, Rawls's theory contains a relatively strong Hegelian element – at least if we follow James Gledhill's interpretation of the role of the Kantian generalization principle in the 'original position'.

On this interpretation, the substantive concepts that result from 'reflective equilibrium' – that is, from reflection on the common sense of the citizens of a liberal political culture – certainly transcend any particular context of origin, because the universal 'sense of justice' is reflected in the *reasonable* intuitions and feelings of citizens already used to a liberal tradition. However, this sense of justice, which all persons are supposed to possess *in nuce*, develops out of concrete conditions of life. Moreover, because it is articulated in the institutionally ordered interactions of the social lifeworld, its normative content is not exhausted by the abstract procedure of justification in the original position. It gives rise to substantive concepts as well, such as 'person', 'well-ordered society', 'fair cooperation', etc. This is why Rawls's *Political Liberalism* can begin from these basic concepts without further justification: 'What is the ultimate justification for the substantive reasonable constraints on the Original Position? Rawls describes Justice as Fairness as a theory of moral sentiments, setting out the principles that are regulative of, in the sense of being implicit within, the sense of justice.'[33]

As I understand James Gledhill, it is this assumption that leads him to make an interesting juxtaposition. While Rawls does not derive the normative content of political justice solely from the Kantian concept of autonomy or from a procedure of rational self-legislation, discourse ethics is based exclusively on the translation of autonomy, understood in socio-cognitive terms, into the procedure of redeeming moral validity claims in discourse. This procedure is inherently normative, but it is 'formal' in the same sense as the application of the categorical imperative.[34] To this observation I would like to add, however, that the meaning of *political* justice cannot be captured *completely*, in the same way as can the meaning of *moral* justice, by a discursive procedure of opinion- and will-formation.

Political justice is designed for a constitutional state and has the meaning of the legitimacy of a system of government that is established *by means of modern law*. The practice of constitution-making thus offers an appropriate model for the reasonable construction of a system of rights which is constitutive for such a political system. The discourse of a constituent assembly already presupposes the legal form of the organization of modern states. Therefore, it must take its cue from more specific assumptions than the explanation of the moral point of view. In the political case, it is a matter not just of judging or constructing morally valid norms of action in general but of constituting a political community by a system of rights which empowers free and equal citizens and directs the exercise of political power into legitimate channels. The goal is to construct a voluntary association of citizens who recognize each other both as democratic fellow legislators and as private subjects of equal individual rights (which have equal value for everybody as well).

In spite of this complex goal, even such a specific concept of political justice exhibits procedural features. It consists of a 'system of rights' which at first serves only to constitute the procedure of democratic law-making. For it must remain the privilege of the democratic legislator to specify the material content of those initially abstract categories of potential basic rights in terms of which an association of free and equal individuals is supposed to take shape. In this respect James Gledhill is completely right when he maintains that, not only for discourse ethics but also for the discourse theory of law and the constitutional state, the normative 'substance resides in the procedure' and not, as in Rawls, 'the procedure in the substance'.

VI Law and Morality

Nobody offers a better account of the ideas of a rational morality or of the relation between autonomy and public justification than Rainer Forst.[35] I relied previously on his advice when I first read the unpublished manuscript of *Political Liberalism*. In 1991 he had just returned from studying with Rawls and was more familiar with the recent development of his theory than I was. Contrary to his assumption, I cannot see any disagreement between us concerning the understanding of religious 'truths'[36] or concerning the shifting boundary between ethical values and the contents of moral beliefs.[37] Only the question of how the co-originality of the principles of popular sovereignty and the 'rule of law' should be understood leads to a genuine controversy, namely, over the relation between morality and law. To the priority accorded democratic self-legislation by republicanism, liberalism objects that a tyrannical majority could violate individual civil rights; to the priority accorded human rights by liberalism, republicanism objects that natural law is paternalistic – who could still claim that their own superior insight gives them the authority to impose constraints on the sovereignty of the united citizenry? The fact that each of the two principles, taken in isolation, can be justified in an equally convincing manner does not resolve this dilemma.

Rainer Forst assumes that the citizens in their role as founders are intrinsically moral persons. *As such* they feel committed to human rights and bring these *morally justified* rights into their constitution-making practice in order to implement them as civil rights and thereby establish the process of democratic legislation, among other things.[38] However, this would amount to translating the liberal priority of human rights into the paternalism of an assembly of morally pre-programmed founders who cannot proceed in a democratic fashion because the system of rights and the democratic procedure first established together with this system would be a product of their antecedent moral wisdom which they bring to bear prior to any political deliberations. In an attempt to avoid this implication, I have proposed a scenario in which the founders of the constitution understand themselves from the outset as political citizens. Before actually implementing the first specific rights, they would have to achieve conceptual clarity concerning their extraordinary role as founders, and hence concerning the complex meaning of their praxis of constitution-making.[39] This would lead them to the realization that an autonomous association of free and equal citizens can be constructed only by means of modern law and on the basis of individual rights that deserve recognition because they are generated by discursive means. In this scenario they would first engage in deliberation concerning the system of necessary rights which *must be made available in concert*, and only then – that is, only in response to the challenge of actual needs for regulation – would they specify the contents of those anticipated categories of rights in detail and back them up with public sanctions.

The first step involves the *conceptual* clarification of the *necessary* system of *potential* rights – that is, of the liberal, political, social and cultural categories of rights. With these basic categories of human rights the assembly becomes aware only of the 'language' in which it can express its democratic will. The democratic constitutional legislator must therefore create this code *uno acto* – it must make it available to itself, as it were – with the first concrete act of lawmaking. In this way we can do justice to the intuition that human rights may not be imposed upon the democratic lawmaker as an external constraint or be instrumentalized merely as a functional requirement for implementing its programmes. Furthermore, this scenario takes into account that human rights, formally speaking, are not moral norms at all but juridical rights with a moral content. Only in modern Europe, under the functional constraints of decentralized markets and a bureaucratic state, did law and morality – albeit on a shared foundation of both individual and communal autonomy – become differentiated out of 'objective', religiously or metaphysically justified bodies of law and develop in different directions.

Through this differentiation, law becomes independent from morality in the sense that, with the individual rights now taking the lead, narrowly specified legal claims replace the moral priority of a 'Thou shalt' that pervades all spheres of life. Individual rights grant legally circumscribed domains of choice – that is, of *action freed from the obligation to justify* – and thereby separate legal domains from the dense network of everyday duties of moral accountability. Moreover, they justify enforceable claims to the mutual recognition of this legal empowerment of subjects to take exclusive responsibility for how they conduct their lives. Human rights and civil rights, which share the form of subjective rights,[40] cannot be justified in the same way as moral norms and, hence, cannot be attributed exclusively to the insight of moral persons. Rather, out of the contents of universalistic morality they select a subset, namely, just those moral contents that can be realized in the medium of coercive and positive law.[41] Therefore, in the discursive justification of human rights, which are intrinsically geared to becoming institutionalized in positive law, the *form* of individual rights functions as a kind of filter. This legal form must be introduced as a separate element into a constitution-making practice that is conducted in accordance with the discourse principle (D).

Rainer Forst, by contrast, wants to trace moral and political justice back to a single 'right to justification'. This right empowers all actors to require each other to justify their actions in the light of norms that 'nobody can reasonably reject'. I appreciate the elegance of a parsimonious, unified construction. But the starting point in a *right* to justification already raises questions. Is it not, rather, the priority of a moral *duty* to justification that can be derived from the discourse-theoretical or (following Thomas M. Scanlon) the contractualist understanding of moral validity claims?[42] As the everyday language games of responsible agency already show, actors are 'responsible' for the consequences of their intentional actions in the sense that they *owe* affected persons a justification. The reciprocity of this duty does not change the general priority of duties over rights. For those affected, it is 'what we owe to each other' that first grounds the *justified* expectation that the others must account for their actions if called upon to do so. The right to justification loses this status as a justified expectation *derived* from *pervasive* moral duties and becomes a political claim only after rational law confronts the brittle religious legitimations of political systems with the idea of human *rights*. The fact that these human rights are conceptualized in intrinsically juridical terms as individual rights that absolve agents from the duty to provide justifications speaks against a monistic construction of law and morality.

VII The Role of Religion in the Secular State

Catherine Audard[43] explains the twofold agenda that I have been pursuing in my recent work on religion.[44] The controversy over the role that religion should play in the public sphere, which is a matter for normative political theory, must not be confused with the metaphilosophical question of how postmetaphysical thinking should understand its relation to religious traditions. Since the seventeenth century, theology has, roughly speaking, lost that connection to contemporary science which until that point had been provided by Aristotle's teleological philosophy of nature. Since then, philosophy has sided with science and more or less ignored theology. At any rate, since that time the onus of proof between religious and secular arguments has been reversed. Even the philosophers of German idealism, who did not ignore but tried to appropriate and *assimilate* the Judeo-Christian heritage, quite naturally claimed the authority to judge what is true and false in the contents of religion. They, too, regarded religion in essence as a hold-over from the past. But is it?

Besides *empirical* evidence that religion remains a *contemporary* intellectual formation, philosophy finds *internal* grounds for this conclusion in its own history. The long-drawn-out process of translating religious contents into philosophical language began in late antiquity – one need only think of the connotations of such concepts as person and individuality, freedom and justice, solidarity and community; a similar osmosis has left its mark on the history of philosophy with concepts such as emancipation, progress, crisis, etc. Today, at any rate, we cannot be certain that the process of assimilating semantic potentials from the religious language games – which remain inaccessible at their core – has been *exhausted* and that it cannot be continued. The conceptual work performed by religious writers and authors – I am thinking of the young Bloch and Benjamin, but also of Levinas and Derrida – tends to suggest that such a philosophical endeavour is still continuing. These circumstances suggest that a form of philosophy which has become fallibilistic should adopt a receptive and dialogical attitude towards *all* religious traditions and should engage in renewed reflection on the position of postmetaphysical thinking *between* science and religion.

This reflection has a twofold thrust. It takes issue, on the one hand, with the scientistic view that philosophy should be assimilated to science. Any assimilation to the paradigm of the hard sciences cancels the reflexive dimension that differentiates the *self-reflective activity* of philosophy from *research*. On the other hand, we should not blur the difference between what it means to take something to be true in the domains of faith and knowledge respectively. Even if reflection on the post-secular situation should lead to a changed attitude to religion, such a revision would do nothing to alter the fact that postmetaphysical thinking is a secular form of thought and must cling to the distinction between faith and knowledge as two essentially different modes of believing in the sense of 'taking-to-be-true'.

This historical perspective raises the question of a complementary learning process. In the West, the Reformation triggered a process of theological reflection on all sides. As a result, religious consciousness became reconciled with the fact of religious and metaphysical pluralism, with the legitimation of a secular state by appealing to human rights, and with the monopoly of institutionalized science over mundane knowledge. Shouldn't this kind of 'modernizing' religious consciousness be matched by a similar advance in reflection on the part of the dogmatic secularistic understanding of the Enlightenment? An Enlightenment aware of its own limits has no need to shut itself off from the possibility of *continuing* the translation of semantic potentials lurking in the major world religions into a publicly accessible language.

These metaphilosophical reflections on shifting mentalities touch upon the historical background of the much narrower issue, namely, what the democratic state must expect from its religious and non-religious citizens as regards the public use of reason. I learned a lot from Rawls about the ethics of democratic citizenship, and I see only a slight disagreement in this regard. Because the liberal state expressly authorizes its citizens to conduct their lives in accordance with their religious faith, it must not strangle religious voices already at the roots of the democratic process in civil society. All citizens who engage in public debates should be free to employ a religious language. They must, on the other hand, accept the proviso that the contents of religious utterances have to be translated into a generally accessible language before they can find their way onto the agendas and into the deliberations of parliaments, courts and public decision-making bodies. An institutional filter between the informal communication in the public sphere and the formal deliberations leading to collectively binding decisions must ensure that all *publicly sanctioned* decisions can be both formulated and *justified* in a universally accessible language. This liberal purpose does not justify restricting the polyphonic plurality of public voices already at the basis. Admittedly, the 'monolingual' contributions of religious citizens are reliant on cooperative efforts of translation by the other side. At the same time, non-religious citizens bear a complementary burden, since they are supposed to remain receptive to the contributions of their religious fellow citizens.

VIII International Law and Cosmopolitanism

What has always fascinated me about Kant's idea of a cosmopolitan condition is that, in it, *national* citizens acquire the additional status of *world* citizens and enjoy the protection of the international community, if necessary even against the failures and crimes of their own governments.[45] Contrary to what Jim Bohman claims,[46] however, I have never entertained a world government as a possible, or even a desirable, aspiration.[47] Since 1998 at the latest, I have employed the formula 'world domestic policy without a world government'[48] and have advocated restricting the functions of the United Nations to the core competences of securing peace and the global implementation of human rights.[49] In this direction, I have taken up the idea proposed by German international lawyers of a progressive *constitutionalization of international law* and have developed the notion – which is more ambitious and more normatively demanding than Rawls's 'law of peoples' – of a global multi-level system, though one which, taken *as a whole*, does not assume the character of the state.[50] This conception is also much more robust from the standpoint of democratic legitimation than Jim Bohman's own rather vague idea of an extension of national chains of legitimation into the global public sphere and a global *civil* society.

I trace the serious misunderstandings (as documented in notes 47–50 above) back to the fact that Jim Bohman clings to the classical concepts of 'sovereignty' and 'legitimacy'.[51] These remain wedded to the model of the nation-state and do not do justice to the complexity of the emerging multicultural world society. Here I can recall only the two corresponding, and by now overdue, conceptual reorientations. The revision of the concept of state sovereignty along Hans Kelsen's lines is by now well established in the resolutions passed by the UN General Assembly. On this unitary reading of international law, 'sovereignty' states that the international community authorizes *and obligates* national governments, which are subject to the prohibition on violence in international law, to safeguard the civil rights of their citizens on their own territory. If they fail to fulfil this obligation, they must expect to meet with sanctions.

The reconceptualization of democratic legitimation is a more complicated matter. Hitherto it has been operationalized in the form of the familiar national institutions and procedures and must now be reconfigured to *governance beyond the nation-state*. In a politically constituted world society, the security and human rights policy pursued at the supranational level is as much in need of democratic legitimation as are the negotiations conducted at the transnational level over questions of global energy, environmental, financial and economic policy (which bear on issues of distribution).[52] Climate change and financial markets running out of control are merely the harbingers of problems which can no longer be managed with the classical international legal instrument of treaties between states but instead call for institutions capable of operating on a global scale. The rapidly growing network of international organizations not only brings home the problems that now call for a new mode of global domestic policy but also points to the need for legitimation that has already arisen but has not yet been met.

These tensions serve as a spur to institutional imagination and justify constructive proposals. Here I cannot discuss my proposed scenario in detail, but I would like to mention two thoughts which are decisive for its construction.[53] On the one hand, the burdens of legitimation can be specified according to competences and tasks and can be distributed among the nested jurisdictions of a multi-level system (which *as a whole* lacks the character of the state) differently than within a nation-state. On the other hand, we must abandon the holistic notion that the state and the democratic constitution are congruent. The three essential elements which are in fact *fused* in the historically successful form of the European nation-state – the state organization, the constitution of an association of free and equal citizens, and the politically and culturally based solidarity among them – would be *disaggregated* in a global multi-level system and would have to form *a new configuration*. Moreover, an international community worthy of the name would have to be constituted both by states and by citizens – or, better, by citizens in their dual role as national and world citizens.

IX Human Rights

Jeffrey Flynn[54] takes up my reflections on the construction of a cosmopolitan condition under the aspect of human rights. I am in agreement with virtually every sentence of his well-thought-out analysis.[55] He correctly identifies the two essential points in which my approach differs from that of Rawls.

- On my conception, the constitution of the international community must be judged fundamentally by the same standards of political justice as the constitutional state; at any rate, the constitutionalization of international law does not require a new, normatively weaker, basis.

- The egalitarian and universalistic content of the system of rights that explicates the concept of political justice endows it with a utopian surplus whose gradual realization becomes the focus of conflicts; and these conflicts have come to a standstill no more at the national than at the global level.

Both of these theses raise questions and are in need of some qualification.

The system of rights that developed in the West found different institutional expression in different states and political cultures. But on the Western understanding they embody the same normative substance that has by now been recognized by all member states of the United Nations – at least according to the letter and in principle. This fact cannot disguise the interpretive conflicts sparked by individual cases in the globally extended circle of cultures and world religions.

In a very rough stylization, one could imagine that the community of Western states is faced with an alternative which casts light on Rawls's and my respective points of departure. One option is that the party characterized for short as 'the West' clings to the existing situation and divides up the rest of the world, as it were, *from the perspective of foreign policy* according to the extent to which other cultures appear to it as more or less 'decent' and should be treated accordingly as coalition partners or as opponents. The alternative is that 'the West' recognizes the need to construct institutions capable of operating on a global scale and is open to an intercultural discourse on the best interpretation of human rights. In contrast to anticipatory resignation in the face of persisting cultural differences, self-confident willingness to engage in discussion harmonizes better with the conviction that the occidental understanding of human rights is *prima facie* well grounded and deserves universal agreement. Notwithstanding its confidence in the power of its own arguments, this would require the Western community of states to enter such an intercultural discourse without reservation and in an awareness of the fallibility of its own interpretation.

If human rights are no longer interpreted one-sidedly from the foreign policy perspective focused on diffusing one's own values but, instead, from the shared standpoint of creating a just global domestic politics, then an unreserved intercultural discourse provides the only forum in which the worldwide acceptability of principles of political justice can be tested. In this forum, all parties must be open to instruction concerning their own blind spots by others. This willingness to learn in no way alters the fact that all participants start from the system of rights which has also been embodied in binding norms in many national constitutions and, in the meantime, also in international law. This first step in the conceptual clarification of principles of political justice which could form the focus of an intercultural consensus corresponds to the first conceptual stage of a constitution-making practice I mentioned earlier; in the real world, it goes hand in hand with the incremental political efforts to consolidate the institutional framework of the international community under the sudden pressure of urgent challenges.

The other difference discussed by Jeffrey Flynn concerns the polemical character of human rights, which were not accidentally the offspring of revolutions. Normatively speaking, human rights acquire positive validity in the shape of civil rights which ground the reciprocally recognized status of democratic citizens. Historically speaking, this still unfinished process was driven by political struggles which were often violent and sometimes revolutionary. This fact is also reflected in the form and content of these unique rights. They guarantee their bearers a *claim* to recognition as subjects of equal rights; their origin in collective outrage over, and revolt against, systematic violations of human dignity leaves behind a trace in this self-conscious character of claims vouched for by *the form of individual rights*. At the same time *their content* also betrays the moral surplus of rights which arose out of moral protests against insults and humiliation and claim universal validity. This moral charge lends the basic rights sanctioned by the state the 'unsaturated' character of a utopian surplus which found expression from the beginning in the dialectical tension between human and civil rights: human rights, by their very meaning, strive for ever more extensive inclusion. But this disruptive moment is expressed not only in the social dimension, in struggles to extend the scope of human rights beyond national frontiers; rather, these struggles enter into communication with substantive conflicts over how to achieve greater protection of human rights within our own democratic nation-states.

In well-established constitutional states, too, political conflicts continue over how rights long since enshrined in positive law *can be further elaborated*. A striking example is the so-called Hartz IV judgement of the German Federal Constitutional Court of 9 February 2010;[56] in the context of a special dispute over the actual standards by which social security benefits should be assessed, the Court 'deduced' a *new* basic right from the first article of the German Basic Law. This new right grants a basic level of social security that goes beyond the economic subsistence minimum and enables the beneficiaries to participate 'in social, cultural and political life' (or enables affected children to prepare for such participation). A minimalistic, abridged interpretation of human rights tailored to foreign policy objectives distracts from this internal dynamic and fails to do justice to the deeper meaning of the constitutional revolutions of the eighteenth century.

The translation of the first human right into positive law gave rise to a *legal duty* to realize exacting moral requirements that has become engraved in the collective memory of humanity. Human rights constitute a *realistic* utopia insofar as they no longer paint deceptive images of a social utopia which guarantees collective *happiness* but anchor the *claim to a just society* in the institutions of constitutional states themselves.[57]

10

RELIGION IN THE PUBLIC SPHERE OF 'POST-SECULAR' SOCIETY

In a single weekend in 2007 it was reported that the Archbishop of Canterbury had recommended that the British parliament should adopt parts of Sharia family law for its domestic Muslim population; that French President Nicolas Sarkozy had dispatched 4,000 additional policemen to the notorious Parisian *banlieues* afflicted by rioting Algerian youths; and that a fire had broken out in an apartment block in the German city of Ludwigshafen in which nine Turks, among them four children, met their deaths, prompting deep suspicion and outrage in the Turkish media despite the fact that the cause of the fire remained unclear; this prompted the Turkish prime minster to make a visit to Germany and his ambivalent campaign speech in a stadium in Cologne in turn triggered a strident response in the German press. These news stories document the scale of the threat to cohesion within supposedly secular societies – and how urgently we need to ask whether we are now dealing with a 'post-secular' society and, if so, in what sense.

I European 'Exceptionalism' or Doubts about the Secularization Thesis

A society can be described as 'post-secular' only if at some point in the past it had been 'secular'. Therefore, this controversial term can be applied only to the affluent societies of Europe or to countries such as Canada, Australia and New Zealand, where people's religious ties have steadily loosened, quite dramatically so since the end of Second World War. These regions had witnessed a more or less universal spread of the awareness among their citizens of living in a secularized society. As measured by the usual sociological indicators, however, the religious behaviour and convictions of the local populations have by no means changed to such an extent as to justify labelling these societies 'post-secular'. In Germany, even trends towards new, de-institutionalized forms of religiosity and spirituality cannot offset the tangible losses suffered by the major religious communities.[1] Nevertheless, global changes and the visible conflicts that flare up in connection with religious issues give us reason to doubt whether the relevance of religion has in fact waned. The hypothesis that there is close linkage between the modernization of society and the secularization of the population, which for a long time went unchallenged, is steadily losing support among sociologists.[2]

This hypothesis rests on three, at first sight, plausible considerations. First, progress in science and technology promotes an *anthropocentric understanding* of the 'disenchanted' world because all empirical states and events can be explained in causal terms; and a scientifically enlightened mind cannot be easily reconciled with theocentric and metaphysical worldviews. Second, with the functional *differentiation of social subsystems*, the churches and other religious organizations lose their influence over law, politics, public welfare, culture, education and science; they confine themselves to their proper function of administering the means of salvation, turn the exercise of religion into a more or less private matter, and in general lose public influence and relevance. Finally, the development from agrarian to industrial and post-industrial societies leads to higher average levels of welfare and increasing social security; and, with the easing of everyday risks and growing existential security, individual human beings have less need for a practice that promises to master uncontrolled contingencies through communication with a 'higher' or cosmic power.

Although the secularization thesis seems to be confirmed by developments in the affluent European societies, it has been a source of controversy among professional sociologists for over two decades.[3] Lately, in the wake of the not unfounded criticism of a narrow Eurocentric perspective, there has even been talk of the 'end of secularization theory'.[4] The United States, notwithstanding the undiminished vibrancy of its religious communities and its unchanging proportion of religiously committed and active citizens, remains at the forefront of modernization. It was long regarded as the great exception to the secularizing trend; yet informed by a *globally extended* perspective on other cultures and world religions, the United States now looks more like the normal case. From this revisionist perspective, the European development, whose occidental rationalism was once supposed to serve as a model for the rest of the world, is actually the exception or deviant path [*Sonderweg*] rather than the norm.[5]

II The Vitality of the Religious

Above all, three overlapping phenomena converge to create the impression of a worldwide 'resurgence of religion': (a) the missionary expansion of the major world religions, (b) their fundamentalist radicalization, and (c) the political instrumentalization of their innate potential for violence.

(a) A first sign of vibrancy is that orthodox, or at least conservative, groups within the established religious organizations and churches are on the advance everywhere. This holds for Hinduism and Buddhism as much as it does for the three monotheistic religions. Most striking of all is the regional spread of these established religions in Africa and in the countries of East and Southeast Asia. The success of these missionary efforts seems to depend, among other things, on the flexibility of the corresponding forms of organization. The transnational and multicultural Roman Catholic Church is adapting better to the trend towards globalization than are the Protestant churches organized at the national level, which are the principal losers. Most dynamic of all are the decentralized networks of Islam (especially in sub-Saharan Africa) and the Evangelicals (especially in Latin America). Their distinguishing feature is an ecstatic form of religiosity inspired by individual charismatic leaders.

(b) As to fundamentalism, the fastest-growing religious movements, such as the Pentecostals and the radical Muslims, can be described most readily as 'fundamentalist'. They either combat the modern world or isolate themselves from it. Their forms of worship combine spiritualism and eschatological adventism with rigid moral conceptions and literal adherence to holy scripture. By contrast, the 'new religious movements' which have mushroomed since the 1970s are marked by 'Californian' syncretism, though they share with the Evangelicals a de-institutionalized form of religious observance. In Japan, approximately 400 such sects have arisen, which combine elements of Buddhism and popular religion with pseudoscientific and esoteric doctrines. In China, the political repression of the Falun Gong sect has focused attention on the large number of 'new religions' in that country, whose followers are estimated to number some 80 million.[6]

(c) Finally, the mullah regime in Iran and Islamist terrorism are merely the most spectacular examples of a political unleashing of the potential for violence innate in religion. Smouldering conflicts that are profane in origin are often first ignited when they are encoded in religious terms. This is true of the 'desecularization' of the Middle East conflict, the politics of Hindu nationalism, the enduring conflict between India and Pakistan,[7] and the mobilization of the religious right in the United States before and during the invasion of Iraq.

III Post-Secular Society: Religious Communities in a Secular Environment

I cannot discuss in detail the controversy among sociologists concerning the supposed exceptionalism of the secularized societies of Europe in the midst of a religiously mobilized world society. My impression is that the data collected globally still provide surprisingly robust support for the defenders of the secularization thesis.[8] In my view, the weakness of the theory of secularization is due rather to rash inferences which betray an imprecise use of the concepts of 'secularization' and 'modernization'. It remains true that, in the course of the differentiation of functional social systems, churches and religious communities increasingly confined themselves to their core function of pastoral care and had to renounce their extensive competencies in other areas of society. At the same time, the practice of faith assumed more personal or subjective forms. There is a correlation between the functional specification of the religious system and the individualization of religious practice.

However, as José Casanova correctly points out, the loss of function and the trend towards individualization do not necessarily imply that religion *loses influence and relevance* either in the public arena and the culture of any given society or in the personal conduct of life.[9] Quite apart from their numerical weight, religious communities can still claim a 'setting' even in the life of societies that are largely secularized. Today the description 'post-secular society' can be applied to public consciousness in Europe to the extent that, for the present, it has to adjust itself 'to the fact that religious communities continue to exist in a context of ongoing secularization'.[10] The revised reading of the secularization thesis relates less to its substance and more to the associated predictions concerning the future role of 'religion'. The new description of modern societies as 'post-secular' refers to a *change in consciousness* that I attribute above all to three phenomena.

First, the broad perception of global conflicts, which are often presented in the media as hinging on religious strife, changes public consciousness. The majority of European citizens do not even need the presence of obtrusive fundamentalist movements and the fear of terrorism veiled in religious terms to make them aware of the relativity of their secular mentality within the global horizon. This undermines the secular*istic* belief that religion *is destined to disappear* and purges the secular understanding of the world of any triumphalism. The awareness of living in a secular society is no longer bound up with the *certainty* that cultural and social modernization can advance only at the cost of the public influence and personal relevance of religion.

Second, the influence of religion is growing not only worldwide but also within national public spheres. I am thinking not so much of the skilful public relations of the churches as of the fact that religious organizations are increasingly assuming the role of 'communities of interpretation' in the political life of secular societies.[11] They can exercise influence on the formation of public opinion and political will by making relevant contributions on key issues, irrespective of whether their arguments are convincing or objectionable. Our pluralist societies are a responsive sounding board for such interventions because, increasingly often, they are split over value conflicts requiring political regulation. Be it the dispute over the legalization of abortion or of voluntary euthanasia, over bioethical issues of reproductive medicine, or over questions of animal protection or climate change – in these and similar disputes the key premises are so opaque that it is by no means settled from the outset which party can draw upon the more convincing moral intuitions.

As it happens, the visibility and vibrancy of immigrant religious communities also enhance the influence of secular societies' own churches and congregations. The Muslims next door, if I may take an example of relevance for both the Netherlands and Germany, force the Christian citizens to confront the practice of a rival faith. They also give the secular citizens a keener awareness of the phenomenon of the public presence of religion.

The third stimulus for a change of consciousness among the population is the immigration of 'guest-workers' and refugees, in particular from countries with traditional cultural backgrounds. Since the sixteenth century, Europe has had to contend with *confessional* schisms within its own culture and society. As a result of immigration, the more strident dissonances between different *religions* are combining with the challenge of a *pluralism of ways of life* typical of immigrant societies, which is more far-reaching than the challenge posed by a *pluralism of religious orientations*. In European

societies which are still caught in the painful process of transformation into postcolonial immigrant societies, the issue of the tolerant
coexistence between different religious communities is made harder
by the difficult problem of how to integrate immigrant cultures into
the host society. While coping with the pressure of globalized labour
markets, social integration must succeed even under the humiliat-
ing conditions of increasing social inequality. But that is a different
story.

IV The Process of the 'Separation of Church and State'

I have thus far taken the viewpoint of a sociological *observer* in
trying to answer the question of why largely secularized societies
can nevertheless be described as 'post-secular'. In these societies,
religion maintains its public influence and relevance, while the
secularistic certainty that religion will disappear everywhere in the
world as modernization accelerates is losing ground. If we henceforth adopt the perspective of *participants*, we face a quite different,
namely, a normative question: How *should* we understand ourselves
as members of a post-secular society and what *must* we expect from
one another in order to ensure that, in firmly entrenched nation-
states, social relations remain civil even under conditions of cultural
and religious pluralism?

These debates over how we should understand ourselves have
assumed a sharper tone since the terrorist attacks of 11 September
2001. In the Netherlands, the murder of Theo van Gogh on 2
November 2004 kindled a passionate public discussion not only
about the victim but also about Mohammed Bouyeri, the assassin,
and Ayaan Hirsi Ali, the actual target of the hatred.[12] That debate
assumed a quality of its own, its ripples spreading beyond national
borders to unleash a European-wide debate.[13] I am interested in
the background assumptions that render this discussion on 'Islam
in Europe' so explosive. But before I can address the philosophical
core of the mutual recriminations, I would like to outline in greater
detail the shared starting point of the parties to the conflict, namely,
the commitment to the separation of church and state.

The secularization of state power was the appropriate response
to the confessional wars of the early modern period. The principle
of the 'separation of church and state' was realized only gradually and took a different form in each national body of law. To
the extent that political authority assumed a secular character, the
religious minorities, which were at first merely tolerated, progressively acquired more extensive rights – first the freedom to practise

their own religion in private, then the right of religious expression, and finally equal rights to exercise their religion in public. A historical review of this protracted process that lasted into the twentieth century can teach us something about the *preconditions* for this precious achievement, namely, inclusive religious freedom extended to all citizens alike.

After the Reformation, the state initially faced the basic task of pacifying a society divided along confessional lines – in other words, of creating a condition of public peace. In the context of the present debate, the Dutch writer Margriet de Moor reminds her fellow citizens of these beginnings:

> Tolerance is often mentioned in the same breath as respect, yet our version of tolerance, which has its roots in the sixteenth and seventeenth centuries, is not based on respect. On the contrary, we used to hold a deep hatred of other people's religion. Catholics and Calvinists did not have an ounce of respect for the views of the other side, and our Eighty Years' War was not just an uprising against Spain but a bloody Jihad of Orthodox Calvinists against Catholicism.[14]

It remains to be seen what Margriet de Moor means here by 'respect'.

As regards peace and order, governments had to assume a neutral stand even when they remained intertwined with the prevailing religion in the country. The state had to disarm the quarrelling parties, invent arrangements for a peaceful coexistence of the inimical confessions, and monitor their precarious coexistence. At the social level, the opposing subcultures could settle into niches of their own so that they remained estranged *from one another*. It was precisely this *modus vivendi* (and this is the point I would like to stress) that proved to be insufficient when the constitutional revolutions of the late eighteenth century spawned a new political order that subjected the completely secularized powers of the state to the rule of law and at the same time to the democratic will of the people.

V Religious Freedom and the Principle of Toleration

This constitutional state is able to guarantee its citizens equal freedom of religion only under the proviso that they no longer barricade themselves within the self-enclosed lifeworlds of their religious communities and seal themselves off from one another. All subcultures, whether religious or not, are expected to free their individual members from their embrace so that the citizens can recognize one another *reciprocally* in civil society – that is, as members of *one and the same* political community. As democratic citizens they give themselves laws under which, as *private citizens*, they can preserve their identity in the context of their own particular culture and worldview and respect each other. This new relation between democratic government, civil society and subcultural self-sufficiency is the key to correctly understanding the two motives that compete with each other today even though they are meant to complement each other. For the universalist project of the political Enlightenment by no means contradicts the particularist sensibilities of multiculturalism, provided that this project is understood in the correct way.

The *liberal* rule of law already guarantees religious freedom as a basic right, meaning that the fate of religious minorities no longer depends on the benevolence of a more or less tolerant state authority. Yet it is the *democratic* state that first makes it possible to apply this principle in an impartial way.[15] In particular cases – for example, when Turkish communities in Berlin, Cologne or Frankfurt want to move their places of worship out of backyards by building mosques which are visible from afar – the issue is no longer the principle per se, but its fair application. However, plausible reasons for defining what should or should not be tolerated can only be ascertained by means of the deliberative and inclusive procedures of democratic will-formation. The principle of toleration is freed from the suspicion of merely expressing condescension only when the conflicting parties meet on an equal footing in the process of reaching an agreement *with one another*.[16] It is always a matter of controversy how, in a particular case, the boundary between positive freedom of religion (that is, the right to exercise your own faith) and the negative freedom not to be encumbered by the religious practices of people of other faiths should be drawn. But in a democracy, those affected, however indirectly, are themselves involved in the decision-making process.

'Toleration' is, of course, not only a question of enacting and applying laws; it must be practised in everyday life. Toleration means that believers of one faith, believers of a different faith and non-believers must acknowledge each other's right to those convictions, practices and ways of life that they themselves reject. This concession must be supported by a shared basis of mutual recognition which makes it possible to overcome repugnant dissonances. The kind of recognition required must not be confused with *esteem* for an alien culture and way of life or for the convictions and practices that are rejected.[17] We need to show tolerance only vis-à-vis worldviews that we consider wrong and vis-à-vis habits that we do not like. Therefore, the basis of recognition is not esteem for this or that characteristic or achievement but the awareness that one is a member of an inclusive community of citizens endowed with equal rights, in which each individual is accountable to the others for her political utterances and actions.[18]

Now that is easier said than done. The equal inclusion of *all* citizens in civil society requires not only a political culture that prevents liberal attitudes from being confused with indifference; inclusion can be achieved only if certain material conditions are also fulfilled. Among these are full integration in kindergartens, schools and universities to offset social disadvantages and equal opportunities when it comes to accessing the labour market.

What is most important to me in the present context, however, is the image of an inclusive civil society in which equal citizenship and cultural difference complement each other in the right way. For example, as long as a considerable portion of German citizens of Turkish origin and Muslim faith have stronger political ties to their old homeland than to their new one, the corrective voices and votes required to *expand* the range of values of the dominant political culture will be lacking in the public sphere and at the ballot boxes. Without the inclusion of minorities in civil society, the two complementary processes will not be able to develop hand in hand, namely, the opening of the political community to a difference-sensitive inclusion of foreign minority cultures, on the one hand, and the liberalization of these subcultures to a point where they encourage their individual members to exercise their equal rights to participate in the democratic process, on the other.

VI 'Enlightenment Fundamentalism' versus 'Multiculturalism': The New *Kulturkampf* and its Slogans

In answering the question of how we should understand ourselves as members of a post-secular society, we can take our cue from these two *interlocking* processes. But the ideological parties that confront each other in public debates today pay scant attention to how the two processes intermesh. The party of the multiculturalists appeals to the protection of collective identities and accuses the other side of being 'Enlightenment fundamentalists', whereas the secularists insist on the uncompromising inclusion of minorities in the existing political culture and charge their opponents with 'multiculturalist betrayal' of the core values of the Enlightenment.

So-called multiculturalists fight for an even-handed adjustment of the legal system to the cultural minorities' claim to equal treatment. They warn against a policy of enforced assimilation which would uproot minorities from their cultural background. The secular state, they claim, must not pursue such a robust policy of integrating minorities into the egalitarian community of citizens that individuals would be torn out of the contexts in which they form their identities. From this communitarian perspective, a policy of abstract integration is open to the suspicion that it subjects minorities to the imperatives of the majority culture. Today, however, the multiculturalists are on the defensive: 'Not just academics but politicians and paper columnists saw the Enlightenment as the fortress to be defended against Islamist extremism.'[19] This reaction, in turn, brings a critique of 'Enlightenment fundamentalism' into play. For example, Timothy Garton Ash argues in the *New York Review of Books* that 'even Muslim women contradict the way in which Hirsi Ali attributes her oppression to Islam instead of the respective national, regional or tribal culture.'[20] In fact, Muslim immigrants cannot be integrated into a Western society in defiance of their religion – only with it.

On the other hand, the secularists fight for a colour-blind political inclusion of all citizens, irrespective of their cultural origin and religious membership. This side warns against the consequences of a 'politics of identity' that goes too far in adapting the legal system to the claims that the intrinsic characteristics of minority cultures should be preserved. From this 'laicistic' point of view, religion must remain exclusively a private matter. Thus, Pascal Bruckner rejects cultural rights because these supposedly give rise to parallel societies – to 'small, self-isolated social groups, each of which adheres to a different norm'.[21] Bruckner roundly condemns multiculturalism as 'anti-racist racism', though his attack applies at most to those extremist multiculturalists who advocate the introduction of collective cultural rights. Such a form of 'species protection' for entire cultural groups would in fact curtail the right of their individual members to choose a way of life of their own.[22] Thus, the conflicting parties both pretend to fight for the same purpose: a liberal society that allows autonomous citizens to coexist in a civilized manner. Yet they are locked in a *Kulturkampf* which resurfaces with every new political pretext. Although it is clear that both aspects are interlinked, they argue bitterly over whether the preservation of cultural identity should be accorded priority over enforcing shared citizenship or vice versa. The discussion acquires its polemical edge from contradictory philosophical premises which the opponents rightly or wrongly attribute to one another. Ian Buruma has made the interesting observation that, following 9/11, an academic debate on the Enlightenment, on modernity and postmodernity, migrated from the university to the marketplace.[23] The debate was stoked by problematic background assumptions, namely, a form of cultural relativism pepped up with a critique of reason, on the one side, and a rigid version of secularism fixated on criticizing religion, on the other.

VII The Relativism of Radical Multiculturalists

The radical reading of multiculturalism often relies on a false notion of the 'incommensurability' of worldviews, discourses or conceptual schemes. From this contextualist perspective, cultural ways of life appear to be semantically closed universes, each of which insists on its own unique standards of rationality and truth claims. Therefore, each culture is supposed to exist for itself as a semantically impervious whole, cut off from dialogues with other cultures. With the exception of precarious compromises, submission or conversion are supposed to be the only alternatives for terminating conflicts between such cultures. Given this premise, universalist validity claims, such as the arguments for the universality of democracy and human rights, are, for radical multiculturalists, nothing but the imperialist power claim of a dominant culture.

Ironically, this relativistic reading inadvertently robs itself of the standards for a critique of the unequal treatment of cultural minorities. In our postcolonial immigrant societies, discrimination against minorities is usually rooted in prevailing cultural prejudices that lead to a selective application of established constitutional principles. If one then does not even take the universalist thrust of these principles seriously, there is no vantage point from which one could uncover the illegitimate entanglement of the interpretation of the constitution with the prejudices of the majority culture.

Here I do not need to address the philosophical issue of why cultural relativism, based on a postmodern critique of reason, is an untenable position.[24] However, this position is interesting for another reason, namely, it explains a peculiar switch of political allegiances. When faced with Islamist terrorism, some of the leftist 'multiculturalists' turned into war-hungry liberal hawks and even formed an unexpected alliance with neoconservative 'Enlightenment fundamentalists'.[25] In the battle against Islamic fundamentalists, these converts were evidently able to embrace the culture of the Enlightenment they had previously combated (like the conservatives) as their own 'Western culture' all the more easily because they had always rejected its universalist claims: 'The Enlightenment has a particular appeal to some conservatives because its values are not just universal, but more importantly, "ours", that is, European, Western values.'[26]

Needless to say, this critique does not apply to those laicist intellectuals of French origin for whom the pejorative term 'Enlightenment fundamentalists' was originally coined. However, a certain militancy on the part of these guardians of a universalist Enlightenment tradition can also be explained in terms of a dubious philosophical background assumption. From their viewpoint, religion must withdraw from the political sphere into the private domain because, cognitively speaking, it represents a historically obsolete 'intellectual formation' (a past *Gestalt des Geistes*, in Hegelian terms). From the normative standpoint of a liberal constitution, religion must be tolerated but it cannot claim to provide a cultural resource for the self-understanding of any truly modern mind.

This philosophical position does not depend on how one judges the empirical observation that religious citizens and communities, too, continue to make relevant contributions to the formation of public opinion and political will even in largely secularized societies. Whether or not one considers the predicate 'post-secular' appropriate for describing Western European societies, one can be convinced, on philosophical grounds, that religious communities owe their enduring influence exclusively to an obstinate survival of pre-modern modes of thought which can be explained in sociological terms. Either way, the substance of faith is scientifically discredited from the standpoint of secularism. This provokes secularists into adopting a polemical stance in discussions with religious traditions and religious believers who still lay claim to a significant public role.

VIII Secular or Secularist

When it comes to terminology, I distinguish between 'secular' and 'secularist'. Unlike the neutral stance of a secular or unbelieving person who takes an agnostic position on religious validity claims, secularists adopt a polemical stance towards religious doctrines that still exert a certain public influence despite the fact that their claims cannot be scientifically justified. Today secularism is often based on a 'hard' version of naturalism – that is, one justified in scientific terms. Unlike the case of cultural relativism, here I do not need to comment on the philosophical background.[27] For what interests me in the present context is whether a secularist devaluation of religion, if it were one day to be shared by the vast majority of secular citizens, is in any way compatible with the post-secular balance between shared citizenship and cultural difference which I have outlined. Or would the secularistic mindset of a relevant portion of the citizenry be just as unappetizing for the normative self-understanding of a post-secular society as the fundamentalist leaning of a mass of religious citizens? This question touches on deeper roots of the present unease than any 'multiculturalist drama'.

It is to the credit of the secularists that they, too, vehemently insist on the indispensability of including all citizens as equals in civil society. Because a democratic order cannot simply be *imposed* on its authors, the constitutional state expects that its citizens should adhere to an ethics of citizenship that goes beyond mere obedience to the law. Religious citizens and communities must do more than merely adjust to the constitutional order in a superficial way. They are expected to assimilate the secular legitimation of constitutional principles under the premises of their own faith.[28] As is well known, it was only with the Second Vatican Council in 1965 that the Catholic Church embraced liberalism and democracy. And it was no different with the Protestant churches in Germany. Many Muslim communities still have this painful learning process ahead of them. Certainly, the insight is also growing in the Islamic world that today a historical-hermeneutic approach to the teachings of the Quran is required. However, the discussion over a desired Euro-Islam draws our attention once again to the fact that it is the religious communities that will themselves decide whether they can recognize in a reformed faith their 'true faith'.[29]

When we think of such a shift from a traditional to a more reflexive form of religious consciousness, what springs to mind is the model of the post-Reformation change in epistemic attitudes that took place within the Christian churches of the West. But such a change in mentality cannot be prescribed, nor can it be politically manipulated or pushed through by law; it is at best the result of a learning process. And it appears as a 'learning process' only from the viewpoint of a secular self-understanding of modernity. Such cognitive presuppositions of an ethics of democratic citizenship show us the limits of a normative political theory that can justify only rights and duties. Learning processes can be fostered, but they cannot be morally or legally stipulated.[30]

IX Dialectic of Enlightenment: Secularization as a Complementary Learning Process

But shouldn't we turn the question around? Is a learning process necessary only on the side of religious traditionalism and not on that of secularism as well? Do the self-same normative expectations that we have of an inclusive civil society not prohibit a secularistic devaluation of religion just as they prohibit, for example, the religious rejection of the equal status of men and women? A *complementary* learning process is necessary on the secular side, at any rate, as long as we do not confuse the neutrality of the secular state towards competing religious worldviews with banishing all religious contributions from the political public sphere.

Certainly, the domain of the state, which controls the means of legitimate coercion, should not be opened up to the strife between diverse religious communities, for otherwise the government could become the executive arm of a religious majority that imposes its will on the opposition. In a constitutional state, it must be possible to formulate and publicly justify all legally *enforceable* norms in a language that all of the citizens understand. Yet the state's neutrality does not preclude the permissibility of religious utterances within the political public sphere, as long as the institutionalized processes of consultation and decision-making at the parliamentary, judicial, ministerial and administrative levels remain clearly separated from the informal flows of political communication and opinion-formation among the broader public of citizens. The 'separation of church and state' calls for a filter between these two spheres – a filter through which only 'translated' – that is, secular – contributions may pass from the confused din of voices within the public sphere into the formal agendas of state institutions.

Two reasons speak in favour of such liberal practice. First, those who are neither willing nor able to divide their moral convictions and their vocabulary into profane and religious strands must be permitted to take part in political will-formation even if they use religious language. Second, the democratic state should not rashly reduce the polyphonic complexity of the diverse public voices, because it cannot know whether to do so would be to cut society off from scarce resources for generating meanings and shaping identities. In particular, with regard to vulnerable social relations, religious traditions have the power to convincingly articulate moral sensitivities and solidaristic intuitions. Then what causes difficulties for secularism is the expectation that secular citizens in civil society and the public sphere should meet their religious fellow citizens on an equal footing.

Were secular citizens to encounter their fellow citizens with the reservation that the latter, because of their religious mindset, cannot be taken seriously as modern contemporaries, they would revert to the level of a mere *modus vivendi* and would thereby relinquish the very basis of mutual recognition which is constitutive for shared citizenship. *A fortiori*, secular citizens may not exclude the possibility that religious utterances contain semantic contents, and even secret intuitions of their own, that can be translated and introduced into secular discourse. So, if all is to go well, both sides, each from its own perspective, must accept an interpretation of the relation between faith and knowledge that enables them to live together in a self-reflective manner.

SOURCES OF THE TEXTS

Sources of the German original texts are followed by references to existing English translations where applicable. All existing translations have been fully revised for this volume.

Chapter 1: First published in German as 'Von den Weltbildern zur Lebenswelt', in *Kritik der Vernunft, Philosophische Texte*, Vol. 5 (Frankfurt am Main: Suhrkamp, 2009), pp. 203–70. This version follows the extensively revised reprint in C. F. Gethmann (ed.), *Lebenswelt und Wissenschaft* (Hamburg: Felix Meiner, 2011), pp. 63–88.

Chapter 2: 'Die Lebenswelt als Raum symbolisch verkörperter Gründe', first published in German in this volume.

Chapter 3: 'Eine Hypothese zum gattungsgeschichtlichen Sinn des Ritus', first published in German in this volume.

Chapter 4: First published in German as 'Ein neues Interesse der Philosophie an Religion: Ein Interview', *Deutsche Zeitschrift für Philosophie* 58 (2010): 3–16. First published in English, trans. Matthias Fritsch, by the Immanent Frame (http://blogs.ssrc.org/tif/).

Chapter 5: 'Religion und nachmetaphysisches Denken: Eine Replik', first published in German in this volume. First published in English as 'Reply to My Critics', in Craig Calhoun, Eduardo Mendieta and Jonathan VanAntwerpen (eds), *Habermas and Religion*, trans. Ciaran Cronin (Cambridge: Polity, 2013), pp. 347–90.

Chapter 6: First published in German as 'Ein Symposion über Glauben und Wissen: Replik auf Einwände, Reaktion auf

Anregungen', in Rudolf Langthaler and Herta Nagl-Docekal (eds), *Glauben und Wissen: Ein Symposium mit Jürgen Habermas* (Vienna: Oldenbourg Akademieverlag, 2007), pp. 366–414.

Chapter 7: 'Das Politische – Der vernünftige Sinn eines zweifelhaften Erbstücks der Politischen Theologie', first published in German in this volume. First published in English in Eduardo Mendieta and Jonathan VanAntwerpen (eds), *The Power of Religion in the Public Sphere*, trans. Ciaran Cronin (New York: SSRC/Columbia University Press, 2011), pp. 15–33.

Chapter 8: First published in German as 'Das "gute Leben" eine "abscheuliche Phrase": Welche Bedeutung hat die religiöse Ethik des jungen Rawls für dessen Politische Theorie?', an afterword to Joshua Cohen and Thomas Nagel (eds), John Rawls, *Über Sünde, Glaube und Religion* (Berlin: Suhrkamp, 2010), pp. 315–36. First published in English, trans. Ciaran Cronin, in Joseph K. Schear (ed.), *European Journal of Philosophy* 18/3 (Oxford/Malden: Blackwell, 2010), pp. 443–54.

Chapter 9: 'Rawls' Politischer Liberalismus: Replik auf die Wiederaufnahme einer Diskussion', first published in German in this volume. First published in English in James Gordon Finlayson and Fabian Freyenhagen (eds), *Habermas and Rawls: Disputing the Political*, trans. Ciaran Cronin (New York: Routledge, 2011), pp. 283–304.

Chapter 10: First published in German under the title 'Die Dialektik der Säkularisierung', *Blätter für deutsche und internationale Politik* 4 (2008): 33–46. First published in English under the title 'What is Meant by a "Post-Secular Society?" A Discussion on Islam in Europe', in *Europe: The Faltering Project*, trans. Ciaran Cronin (Cambridge: Polity, 2009), pp. 59–77. A different translation appeared under the title 'Notes on Post-Secular Society', in Nathan Gardels (ed.), *New Perspectives Quarterly* 25/4 (Oxford/Malden: Blackwell 2008): 17–29.

Notes

Preface

1 Habermas, *Postmetaphysical Thinking: Philosophical Essays*, trans. William Mark Hohengarten (Cambridge: Polity, 1992).
2 Herbert Schnädelbach, *Was Philosophen wissen und was man von ihnen lernen kann* (Munich: C. H. Beck, 2012).
3 See Robert Spaemann's self-confident retrospective account of his intellectual biography in *Über Gott und die Welt: Eine Autobiographie in Gesprächen* (Stuttgart: Klett-Cotta, 2012) and *Schritte über uns hinaus: Gesammelte Reden und Aufsätze* (Stuttgart: Klett-Cotta, 2010).
4 Dieter Henrich has continued to pursue his programme with impressive rigour: Henrich, *Denken und Selbstsein: Vorlesungen über Subjektivität* (Frankfurt am Main: Suhrkamp, 2007) and *Werke im Werden: Über die Genesis philosophischer Einsichten* (Munich: C. H. Beck, 2011).
5 Hent de Vries, *Philosophy and the Turn to Religion* (Baltimore: Johns Hopkins University Press, 1999).
6 Habermas, *Between Naturalism and Religion: Philosophical Essays*, trans. Ciaran Cronin (Cambridge: Polity, 2008).
7 Michael Tomasello, *Origins of Human Communication* (Cambridge, MA: MIT Press, 2008).
8 See the introduction to Habermas, *Rationalitäts- und Sprachtheorie, Philosophische Texte*, Vol. 2 (Frankfurt am Main: Suhrkamp, 2009), pp. 9–28.
9 Habermas, 'Toward a Critique of the Theory of Meaning', in *Postmetaphysical Thinking*, pp. 57–87.
10 The distinction between normatively freestanding and normatively embedded requests and proclamations compelled me to make corresponding differentiations between the use of language 'oriented towards agreement' and the use of language 'oriented towards reaching understanding' and between 'strong' and 'weak' communicative action. See Habermas, 'Some Further Clarifications of the Concept of Communicative Rationality', in *On the Pragmatics of Communication*,

ed. Maeve Cooke (Cambridge: Polity, 1999), pp. 307–42, here pp. 320ff. and pp. 326ff.

11 Habermas, *The Theory of Communicative Action*, Vol. 2, trans. Thomas McCarthy (Boston: Beacon Press, 1987), p. 77.

12 Michael Tomasello, *Constructing a Language: A Usage-Based Theory of Language Acquisition* (Cambridge, MA: Harvard University Press, 2003).

13 I use the term 'linguistic' to refer to the communicative exchange of conventionalized symbols employed with identical meanings within the linguistic community.

14 Merlin Donald, *Origins of the Modern Mind: Three Stages in the Evolution of Culture and Cognition* (Cambridge, MA: Harvard University Press, 1991).

15 From this formal perspective, a similar relationship between philosophy and science can still be found even in the postmetaphysical understanding of ourselves and the world. This is true, at any rate, as long as philosophy regards it as its classical task, as it were, to rationally reconstruct the most general features of the intuitive knowledge of knowing, speaking and acting subjects about how to form and justify judgements, pursue and realize intentional goals, and form linguistic expressions and use them for communicative purposes.

16 I have defended this conception a number of times against the concerns expressed by theologians that it involves a functionalist understanding of religion. See, among others, my 'Reply', in Michael Reder and Josef Schmidt (eds), *An Awareness of What is Missing: Faith and Reason in a Post-Secular Age*, trans. Ciaran Cronin (Cambridge: Polity, 2010), pp. 72–83.

Chapter 1 From Worldviews to the Lifeworld

1 Martin Heidegger, 'The Age of the World Picture', in Heidegger, *Off the Beaten Track*, ed. and trans. Julian Young and Kenneth Haynes (Cambridge: Cambridge University Press, 2002), pp. 57–85.

2 In what follows, I will use the term 'worldview' as long as the context does not explicitly require emphasizing the process aspect.

3 See the article 'Welt' in Joachim Ritter et al. (eds), *Historisches Wörterbuch der Philosophie*, Vol. 10 (Darmstadt: Wissenschaftliche Buchgesellschaft, 1992), pp. 408–46.

4 On the following, see Habermas, 'Actions, Speech Acts, Linguistically Mediated Interactions, and the Lifeworld', in *On the Pragmatics of Communication*, ed. and trans. Maeve Cooke (Cambridge: Polity, 2000), pp. 215–55.

5 See, especially, the classics of Anglo-American social and cultural anthropology and those of structural anthropology following Lévi-Strauss.

6 Marcel Gauchet treats shamanism as an example of this monistic world inhabited by the living and the dead alike:

Here we have specialists who initiate communication with the spirit world and manipulate its representatives, but who, despite the considerable prestige and fears they inspire, are steadfastly confined to the common lot of their society. This is because the visible and the invisible is intertwined in a single world . . . The shaman remains a technician endowed with a special ability to move between the living and the dead, between spirits and magical forces. He is in no way an incarnating force creating a permanent union between the human world and its creator or ruler. (Gauchet, *The Disenchantment of the World* [Princeton, NJ: Princeton University Press, 1997], p. 31)

7 Karl Jaspers, *The Origin and Goal of History*, trans. Michael Bullock (London: Routledge, 1953), pp. 1–21.

8 Johann P. Arnason, Shmuel N. Eisenstadt and Björn Wittrock (eds), *Axial Civilizations and World History* (London and Boston: Brill, 2005).

9 On Abelard, see, for example, Kurt Flasch, *Kampfplätze der Philosophie: Große Kontroversen von Augustin bis Voltaire* (Frankfurt am Main: Klostermann, 2008), pp. 125–40.

10 Ludger Honnefelder, *Duns Scotus* (Munich: C. H. Beck, 2005); on the medieval origins of modern thought in general, see Honnefelder, *Woher kommen wir? Ursprünge der Moderne im Mittelalter* (Berlin: Berlin University Press, 2008).

11 On the epistemology of the practical sciences in the thirteenth and fourteenth centuries, see Matthias Lutz-Bachmann and Alexander Fidora (eds), *Handlung und Wissenschaft: Die Epistemologie der praktischen Wissenschaften im 13. und 14. Jahrhundert* (Berlin: De Gruyter, 2008).

12 Habermas, *Between Naturalism and Religion: Philosophical Essays*, trans. Ciaran Cronin (Cambridge: Polity, 2008).

13 Kant, *Religion within the Boundaries of Mere Reason*, ed. Allen Wood and George di Giovanni (Cambridge: Cambridge University Press, 1998), p. 81 (6:63). (Citations of Kant's works in parentheses refer to the volume and page numbers of the edition of the Königlich-Preußische Akademie der Wissenschaften (1903–11) [Berlin: de Gruyter, 1968].)

14 Thomas Nagel, 'What Is it like to Be a Bat?', in Nagel, *Mortal Questions* (Cambridge: Cambridge University Press, 1979), pp. 165–80.

15 Thomas Hobbes, 'Second Objection', in René Descartes, *The Philosophical Writings of Descartes*, Vol. 2, trans. John Cottingham et al. (Cambridge: Cambridge University Press, 1984), p. 122.

16 Richard Rorty, *Philosophy and the Mirror of Nature* (Princeton, NJ: Princeton University Press, 1979).

17 Against Hobbes, Descartes appeals to the consciousness-transcending generality of propositions: 'Who doubts that a Frenchman and a German can reason about *the same things*, despite the fact that the words that they think of are completely different?'

18 Robert B. Pippin, 'Kant on the Spontaneity of Mind', in Pippin, *Idealism as Modernism: Hegelian Variations* (Cambridge: Cambridge University Press, 1997), pp. 29ff.

19 Immanuel Kant, *Critique of Pure Reason*, trans. and ed. Paul Guyer

and Allen W. Wood (Cambridge: Cambridge University Press, 1998), p. 117 (B xxx) (emphasis in original).

20 On this interpretation of the postulates of practical reason, see Ulrich Anacker, *Natur und Intersubjektivität* (Frankfurt am Main: Suhrkamp, 1974), Part II.

21 Thomas McCarthy, *Ideals and Illusions* (Cambridge, MA: MIT Press, 1992), pp. 16ff.; Habermas, 'Communicative Reason and the Detranscendentalized Use of Reason', in *Between Naturalism and Religion*, pp. 24–76.

22 See my reply in Axel Honneth and Hans Joas (eds), *Communicative Action* (Cambridge, MA: MIT Press, 1991), pp. 214–64.

23 This restriction to nomological natural sciences, on the one hand, and the humanities and social sciences, on the other, involves a simplification which is a consequence of the perspective of the question I am posing. In making such a rough contrast I am neglecting not only specific features of the biological sciences and psychology which become relevant in other contexts but also the manifold differences within the two major domains of the 'natural' and the 'human' sciences characterized *only by their mode of access* to their respective object domains.

24 I am grateful to Lutz Wingert for this clarification.

25 Not even versions of systems theory in social science that strive to eliminate all normative traits from their object domain can dispense with hermeneutic access to their symbolic objects and with 'meaning' as a basic concept.

26 Ernst Cassirer's 'theory of symbolic forms' sees itself as a direct defence of Kant's transcendental philosophy against this historicist critique.

27 Habermas, *Postmetaphysical Thinking: Philosophical Essays*, trans. William Mark Hohengarten (Cambridge: Polity, 1992); Habermas, *The Theory of Communicative Action*, Vol. 1, trans. Thomas McCarthy (Boston: Beacon Press, 1987), pp. 24–8.

28 Whether the 'original' image of man can be completely assimilated by the 'scientific image of man' is discussed by Wilfrid Sellars in 'Philosophy and the Scientific Image of Man' (1960), in Sellars, *Science, Perception and Reality* (Atascadero, CA: Ridgeview, 1963), pp. 1–40.

29 Maxwell Bennett, Daniel Dennett, Peter Hacker and John Searle, *Neuroscience and Philosophy: Brain, Mind, and Language* (New York: Columbia University Press, 2007).

30 Habermas, 'Reconstruction and Interpretation in the Social Sciences', in Habermas, *Moral Consciousness and Communicative Action*, trans. Christian Lenhardt and Shierry Weber Nicholsen (Cambridge: Polity, 1992), pp. 21–42.

31 Lutz Wingert, 'Lebensweltliche Gewißheit versus wissenschaftliches Wissen?', in Peter Janich (ed.), *Naturalismus und Menschenbild* (Hamburg: Felix Meiner, 2008), pp. 288–309.

32 Lutz Wingert, 'Grenzen der naturalistischen Selbstobjektivierung', in Dieter Sturma (ed.), *Philosophie und Neurowissenschaften* (Frankfurt am Main: Suhrkamp, 2006), pp. 240–60.

33 Michael Pauen, 'Ratio und Natur: Warum unsere Fähigkeit, nach Gründen zu handeln, auch durch reduktive Ansätze in Frage gestellt werden kann', in Hans-Peter Krüger (ed.), *Hirn als Subjekt?*

Philosophische Grenzfragen der Neurobiologie (Berlin: Akademie, 2007), pp. 417–29; for a recent account, see Ansgar Beckermann, *Gehirn, Ich, Freiheit: Neurowissenschaften und Menschenbild* (Paderborn: Mentis, 2008); for my critique of compatibilism, see Habermas, 'The Language Game of Responsible Agency and the Problem of Free Will: How Can Epistemic Dualism be Reconciled with Ontological Monism?', *Philosophical Explorations* 10/1 (2007): 13–50.
34 See ibid.
35 Arno Ros, *Materie und Geist: Eine philosophische Untersuchung* (Paderborn: Mentis, 2005).
36 The advantage of the constructivism of the Erlangen and Marburg school is that it takes the pragmatic dimension of research seriously as a context of action and reconstructs the performative aspects of research. See Peter Janich, 'Naturwissenschaften vom Menschen versus Philosophie', in Janich (ed.), *Naturalismus und Menschenbild*, p. 45: 'The inclusion of the performative perspective in fact constitutes the most important difference between a philosophy of science that remains at the level of mere description and the methodological reconstructions of methodological-culturalistic approaches.' See also Janich, *Kleine Philosophie der Naturwissenschaften* (Munich: C. H. Beck, 1997); Janich, *Kultur und Methode: Philosophie in einer wissenschaftlich geprägten Welt* (Frankfurt am Main: Suhrkamp, 2006). However, restricting images of the world which are constitutive of object domains to 'determinations of aims' involves a narrowing down based on an inadmissible reduction of linguistic behaviour to teleological action. The background of communicative action in the lifeworld is much more complex than the background of actions analysed solely under the aspect of instrumental rationality, on which Janich focuses exclusively (see, inter alia, 'Naturwissenschaft vom Menschen versus Philosophie', p. 47). As a result, the world-disclosing element of language, which Heidegger accorded independent status at the expense of inner-worldly learning processes, is sacrificed in favour of a Fichtean stress on voluntarist 'positings'.
37 Among these approaches is also the theory of cognitive interests that I developed together with Karl-Otto Apel. See also Christoph Hubig and Andreas Luckner, 'Natur, Kultur und Technik als Reflexionsbegriffe', in Janich (ed.), *Naturalismus und Menschenbild*, pp. 52–66.
38 Richard Rorty, *Philosophy and Social Hope* (London: Penguin, 1999), pp. 23–92.
39 Thomas Rentsch, *Gott* (Berlin: de Gruyter, 2005); Hans Julius Schneider, *Religion* (Berlin: de Gruyter, 2008); see also the contributions in Hent de Vries (ed.), *Religion: Beyond a Concept* (New York: Fordham University Press, 2008).
40 Dieter Henrich, *Denken und Selbstsein: Vorlesungen über Subjektivität* (Frankfurt am Main: Suhrkamp, 2007).
41 Christoph Demmerling, 'Welcher Naturalismus? Von der Naturwissenschaft zum Pragmatismus', in Janich (ed.), *Naturalismus und Menschenbild*, pp. 240–56.
42 Karl-Otto Apel speaks in this sense of a postulate of the 'self-recovery of the mind' [*Selbsteinholung des Geistes*]. Janich ('Naturwissenschaft

vom Menschen versus Philosophie', p. 41) radicalizes this requirement into the methodological principle that the 'natural sciences of the
human' *may* claim validity only for those results which are compatible
with the fact that these findings were obtained by human beings *as
investigating subjects.*

43 This condition meets the objection raised by Hubig and Luckner
('Natur, Kultur und Technik als Reflexionsbegriffe', p. 57) that the
search for an 'evolution' that encompasses both nature and culture
represents a regression to a 'lower level of reflection'.

44 The synthetic materialism of Arno Ros, *Materie und Geist* seems
ultimately to boil down to a form of perspectivism of the conceptual
systems employed with which the same phenomena can be classified in
narrower or broader spatiotemporal contexts respectively.

Chapter 2 The Lifeworld as a Space of Symbolically Embodied Reasons

1 For a critique of a 'separatist conception of the space of reasons',
see Lutz Wingert, 'Was geschieht im Raum der Gründe?', in Dieter
Sturma (ed.), *Vernunft und Freiheit: Zur praktischen Philosophie von
Julian Nida-Rümelin* (Berlin: de Gruyter, 2012). See also the references
provided there to the relevant analyses of Donald Davidson, Julian
Nida-Rümelin and John Searle.

2 Robert B. Brandom, *Making it Explicit: Reasoning, Representing, and
Discursive Commitment* (Cambridge, MA: Harvard University Press,
1998).

3 The content of a speech act is itself a reason for the addressees and
cannot be reduced to an intention that a speaker wants to reveal to a
hearer. Julian Nida-Rümelin uses this argument against an abridged
empiricist version of intentionalism; see Nida-Rümelin, 'Grice, Gründe
und Bedeutung', in Nida-Rümelin, *Philosophie und Lebensform*
(Frankfurt am Main: Suhrkamp, 2009), pp. 135–54. In the space of
reasons, what is said is not exhausted by what is intended. I previously
argued along these lines in Habermas, 'Intentionalistische Semantik'
(1975/76), in Habermas, *Vorstudien und Ergänzungen zur Theorie des
kommunikativen Handelns* (Frankfurt am Main: Suhrkamp, 1984), pp.
332–52.

4 On my approach in terms of a pragmatics of language, see the studies in
Habermas, *Rationalitäts- und Sprachtheorie, Philosophische Texte*, Vol.
2 (Frankfurt am Main: Suhrkamp, 2009).

5 On the following, see the studies in Habermas, *Sprachtheoretische
Grundlegung der Soziologie, Philosophische Texte*, Vol. 1 (Frankfurt am
Main: Suhrkamp, 2009).

6 On the importance of Peirce for the paradigm shift from the philosophy of consciousness to the philosophy of language, see the essay
by Karl-Otto Apel, 'Metaphysik und die transzendentalphilosophis-
chen Paradigmen der Ersten Philosophie', in Apel, *Paradigmen der
Ersten Philosophie: Zur reflexiven – transzendentalpragmatischen –
Rekonstruktion der Philosophiegeschichte* (Berlin: Suhrkamp, 2011), pp.
164–90.

7 Michael Tomasello, *The Cultural Origins of Human Cognition* (Cambridge, MA: Harvard University Press, 1999).

8 Here I am using the term 'egocentric' in a metaphorical sense because the relations to self that permit talk of an 'I' develop only after the level of linguistic communication has been reached. The 'I' is a social construct (which is why the search by neurobiology for a central instance in the midst of decentrally networked brain waves is also condemned to failure). On the genesis of the self as the result of social interactions, see Habermas, 'The Language Game of Responsible Agency and the Problem of Free Will: How Can Epistemic Dualism be Reconciled with Ontological Monism?', *Philosophical Explorations* 10/1 (2007): 13–50.

9 Michael Tomasello, *Origins of Human Communication* (Cambridge, MA: MIT Press, 2008).

10 However, Michael Tomasello himself presents the explanatory reasons in a different evolutionary sequence when he adopts a mentalist strategy of explanation by tracing the symbolic meanings back to shared perceptions and intentions. But how can the mental abilities take precedence in the order of explanation over communication if the interconnection between the interpersonal relationship and intentionality (in the sense of the objectifying attitude towards the world) cannot be explained without an intervening gesture? I tend to assume the co-originality of the three human monopolies – namely, the use of symbols, reciprocal perspective-taking, and the intentional attitude towards objects. As regards the conceptual analysis, this means that these characteristic faculties form a system. Co-originality in the genetic sense draws attention to the highly contingent character of an improbable initial constellation in the horde life of our immediate biological ancestors – of a situation, for example, in which environmentally conditioned pressures to cooperate *meet with* a high level of practical cognitive maturity and favour a functional change in the non-intentional expressive movements, which signifies *simultaneously* a socialization of cognition, a new form of symbolically mediated communication, and the communalization of motives. In contrast, Tomasello (see note 11 below) postulates an improbable moral revolution of motives as the beginning of anthropogenesis.

11 Michael Tomasello and Hannes Rakoczy, 'What Makes Human Cognition Unique? From Individual to Shared to Collective Intentionality', *Mind and Language* 18/2 (2003): 121–47.

12 Wilfrid Sellars offers an epistemological defence of this *order of explanation* in *Empiricism and the Philosophy of Mind* (Cambridge, MA: Harvard University Press, 1997) (with an instructive introduction by Richard Rorty and a study guide by Robert Brandom).

13 On this objection, see Wolfgang Detel, 'Sprachliche Fähigkeiten', *Deutsche Zeitschrift für Philosophie* 59 (2011): 147–52.

14 Lutz Wingert, 'Die elementaren Strukturen der menschlichen Sozialität', *Deutsche Zeitschrift für Philosophie* 59 (2011): 158–63. Hans Bernhard Schmid, 'Am Ursprung der Freundlichkeit', *Deutsche Zeitschrift für Philosophie* 59 (2011): 153–7.

15 This is also why socio-ontological attempts to explain social obligations

in terms of collective intentionality fail; see the overview of the debate in Hans Bernhard Schmid and David P. Schweikard (eds), *Kollektive Intentionalität* (Frankfurt am Main: Suhrkamp, 2009). A good example is the approach of John Searle, who traces deontological obligations back to the declarative act of conferring or creating a social status. The performance of declarative speech acts (through which, for example, marriages are concluded, presidents appointed or currencies declared to be valid) presupposes the institutions they are supposed to explain. See John R. Searle, *The Construction of Social Reality* (New York: Free Press, 1995), and Searle, *Making the Social World: The Structure of Human Civilization* (New York: Oxford University Press, 2010).

16 Michael Tomasello can discreetly brush this conceptual difficulty aside in the relevant chapter from *Origins of Human Communication* ('From Ape Gestures to Human Language', pp. 319–46) because he assumes that our species is distinguished from the outset by an unusual degree of prosocial behaviour. From an empirical point of view, however, the evolution of human communication would then ultimately have to be attributed to an improbable 'moral mutation' (Detel).

17 For a summary of his theory of the episodic, mimetic, mythical and theoretical stages of cultural development, see Merlin Donald, *A Mind So Rare: The Evolution of Human Consciousness* (New York: W. W. Norton, 2001), chs 7 and 8.

18 Martin Riesebrodt, *The Promise of Salvation: A Theory of Religion*, trans. Stephen Rendall (Chicago: University of Chicago Press, 2009).

19 Riesebrodt, *The Promise of Salvation*, defines religious practices in general as practices of dealing with powers of salvation and misfortune [*Mächten des Heils und des Unheils*].

20 On the formation of canons, see Jan Assmann, *Religion and Cultural Memory: Ten Studies*, trans. Rodney Livingstone (Stanford, CA: Stanford University Press, 2006), pp. 37ff.

21 Philosophically speaking, I am interested only in reasons for stabilizing behavioural expectations which are in principle accessible, either consciously or unconsciously, to the members of the society themselves, not in the latent functions of social structures, which are often discernible only from the observer perspective of social science.

22 Robert N. Bellah, *Religion in Human Evolution: From the Paleolithic to the Axial Age* (Cambridge, MA: Belknap Press, 2011).

23 Ludger Honnefelder, *Woher kommen wir? Ursprünge der Moderne im Denken des Mittelalters* (Berlin: Berlin University Press, 2008).

24 I described the rationalization of the lifeworld from this perspective in Habermas, *The Theory of Communicative Action*, 2 vols, trans. Thomas McCarthy (Boston: Beacon Press, 1984, 1987).

25 Emil Angehrn, *Sinn und Nicht-Sinn: Das Verstehen des Menschen* (Tubingen: Mohr Siebeck, 2010), pp. 178–223; on this, see Albrecht Wellmer, 'Eine hermeneutische Anthropologie', *Deutsche Zeitschrift für Philosophie* 59/3 (2011): 455–65.

26 On aesthetic meaning and criticism, see Martin Seel, *Die Kunst der Entzweiung: Zum Begriff der ästhetischen Rationalität* (Frankfurt am Main: Suhrkamp, 1985), pp. 180ff.

27 On the controversy between Dieter Schnebel and Adorno concern-

ing the proximity and distance of music to language, see the excellent analysis in Wellmer, *Versuch über Musik und Sprache* (Munich: Hanser, 2009), pp. 9–124.

Chapter 3 A Hypothesis concerning the Evolutionary Meaning of Rites

1 Martin Riesebrodt, *The Promise of Salvation: A Theory of Religion*, trans. Stephen Rendall (Chicago: University of Chicago Press, 2009), p. 72: 'In their liturgies, religions usually claim the ability to ward off misfortune, surmount crises, and provide blessings and salvation by communicating with superhuman powers.'

2 Ruth Berger, *Warum der Mensch spricht: Eine Naturgeschichte der Sprache* (Frankfurt am Main: Eichborn, 2008), pp. 110ff.

3 William Robertson Smith, 'Lectures on the Religion of the Semites' (1899), in Robert A. Segal (ed.), *The Myth and Ritual Theory: An Anthology* (Oxford: Blackwell, 1998), pp. 17–34.

4 Claude Lévi-Strauss, *Introduction to a Science of Mythology*, 4 vols, trans. John and Doreen Weightman (Chicago: University of Chicago Press, 1969–81).

5 Lévi-Strauss, *The Savage Mind* (Chicago: University of Chicago Press, 1966).

6 Ibid., pp. 245ff.

7 Robert A. Segal, *Myth: A Very Short Introduction* (2nd edn, Oxford: Oxford University Press, 2015), p. 49.

8 Walter Burkert, *Homo necans: Interpretationen altgriechischer Opferriten und Mythen* (23rd edn, Berlin: de Gruyter, 1997), pp. 39–45.

9 Catherine Bell, *Ritual: Perspectives and Dimensions* (Oxford: Oxford University Press, 1997), pp. 108–20.

10 Émile Durkheim, *The Elementary Forms of Religious Life* (1912) (New York: Free Press, 1995); on this, see Habermas, *The Theory of Communicative Action*, trans. Thomas McCarthy (Boston: Beacon Press, 1987), Vol. 2, pp. 47–62.

11 Arnold van Gennep, *Rites of Passage*, trans. Monika B. Vizedom and Gabriella M. Caffee (Chicago: University of Chicago Press, 1960).

12 Wilhelm Dupré, *Religion in Primitive Cultures: A Study in Ethnophilosophy* (The Hague: Mouton, 1975), pp. 64–5: 'Because we live in and through symbols, we are capable of conceiving the symbol of symbolization. . . . And thus we may ask, is this dimension the source and initial completion of religion, the dimension out of which symbols emerge . . .?'

13 Ibid., p. 247.

14 Michael Tomasello, *The Cultural Origins of Human Cognition* (Cambridge, MA: Harvard University Press, 1999), pp. 13ff.

15 For a detailed account, see chapter 2 ('The Lifeworld as a Space of Symbolically Embodied Reasons') in this volume.

16 Habermas, 'Actions, Speech Acts, Linguistically Mediated Interactions, and the Lifeworld', in *On the Pragmatics of Communication*, ed. and trans. Maeve Cooke (Cambridge: Polity, 2000), pp. 215–55.

17 The assumption that the non-linguistic media of art are rooted in such a stage of symbolic communication could explain why we understand works of art without being able to *exhaust* their semantic content in commentaries and explanations. The linguistically opaque core of aesthetic experience can be traced back to the highly sensitive use of media, which make communication between author and public possible without allowing a disaggregation of the communicative contents into propositional and modal components. The superiority of art is founded on the fact that the complex content of sublime moods, of multifaceted, often highly ambivalent feelings and intellectual stirrings, expressing the most refined experiences and responses of the most sensitive minds of an epoch, cannot be expressed adequately in a prosaic language. For propositionally differentiated language severs the semantic threads linking the perceptions which are interwoven and interact in present experiences, on the one hand, and the associated feelings, appeals and behavioural dispositions, on the other. Only a representation in a non-linguistic medium can do justice to this *experience* of interference between the propositional, expressive and appellative semantic components that, as it were, echo each other.

18 For a response to objections, see Tomasello, 'On the different Origins of Symbols and Grammars', in Morten H. Christiansen and Simon Kirby (eds), *Language Evolution* (Oxford: Oxford University Press, 2003), pp. 90–110, here p. 100:

> Nevertheless, chimpanzees still do not use their gestures referentially. This is because (1) they almost invariably use them in dyadic contexts – either to attract the attention of others to the self or to request some behaviour of another toward the self (e.g. play, grooming, sex) – not triadically to attract the attention of others to some outside entity; and (2) they use them exclusively for imperative purposes to request actions from others, not for declarative purposes to direct the attention of others to something simply for the sake of sharing interest in it or commenting on it.

19 Tomasello, *The Cultural Origins of Human Cognition*, pp. 51ff.
20 Tomasello, *Origins of Human Communication* (Cambridge, MA: MIT Press, 2008), pp. 173–85.
21 Merlin Donald, *Origins of the Modern Mind: Three Stages in the Evolution of Culture and Cognition* (Cambridge, MA: Harvard University Press, 1991), p. 168.
22 René Girard, *I See Satan Fall Like Lightning*, trans. James G. Williams (Maryknoll, NY: Orbis Books, 2001); Girard, *Things Hidden since the Foundation of the World*, trans. Stephen Bann and Michael Metteer (Stanford, CA: Stanford University Press, 1987).

Chapter 4 The New Philosophical Interest in Religion

1 The conversation took place in autumn 2009 on Long Island. The questions were posed by Eduardo Mendieta, professor of philosophy

at Stony Brook University. [The present translation is a lightly revised version of a translation by Mattias Fritsch. *Trans.*]

2 See, now, Habermas, 'A Hypothesis concerning the Evolutionary Meaning of Rites', chapter 3 in this volume (though this version does not contain all material in the manuscript discussed in the interview).

3 Charles Taylor, *A Secular Age* (Cambridge, MA: Harvard University Press, 2007).

4 See Habermas, 'What Is Meant by a "Post-Secular Society"? A Discussion on Islam in Europe', in *Europe: The Faltering Project*, trans. Ciaran Cronin (Cambridge: Polity, 2009), pp. 59–77, here p. 65.

5 See chapter 7 in this volume, '"The Political": The Rational Meaning of a Questionable Inheritance of Political Theology', pp. 163–74.

Chapter 5 Religion and Postmetaphysical Thinking

1 My reply refers to contributions to a symposium on my work on the relation between postmetaphysical thinking and religion held on 23–4 October 2009 at New York University at the invitation of Craig Calhoun and Eduardo Mendieta.

2 The sequence in which I present my responses reflects the need to impose a certain systematic order on the various objections. The length of a reply is a function of the opportunity presented for clarifying my thoughts and is not a reflection of the importance that I attach to individual contributions.

3 Professor of Sociology, Georgetown University, Washington, DC.

4 José Casanova, 'Exploring the Postsecular: Three Meanings of "the Secular" and Their Possible Transcendence', in Craig Calhoun, Eduardo Mendieta and Jonathan VanAntwerpen, *Habermas and Religion* (Cambridge: Polity, 3013), pp. 27–48.

5 José Casanova, *Europas Angst vor der Religion*, trans. Rolf Schieder (Berlin: Berlin University Press, 2009), pp. 98ff.

6 Here I am thinking of religions that, when it comes to our mundane knowledge, acknowledge what *can no longer be asserted* within the limits of fallible but scientifically filtered arguments.

7 Jan Assmann, *Religion and Cultural Memory: Ten Studies*, trans. Rodney Livingstone (Stanford, CA: Stanford University Press, 2006), pp. 101ff.

8 Robert N. Bellah, *Religion in Human Evolution: From the Paleolithic to the Axial Age* (Cambridge, MA: Belknap Press, 2011).

9 René Girard, *I See Satan Fall Like Lightning*, trans. James G. Williams (Maryknoll, NY: Orbis Books, 2001).

10 José Casanova, 'Two Dimensions, Temporal and Spatial, of the Secular', in Rosmarie van der Breemer, José Casanova, and Tryvge Wyller (eds), *Secular and Sacred? The Scandinavian Case of Religion in Human Rights, Law and Public Space* (Göttingen: Vandehoeck & Ruprecht, 2014), pp. 21–33, here p. 23.

11 Paul Veyne, *L'Empire gréco-romain* (Paris: Seuil, 2005).

12 Jan Assmann, *The Price of Monotheism*, trans. Robert Savage (Stanford, CA: Stanford University Press, 2010), chs 1 and 3.

238 Notes to pp. 81–87

13 Harold J. Berman, *Law and Revolution: The Formation of the Western Legal Tradition* (Cambridge, MA: Harvard University Press, 1983).
14 Ludger Honnefelder, *Woher kommen wir? Ursprünge der Moderne im Denken des Mittelalters* (Berlin: Berlin University Press, 2008).
15 See the introduction to Habermas, *Kritik der Vernunft, Philosophische Texte*, Vol. 5 (Studienausgabe, Frankfurt am Main: Suhrkamp, 2009).
16 Thomas McCarthy, *Ideals and Illusions* (Cambridge, MA: MIT Press, 1991).
17 Professor of Philosophy, Universidad Nacional Autónoma de México.
18 Maria Herrera Lima, 'The Anxiety of Contingency: Religion in a Secular Age', in Calhoun, Mendieta and VanAntwerpen (eds), *Habermas and Religion*, pp. 49–71.
19 See the commentaries on Maria Pia Lara and Amy Allen below.
20 Theodor W. Adorno, 'Reason and Revelation', in Adorno, *Critical Models: Interventions and Catchword*, trans. Henry W. Pickford (New York: Columbia University Press, 1998), p. 136.
21 Charles Taylor, *A Secular Age* (Cambridge, MA: Harvard University Press, 2007), pp. 594ff.
22 Martin Riesebrodt, *The Promise of Salvation: A Theory of Religion*, trans. Stephen Rendall (Chicago: University of Chicago Press, 2009), p. 72.
23 Norman Birnbaum, *After Progress: American Social Reform and European Socialism in the Twentieth Century* (New York: Oxford University Press, 2001).
24 On the following, see Habermas, 'The Language Game of Responsible Agency and the Problem of Free Will', *Philosophical Explorations* 10/1 (2007): 13–50, here pp. 15ff.
25 I am thinking not only of the social crises involved in the transition from national societies to a multicultural world society which cannot be held together by markets and electronic networks alone but requires a political constitution. An even more profound moral and political challenge is posed by the eugenic options towards which economic interests are driving the development of 'converging technologies'. 'Human enhancement' is being pursued under a premise for which Carl Schmitt once coined an apt phrase in a different context: 'Homo homini res mutanda' [man is something changeable for man].
26 Karl Löwith, *Meaning in History: The Theological Implications of the Philosophy of History* (Chicago: University of Chicago Press, 1949).
27 Jacques Derrida, 'Faith and Knowledge', in Derrida and Gianni Vattimo (eds), *Religion* (Stanford, CA: Stanford University Press, 2001), p. 14: 'How then to think – within the limits of reason alone – a religion which, without again becoming natural religion, would today be effectively universal? And which, for that matter, would no longer be restricted to a paradigm that was Christian or even Abrahamic?'
28 Habermas, 'The Boundary between Faith and Knowledge: On the Reception and Contemporary Importance of Kant's Philosophy of Religion', in *Between Naturalism and Religion*, trans. Ciaran Cronin (Cambridge: Polity, 2008), pp. 209–47, especially pp. 243ff.
29 New School for Social Research, New York.

30 Maria Pia Lara, 'Is the Postsecular a Return to Political Theology?', in Calhoun, Mendieta and VanAntwerpen (eds), *Habermas and Religion*, pp. 72–91.
31 Otto Marchart, *Die politische Differenz: Zum Denken bei Nancy, Lefort, Badiou, Laclau und Agamben* (Berlin: Suhrkamp, 2010); Thomas Bedorf and Kurt Rötthers (eds), *Das Politische und die Politik* (Berlin: Suhrkamp, 2010).
32 On this, see chapter 7 in the present volume.
33 Hans Blumenberg, *The Legitimacy of the Modern Age*, trans. Robert M. Wallace (Cambridge, MA: MIT Press, 1983), pp. 13ff. This is a translation of the revised German edition which appeared in three volumes in 1973, 1974 and 1976.
34 Ibid., p. 86 (translation amended).
35 Hans Blumenberg, Carl Schmitt, *Briefwechsel 1971–1978* (Frankfurt am Main: Suhrkamp, 2007).
36 Blumenberg even follows Schmitt's interpretation of the political idea of progress when, arm in arm with Reinhart Koselleck, he takes 'progress' to be an expression of the political deficit of the Enlightenment's moralizing critique of history: Blumenberg, *The Legitimacy of the Modern Age*, p. 31. Here he refers to Koselleck, *Critique and Crisis: Enlightenment and the Pathogenesis of Modern Society* (Cambridge, MA: MIT Press, 1988).
37 Professor of Philosophy, Dartmouth College.
38 Imre Lakatos and Alan Musgrave, *Criticism and the Growth of Knowledge* (Cambridge: Cambridge University Press, 1974); on this, see Werner Diederich (ed.), *Theorien der Wissenschaftsgeschichte: Beiträge zur diachronischen Wissenschaftstheorie* (Frankfurt am Main: Suhrkamp, 1974).
39 Amy Allen, 'Having One's Cake and Eating it Too: Habermas's Genealogy of Postsecular Reason', in Calhoun, Mendieta and VanAntwerpen (eds), *Habermas and Religion*, pp. 132–53.
40 Hugo Ott, *Martin Heidegger: A Political Life*, trans. Allan Blunden (London: HarperCollins, 1993).
41 Following Nietzsche, and appealing to the 'original' truth of the Presocratics or alluding to Hölderlin's plural gods ('only a (!) God can save us', as he put it in his final interview, published posthumously in *Der Spiegel*), Heidegger embraced nationalistic neo-pagan sentiments, or at least made use of them. From the Nazi period onwards, his 'mythological' conversation with Hölderlin was intended to promote the 'dream' of a national religious 'reconnection with the gods' of 'holy Germany'. See Christian Sommer, 'Rückbindung an die Götter: Heideggers Volksreligion (1934/35)', *Internationales Jahrbuch für Hermeneutik*, Vol. 9 (Tubingen: Siebeck, 2010), pp. 283–310.
42 Klaus Heinrich, *Parmenides und Jona: Vier Studien über das Verhältnis von Philosophie und Mythologie* (Frankfurt am Main: Suhrkamp, 1966); Henrich, *Tertium datur: Dahlemer Vorlesungen* (Frankfurt am Main: Stroemfeld/Roter Stern, 1981).
43 Amy Allen explicitly endorses this reading in her text. See Allen, 'Having One's Cake and Eating it Too', n. 20, p. 148.
44 Professor of Philosophy, New School for Social Research, New York.

45 J. M. Bernstein, 'Forgetting Isaac: Faith and the Impossibility of a Postsecular Society', in Calhoun, Mendieta and VanAntwerpen (eds), *Habermas and Religion*, pp. 154–75, here p. 160.
46 Ibid. (emphasis added).
47 On the analysis of religious validity claims, see Edmund Arens, *Gottesverständigung: Eine kommunikative Religionstheologie* (Freiburg: Herder, 2007), pp. 239ff.
48 I fear that this accentuation has more to do with present-day Islamophobia, which inadvertently aligns Bernstein with certain Christian agitators.
49 Bernstein, 'Forgetting Isaac', p. 170.
50 Moses proclaims to his people:

> When you come into the land that the Lord your God is giving you, you must not learn to imitate the abhorrent practices of those nations. No one shall be found among you who makes a son or daughter pass through fire, or who practises divination, or is a soothsayer, or an augur, or a sorcerer, or one who casts spells, or who consults ghosts or spirits, or who seeks oracles from the dead. For whoever does these things is abhorrent to the Lord. (Deut. 18: 9–12)

51 Troels Norager, *Taking Leave of Abraham: An Essay on Religion and Democracy* (Aarhus: Aarhus University Press, 2008).
52 Søren Kierkegaard, *Fear and Trembling*, in Kierkegaard, *Fear and Trembling; Repetition*, trans. Howard V. Hong and Edna H. Hong (Princeton, NJ: Princeton University Press, 1983), pp. 64ff.
53 Benjamin Uffenheimer, 'Myth and Reality in Ancient Israel', in Shmuel Noah Eisenstadt (ed.), *The Origins and Diversity of Axial Age Civilizations* (Albany: State University of New York Press, 1986), pp. 135–68, here pp. 143–9.
54 'Whoever comes to me and does not hate father and mother, wife and children, brothers and sisters, yes, and even life itself, cannot be my disciple.'
55 Department of Philosophy, Concordia University, Montreal.
56 Matthias Fritsch, 'Sources of Morality in Habermas's Recent Work on Religion and Freedom', in Calhoun, Mendieta and VanAntwerpen (eds), *Habermas and Religion*, pp. 277–300, here p. 279.
57 Professor of Philosophy, Northwestern University, Evanston.
58 Cristina Lafont, 'Religion and the Public Sphere: What are the Deliberative Obligations of Democratic Citizenship?' in Calhoun, Mendieta and VanAntwerpen (eds), *Habermas and Religion*, pp. 230–48, here p. 231. The further objection that the proposed expectation could tempt secular citizens into insincerity carries no weight on a discourse-theoretical understanding of the democratic process. Aside from the fact that voters' *de facto* motives may not in any case be exposed to any form of regulation, only public utterances – that is, actual contributions to the formation of opinions and consensus-building – not mindsets, have a bearing on the legitimizing power of democratic discourses.
59 Habermas, 'Religion in the Public Sphere: Cognitive Presuppositions

for the "Public Use of Reason" by Religious and Secular Citizens', in *Between Naturalism and Religion*, pp. 114–47, here pp. 146–7.
60 Lafont, 'Religion and the Public Sphere', p. 239.
61 Professor of Philosophy, University College, Dublin.
62 This passage does not appear in the published version of Cooke's paper; see Maeve Cooke, 'Violating Neutrality? Religious Validity Claims and Democratic Legitimacy', in Calhoun, Mendieta and VanAntwerpen (eds), *Habermas and Religion*, pp. 249–74. Here I disregard the asymmetry between the interlocutors. The interlocutors of the people of faith are secular *citizens*, not secularly minded philosophers who study the epistemic attitudes and the nature of the arguments exchanged.
63 Habermas, *Politische Theorie* (Frankfurt am Main: Suhrkamp, 2009), Section IV: Konstitutionalisierung des Völkerrechts?, pp. 298–424.
64 Professor of Philosophy and International Studies, Washington University, St Louis.
65 James Bohman, 'A Post-Secular Global Order? The Pluralism of Forms of Life and Communicative Freedom', in Calhoun, Mendieta and VanAntwerpen (eds), *Habermas and Religion*, pp. 179–202, here p. 197.
66 Emeritus Professor of Philosophy, Northwestern University, Evanston.
67 Thomas McCarthy, 'The Burdens of Modernized Faith and Postmetaphysical Reason in Habermas's "Unfinished Project of Enlightenment"', in Calhoun, Mendieta and VanAntwerpen (eds), *Habermas and Religion*, pp. 115–31.
68 I suspect that lurking behind *this* disagreement is the more far-reaching antithesis between philosophical cultures that go back to Hume and Kant respectively. The antagonism was initially sparked by opposed strategies for addressing the fundamental epistemological problem of the application of concepts (understood in the nominalistic terms) to the given (whatever it may be), namely, whether to proceed from the sensory input or from the concept. Pragmatism goes beyond these alternatives by appealing to the *practice* of employing concepts. The gap between concept and the given, when we become aware of it in the functional domain of established practices, has 'always already' been bridged by practice. But because the intra-subjective approach of pragmatism makes it responsive to the pluralism of participants in shared practices, the problem of bridging differences reappears within pragmatism in the guise of a pluralism of perspectives. How can we bridge the differences between the conceptions of different participants that emerge in the process of applying the same analytical distinctions from their various particular contexts of origin? The answer suggested by the Kantian strategy is that the conceptual structure of the shared practice of discourse equips the practised participants with a sufficiently convergent *prior* understanding to be able to clarify those differences that emerge in the course of applying the same concepts through the give and take of reasons. The most uncompromising pragmatist version of Hume's opposing nominalistic strategy is the one developed by Richard Rorty.
69 McCarthy, 'The Burdens of Modernized Faith and Postmetaphysical Reason', p. 121; see McCarthy, *Ideals and Illusions* (Cambridge, MA: MIT Press, 1993), pp. 181–99.

70 See the excellent account of this transition in Herbert Marcuse, *Reason and Revolution* (Boston: Beacon Press, 1960).

71 Professor of Philosophical Theology, Yale University.

72 See the relevant essays in Habermas, *Postmetaphysical Thinking: Philosophical Essays*, trans. William Mark Hohengarten (Cambridge: Polity, 1992).

73 I fail to understand Wolterstorff's laborious attempt to construct a so-called Kant-rationality; see Nicholas Wolterstorff, 'An Engagement with Jürgen Habermas on Postmetaphysical Philosophy, Religion, and Political Dialogue', in Calhoun, Mendieta and VanAntwerpen (eds), *Habermas and Religion*, pp. 92–111, here p. 98. From my perspective, all we need is the procedural concept of 'communicative rationality', which, as I have explained at length, is intended to take the place of the traditional substantive concept of reason. For an introduction, see Habermas, 'The Unity of Reason in the Diversity of its Voices', in *Postmetaphysical Thinking*, pp. 115–48; Habermas, 'Communicative Reason and the Detranscendentalized "Use of Reason"', in *Between Naturalism and Religion*, pp. 24–76.

74 This, as it happens, is my *general* objection to a reformed epistemology that, if I am not mistaken, wants to cancel the distinction between the modalities of taking-to-be-true involved in religious and secular assertions respectively.

75 Professor of Religion, Politics and Ethics, University of Nottingham.

76 John Milbank, 'What Lacks is Feeling: Hume versus Kant and Habermas', in Calhoun, Mendieta and VanAntwerpen (eds), *Habermas and Religion*, pp. 322–46, here p. 342.

77 Ibid., p. 331.

78 Ibid., p. 334.

79 P. F. Strawson, 'Freedom and Resentment', *Proceedings of the British Academy* 48 (1964): 1–25.

80 Milbank, 'What Lacks is Feeling', p. 343.

81 Director of the Humanities Center, Johns Hopkins University, Baltimore.

82 Michael Theunissen's plea points in the same direction, though, in my opinion, with stronger arguments: Theunissen, 'Philosophie der Religion oder religiöse Philosophie', *Information Philosophie* (December 2003): 7–15.

83 Hent de Vries, 'Global Religion and the Postsecular Challenge', in Calhoun, Mendieta and VanAntwerpen (eds), *Habermas and Religion*, pp. 203–29, here p. 215.

84 Professor of Philosophy, Binghamton University.

85 Max Pensky, 'Solidarity with the Past and the Work of Translation: Reflections on Memory Politics and the Post-Secular', in Calhoun, Mendieta and VanAntwerpen (eds), *Habermas and Religion*, pp. 301–21, here p. 319.

86 Lutz Wingert, 'Haben wir moralische Verpflichtungen gegenüber früheren Generationen? Moralischer Universalismus und erinnernde Solidarität', *Babylon – Beiträge zur jüdischen Gegenwart* 9 (1991): 78–94.

87 Pensky, 'Solidarity with the Past and the Work of Translation', p. 312.

88 Adorno spoke in this sense of 'Heine the Wound' [*die Wunde Heine*].

Chapter 6   A Symposium on Faith and Knowledge

1 On 23–24 September 2005, a closed meeting of philosophers and theologians took place at the University of Vienna at the invitation of Rudolf Langthaler and Herta Nagl-Docekal at which distinguished colleagues kindly engaged with my views on the relationship between faith and knowledge. The present reply to the insightful and stimulating contributions of the participants is taken from Rudolf Langthaler and Herta Nagl-Docekal (eds), *Glauben und Wissen* (Vienna: Oldenbourg, 2007), pp. 366–414.

2 Professor of Systematic Theology at the University of Vienna.

3 Christian Danz, 'Religion zwischen Aneignung und Kritik', in Langthaler and Nagl-Docekal (eds), *Glauben und Wissen*, pp. 9–31.

4 Immanuel Kant, *Critique of the Power of Judgement*, ed. Paul Guyer, trans. Paul Guyer and Eric Matthews (Cambridge: Cambridge University Press, 2000), p. 310 (5:444). Citations of Kant's works in parentheses refer to the volume and page numbers of the edition of the Königlich-Preußische Akademie der Wissenschaften (1903–11) (Berlin: de Gruyter, 1968).

5 Markus Knapp, *Verantwortetes Christsein heute: Theologie zwischen Metaphysik und Postmoderne* (Freiburg: Herder, 2006), p. 247.

6 Danz, 'Religion und Theologie unter den Bedingungen pluraler Gesellschaften', in Klaus Dethloff et al. (eds), *Orte der Religion im philosophischen Diskurs der Gegenwart* (Berlin: Parerga, 2004), pp. 341–62, here pp. 356–7.

7 Ibid., p. 359.

8 Professor of Philosophy, Faculty of Catholic Theology, University of Vienna.

9 Rudolf Langthaler, 'Zur Interpretation und Kritik der kantischen Religionsphilosophie bei Jürgen Habermas', in Langthaler and Nagl-Docekal (eds), *Glauben und Wissen*, pp. 32–92.

10 Kant, *Religion within the Bounds of Mere Reason*, ed. and trans. Allen W. Wood and Giorgio Di Giovanni (Cambridge: Cambridge University Press, 1998), p. 35 n. (6:6).

11 Ibid., p. 35 (6:6).

12 Ibid., p. 34 (6:4–5).

13 Kant, *Critique of Practical Reason*, ed. and trans. Mary Gregor (Cambridge: Cambridge University Press, 1997), p. 92 (5:109).

14 Ibid., p. 92 (5:110).

15 Kant, *Religion*, p. 34 (6:5).

16 Ibid.

17 Ibid.

18 Ibid., p. 36 n. (6:7).

19 Kant, *Critique of Practical Reason*, p. 104 (5:125).

20 Kant, *Religion*, p. 109 (6:98).

21 Kant, 'On the Common Saying: That May be Correct in Theory, but it

is of no Use in Practice,' in Kant, *Practical Philosophy*, ed. and trans. Mary Gregor (Cambridge: Cambridge University Press, 1996), pp. 279–309, here pp. 282–3 (8:279, 280). On this, see Langthaler, 'Zur Interpretation und Kritik der kantischen Religionsphilosophie bei Jürgen Habermas', p. 35, n. 4.

22 Ibid., p. 49.

23 Ibid., p. 46.

24 'According to this reading, Kant's concern was not "to elevate the highest good in the world to the status of a moral duty" [quoted from my text], but solely to rationally demonstrate the justice- and meaning-oriented "final end of practical reason" for "reasonable, finite beings"' (ibid.).

25 In my opinion, there is no basis for this move in the text of Kant's doctrine of virtue. The moral imperative of benevolence, in the sense of the requirement to make 'the well-being of others my *end*' and to promote 'the happiness of others', is one of the positive duties. It fits into the grammatical form of normal duties. Because the degree of fulfilment must remain indeterminate, the claim of positive duties goes beyond negative duties of respect. However, they are by no means extravagant, like the duty to promote the highest good; rather, they call for observance by the individual *within the limits of what is possible*. They do not impose any obligations on individuals which, given the circumstances, they could not fulfil through their own efforts. Langthaler himself highlights the structure of these duties with the following quotation from Kant: 'Putting aside the fact that . . . we can do no more than our obligation, it is also only our duty to do good to the poor.'

26 Kant, *Critique of Judgment*, ed. Paul Guyer, trans. Paul Guyer and Eric Matthews (Cambridge: Cambridge University Press, 2000), p. 336 n. (5:472 n.).

27 See my study on the concept of 'individuality': Habermas, 'Individuation through Socialization: On George Herbert Mead's Theory of Subjectivity', in *Postmetaphysical Thinking: Philosophical Essays*, trans. William Mark Hohengarten (Cambridge: Polity, 1992), pp. 149–204, esp. pp. 153ff.

28 Professor at the Institute of Philosophy of the University of Vienna.

29 Herta Nagl-Docekal, 'Eine rettende Übersetzung? Jürgen Habermas interpretiert Kants Religionsphilosophie', in Langthaler and Nagl-Docekal, *Glauben und Wissen*, pp. 93–119.

30 Kant, *Religion*, p. 106 (6:94).

31 On my interest in this theological theme, see Markus Knapp, *Gottes Herrschaft als Zukunft der Welt* (Würzburg: Echter, 1993).

32 This is the intuition that John Rawls associates with the concept of overlapping consensus.

33 See the brilliant interpretation of Pierre Bayle in Rainer Forst, *Toleration in Conflict: Past and Present*, trans. Ciaran Cronin (Cambridge: Cambridge University Press, 2013), pp. 237–65.

34 On the following, see Habermas, 'Rightness versus Truth: On the Sense of Normative Validity in Moral Judgements and Norms', in *Truth and Justification*, trans. Barbara Fultner (Cambridge: Polity, 2003), pp. 237–76, here pp. 273ff.

35 Professor of Philosophy at the University of Passau.
36 On this, see Richard J. Bernstein, *Beyond Objectivism and Relativism: Science, Hermeneutics, and Praxis* (Philadelphia: University of Pennsylvania Press, 1983).
37 Aside from the question of whether and how this interpretation coheres with Kant's text, I do not altogether understand why a procedural morality which is not committed to final ends should lack content and substantive criteria. On Kant's conception, the person who makes moral judgements allows the contents to be specified in advance in the form of controversial maxims and then tests which of the relevant norms of action is equally good for all.
38 Wilhelm Lütterfelds, 'Der praktische Vernunftglaube und das Paradox der kulturellen Weltbilder', in Langthaler and Nagl-Docekal (eds), *Glauben und Wissen*, pp. 120–54, here p. 138.
39 Ibid.
40 Professor of Theoretical Philosophy at the University of Potsdam.
41 Ludwig Wittgenstein, *Lecture on Ethics*, ed. Edoardo Zamuner et al. (Chichester: Wiley Blackwell, 2014).
42 Hans Julius Schneider, '"Wertstofftrennung"? Zur Habermas'schen Skizze nachkantischer Religionsbegriffe', in Langthaler and Nagl-Docekal (eds), *Glauben und Wissen*, pp. 155–85.
43 Ibid., p. 184.
44 With reference to my essay 'The Boundary between Faith and Knowledge: On the Reception and Contemporary Importance of Kant's Philosophy of Religion', in *Between Naturalism and Religion: Philosophical Essays*, trans. Ciaran Cronin (Cambridge: Polity, 2008), pp. 209–47.
45 Richard J. Bernstein, *Radical Evil: A Philosophical Interrogation* (Cambridge: Polity, 2002).
46 Habermas, *Postmetaphysical Thinking*, pp. 57–112 (Part II: The Turn to Pragmatics); Habermas, 'Hermeneutic and Analytic Philosophy: Two Complementary Versions of the Linguistic Turn', in *Truth and Justification*, pp. 51–82; Habermas, 'Some Further Clarifications of the Concept of Communicative Rationality', in *On the Pragmatics of Communication*, ed. and trans. Maeve Cooke (Cambridge: Polity, 1999), pp. 307–42; Habermas, 'Communicative Reason and the Detranscendentalized "Use of Reason"', in *Between Naturalism and Religion*, pp. 24–76.
47 *Translator's note*: In his famous article 'On Sense and Reference' (trans. Max Black in *Translations from the Philosophical Writings of Gottlob Frege*, ed. Peter Geach and Max Black [Oxford: Blackwell, 1952], pp. 56–78), Gottlob Frege drew a distinction between the 'content' of a linguistic expression or what it designates (which he called its 'reference' [*Bedeutung*]) and the way or 'mode' in which it presents what is designated (which he called its 'sense' [*Sinn*]). To use Frege's famous example, according to this distinction the expressions 'morning star' and 'evening star' have the same reference but a different sense. This explains why the proposition 'The morning star is the evening star' is a substantive statement which tells us something about the world; it is not simply an analytic statement which asserts that a particular celestial

body is identical with itself or a tautological statement about the identical meaning of two linguistic expressions (neither of which would tell us anything about the world).

48 Professor at the Institute of Philosophy of the University of Vienna.

49 Ludwig Nagl, 'Die unerkundete Option: Pragmatistische Denkansätze in der Religionsphilosophie', in Langthaler and Nagl-Docekal (eds), *Glauben und Wissen*, pp. 186–215.

50 English translation: *The Other: Studies in the Social Ontology of Husserl, Heidegger, Sartre and Buber*, trans. Christopher Macann (Cambridge, MA: MIT Press, 1984).

51 Karl-Otto Apel, *Charles S. Peirce: From Pragmatism to Pragmaticism*, trans. John Michael Krois (Cambridge, MA: MIT Press, 1981); Habermas, *Time of Transitions*, trans. Ciaran Cronin (Cambridge: Polity, 2006), Part VI: American Pragmatism and German Philosophy: Three Reviews, pp. 129–46.

52 *Translator's note*: This is a reference to the second edition of Schleiermacher's main work in dogmatic theology, *Der Christliche Glaube* (Berlin: Georg Reimer, 1830), especially §§1–7, where Schleiermacher defines dogmatic theology as the science of the public doctrine of a particular Christian congregation at a particular historical time. English translation: Schleiermacher, *The Christian Faith: English Translation of the Second German Edition*, ed. H. R. Mackintosh and J. S. Stewart (Philadelphia: Fortress Press, 1928).

53 Professor of Philosophical Foundations of Theology at the Faculty of Catholic Theology, Münster University.

54 Benjamin, *The Origin of German Tragic Drama*, trans. John Osborne (London: Verso, 1998), p. 31.

55 Habermas, 'Consciousness-Raising or Redemptive Criticism: The Contemporaneity of Walter Benjamin' (1971), trans. Philip Brewster and Carl Howard Buchner, *New German Critique* 17 (1979): 30–59, here p. 58.

56 Klaus Müller, 'Balancen philosophischer Topographie', in Langthaler and Nagl-Docekal (eds), *Glauben und Wissen*, pp. 216–37.

57 Joseph Cardinal Ratzinger, *Truth and Tolerance: Christian Belief and World Religions* (San Francisco, CA: Ignatius Press, 2004), p. 163. Referring to the encyclical of John Paul II 'Fides et ratio', Magnus Striet (see above, p. 152) plays down this question, observing that the task of rationally justifying faith makes Christian theology dependent on philosophy, but 'without committing [it] to a particular, historically evolved form of metaphysics'.

58 Matthias Lutz-Bachmann, 'Hellenisierung des Christentums?' in Carsten Colpe, Ludger Honnefelder and Lutz-Bachmann (eds), *Spätantike und Christentum: Beiträge zur Religions- und Geistesgeschichte der griechisch-römischen Kultur und Zivilisation der Kaiserzeit* (Berlin: Akademie, 1992), pp. 77–98.

59 In his encyclical 'Deus caritas est', Pope Benedict XVI demonstrates with reference to the range of Greek words for 'love' (*eros, philia* and *agape*) the explosive force of the biblical concept of divine love – the love of the God who 'loved us first' and thus pre-empts the commemoration of God by human beings.

60 I leave aside whether this still holds without qualification for Theunissen – that is, after the publication of his major work on Pindar, *Menschenlos und Wende der Zeit* (Munich: C. H. Beck, 2000); see my introduction to Theunissen, *Schicksal in Antike und Moderne* (Munich: Carl Friedrich von Siemens Stiftung, 2004).

61 Müller's reference to the recent debate between Henrich and Theunissen provides an important clue. Philosophy in Germany has only one advantage over Anglo-Saxon philosophy, which in other respects has overtaken it – namely, its receptivity to the kinds of questions that have not disappeared simply because they can no longer be answered in metaphysical terms. That is certainly a legacy of the tradition extending from Kant to Hegel and Marx; on the other hand, this circumstance per se does not authorize the continuation of this tradition *at the level of speculative thinking*.

62 The interest is not confined to the Catholic side. See, among others, the excellent studies by Hermann Düringer, *Universale Vernunft und partikularer Glaube: Eine theologische Auswertung des Werkes von Jürgen Habermas* (Leuven: Peeters, 1999), and Jens Glebe-Möller, *A Political Dogmatic* (Philadelphia: Fortress Press, 1987).

63 Professor of Dogmatic Theology at the University of Linz.

64 Düringer (1999) takes this as his guideline for interpreting the relationship between the theory of communicative action and the Judeo-Christian tradition as understood by Protestantism.

65 *Translator's note*: A play on Kant's assertion that 'a religion that rashly declares war on reason will not long endure against it.' Kant, *Religion*, p. 38 (6:10).

66 Theodor W. Adorno, 'Reason and Revelation', in Adorno, *Critical Models: Interventions and Catchwords*, trans. Henry W. Pickford (New York: Columbia University Press, 1998), pp. 135–42, here p. 136.

67 Raberger, '"Übersetzung" – "Rettung" des Humanen?', in Langthaler and Nagl-Docekal (eds), *Glauben und Wissen*, pp. 238–58.

68 Kant, *Dreams of a Spirit-Seer*, trans. Emanuel F. Goerwitz (New York: Macmillan, 1900), p. 86 (translation amended).

69 Ibid., p. 253.

70 Professor of Fundamental Theology at the University of Freiburg.

71 Magnus Striet, 'Grenzen der Übersetzbarkeit', in Langthaler and Nagl-Docekal (eds), *Glauben und Wissen*, pp. 259–82.

72 *Translator's note*: The Latin expression *'etsi deus non daretur'* was coined by the seventeenth-century Dutch theologian and legal philosopher Hugo Grotius to express the idea that the principles of rational natural law should hold 'even if God did not exist'.

73 Habermas, *The Future of Human Nature*, trans. Hannah Beister, Max Pensky and William Rehg (Cambridge: Polity, 2003), pp. 37ff.

74 Striet, 'Grenzen der Übersetzbarkeit', p. 277.

75 Ibid., p. 278.

76 Professor of Fundamental Theology at the University of Vienna.

77 Reikerstorfer, 'Eine "Übersetzung", in der "Übersetztes" nicht überflüssig wird', in Langthaler and Nagl-Docekal (eds), *Glauben und Wissen*, pp. 283–98.

78 As Reikerstorfer puts it in his lecture manuscript.

79 Habermas, 'On the Pragmatic, the Ethical, and the Moral Employments of Practical Reason', in *Justification and Application: Remarks on Discourse Ethics*, trans. Ciaran Cronin (Cambridge: Polity, 1993), pp. 1–17. Against this, Lutz Wingert, 'Haben wir moralische Verpflichtungen gegenüber früheren Generationen? Moralischer Universalismus und erinnernde Solidarität', *Babylon* 9 (1991): 78–94.

80 Helmut Peukert, *Wissenschaftstheorie, Handlungstheorie, fundamentale Theologie: Analysen zu Ansatz und Status theologischer Theoriebildung* (Frankfurt am Main: Suhrkamp, 1988).

81 Max Pensky, 'Jürgen Habermas and the Antinomies of the Intellectual', in Peter Dews (ed.), *Habermas: A Critical Reader* (Oxford: Wiley-Blackwell, 1999), pp. 211–37.

82 Jan Philipp Reemtsma, 'Laudatio', in Habermas, *Glauben und Wissen: Friedenspreis des Deutschen Buchhandels 2001* (Frankfurt am Main: Suhrkamp, 2002), p. 47.

83 See the articles in Parts II and IV of Habermas, *Between Naturalism and Religion*.

84 Professor of Philosophy at the Faculty of Catholic Theology, University of Graz.

85 Reinhold Esterbauer, 'Der "Stachel eines religiösen Erbes"', in Langthaler and Nagl-Docekal (eds), *Glauben und Wissen*, pp. 299–321.

86 The empirical trends within the West point towards the Californian individualization of unchurched religiosity (Friedrich Wilhelm Graf, *Die Wiederkehr der Götter: Religion in der modernen Kultur* [Munich: C. H. Beck, 2004]), while worldwide the decentralized networks of the evangelical currents of Protestantism and Islam are on the rise (Peter L. Berger [ed.], *The Desecularization of the World: Resurgent Religion and World Politics* [Grand Rapids, Michigan: W. B. Eerdmans, 1999]).

87 The missionary success currently being enjoyed by globally networked religious communities such as the evangelicals and Islam, and even by Roman Catholicism, in contrast to the nationally organized Protestant churches inspires Hauke Brunkhorst ('Die Wiederkehr alter Probleme: Kapitalismus und Religion in der Weltgesellschaft', MS, 2006) to draw interesting comparisons between present-day problem constellations and those in early modern Europe.

88 Professor of Philosophy of Religion at the Faculty of Catholic Theology, University of Frankfurt.

89 Habermas, 'Religion in the Public Sphere', in *Between Naturalism and Religion*, pp. 114–47.

90 Thomas Schmidt, 'Religiöser Diskurs und diskursive Religion in der postsäkularen Gesellschaft', in Langthaler and Nagl-Docekal (eds), *Glauben und Wissen*, pp. 322–40.

91 Ibid., p. 340.

92 Ibid., pp. 338–9.

93 Professor of Philosophy at University College, Dublin.

94 Maeve Cooke, 'Säkulare Übersetzung oder postsäkulare Argumentation?', in Langthaler and Nagl-Docekal (eds), *Glauben und Wissen*, pp. 341–66, here p. 349.

95 A fourth argument which demands that it should be *possible* to justify political decisions to religious citizens in strong metaphysical terms

presumably rests on a misunderstanding: all political questions are necessarily ‚'penultimate' questions from the perspective of religious citizens.

Chapter 7 'The Political'

1 *Translator's Note*: This translation gratefully incorporates elements from the version published in Judith Butler et al., *The Power of Religion in the Public Sphere* (New York: Columbia University Press, 2011).

2 Otto Marchart, *Die politische Differenz: Zum Denken bei Nancy, Lefort, Badiou, Laclau und Agamben* (Berlin: Suhrkamp, 2010); Thomas Bedorf and Kurt Rötthers (eds), *Das Politische und die Politik* (Berlin: Suhrkamp, 2010).

3 Claude Lefort, 'The Permanence of the Theologico-Political', in Lefort, *Democracy and Political Theory*, trans. David Macey (Cambridge: Polity, 1988), pp. 213–55, here p. 224.

4 On the conditions of the emergence of political power as a medium of social integration, see Habermas, *Between Facts and Norms: Contributions to a Discourse Theory of Law and Democracy*, trans. William Rehg (Cambridge: Polity, 1996), pp. 137–44.

5 Here I am using the term 'religion' in the extended sense that includes myth and magic; see Martin Riesebrodt, *The Promise of Salvation: A Theory of Religion*, trans. Stephen Rendall (Chicago: University of Chicago Press, 2009), p. 72.

6 Claude Lefort speaks in this context of *mise en forme* in the twofold sense of *mise en sens* and *mise en scène*: 'We can say that the advent of a society capable of organizing social relations can come about only if it can institute the conditions of their intelligibility, and only if it can use a multiplicity of signs to arrive at a quasi-representation of itself' (Lefort, 'The Permanence of the Theologico-Political?', p. 219); see also the other essays collected in Lefort, *Democracy and Political Theory*.

7 Robert N. Bellah, *Religion in Human Evolution: From the Paleolithic to the Axial Age* (Cambridge, MA: Belknap Press, 2011).

8 See the 'Vorwort' to the new edition of Schmitt, *Der Begriff des Politischen* (1932) (Berlin: Duncker & Humblot, 1963), pp. 9–19.

9 I trace this distorted view of history back to the fact that Carl Schmitt neglected the origins of modernity in medieval thought. See the recent account by Ludger Honnefelder, *Woher kommen wir? Ursprünge der Moderne im Denken des Mittelalters* (Berlin: Berlin University Press, 2008). Oddly enough, although Schmitt's concept of God was basically shaped by nominalism, he paid no attention to the long-term effects of the so-called nominalist revolution of the thirteenth century on the prevailing intellectual movements of the sixteenth and seventeenth centuries (on the following four points, see also Michael Allen Gillespie, *The Theological Origins of Modernity* [Chicago: University of Chicago Press, 2008]).

   • One path leads to Protestantism. From the nominalist emphasis on divine omnipotence, from the contingency of human destinies

250 Notes to pp. 169–170

at the mercy of God's unfathomable decrees, and from the constitutional weakness of human understanding which relies on empirical knowledge, a path leads directly to the voluntarist conception of God and the Protestant doctrine of grace. The Protestant valorization of subjective faith taps into a spiritual source of individual autonomy which inspired, on the one hand, political indifference and, on the other, resistance to the authority of the state.

- Another path leads from nominalism to modern science. By purging nature of divine ideas and advocating an ontology that attributes existence only to completely determined individual entities, nominalism, viewed in terms of its historical influence, also created the preconditions for the development of empirical natural science. The latter intensified the contrast between faith and knowledge and, in pluralistic societies, promoted the public authority of mundane knowledge as a shared basis for universally accessible knowledge.

- More controversial is the influence of nominalism on Renaissance humanism, which promoted the anthropocentric turn in modern thought, and how the sciences contributed to the development of a rational alternative to the religious worldview.

- By contrast, nominalism clearly played a crucial role in undermining the foundations of Christian natural law. In addition to undermining the religious legitimation of power, nominalism paved the way for a turn in the philosophy of the subject to those two discourses of the theory of knowledge and social contract theory that dominated seventeenth-century philosophy and provided a secular foundation for the legitimation of politics.

10 Thus Mark Lilla, *The Stillborn God: Religion, Politics, and the West* (New York: Knopf, 2007); for a critical response, see Michael Kirwan, *Political Theology: A New Introduction* (London: Darton, Longman & Todd, 2008).
11 Carl Schmitt, *Political Theology: Four Chapters on the Concept of Sovereignty*, trans. George Schwab (Cambridge, MA: MIT Press, 1985), p. 63.
12 Ibid., p. 59.
13 Ibid., p. 66. On Carl Schmitt's political theology, see Heinrich Meier, *The Lesson of Carl Schmitt: Four Chapters on the Distinction between Political Theology and Political Philosophy*, expanded edn, trans. Marcus Brainard (Chicago: University of Chicago Press, 2011).
14 In order to render such a bizarre voluntaristic concept of 'the political' plausible for an expert public, Schmitt takes the concept of state sovereignty in international law as his starting point. No matter how much a democratic constitution may strangle the sovereignty of the people in the domestic sphere, he argues, nation-states can affirm their sovereignty in external relations in accordance with the principles of classical international law as long as the *ius ad bellum* permits them to conduct wars of aggression as they wish. Adopting this perspective of warring nations, Schmitt begins his 1927 work *Constitutional Theory* with a non-normative

concept of the constitution: 'The state does not *have* a constitution . . . The state exists in a certain constitution, in other words, in an actually present condition, occupying a *status* of unity and order.' (Carl Schmitt, *Constitutional Theory*, trans. and ed. Jeffrey Seitzer [Durham, NC: Duke University Press, 2008], p. 60 [translation amended].)

Schmitt does not understand the constituent power of the 'nation' in the usual way as a legally constituted unity of autonomous citizens either but, rather, as a concrete and organic collectivity. National membership is determined by 'common race, belief, common destiny, and tradition' – in other words, by ascriptive features (ibid., p. 258). Accordingly, Schmitt brings a collectivistic and plebiscitary conception of democracy into play which is directed against the egalitarian conception of individual human rights and against a deliberative conception of politics:

> This democratic equality is the *prerequisite* for all other additional equalities, such as equality of the law, equal right to elected office, equal right to vote, general duty of military service, and equal access to all employment. Hence, the general right to elected office is not the content of democratic equality, but rather the consequence of a presupposed equality. Because all members of the state are presupposed as equal, they must have an equal right to elected office or an equal right to vote, etc. (Ibid., p. 259)

But the people can exercise their right of participation only by acclamation; they can 'express their consent or disapproval by . . . celebrating a leader or a suggestion . . . or denying the acclamation by silence or complaining' (ibid., p. 272).

These theoretical moves are the result of a first problematic decision. Schmitt dissects the liberal constitution – against its express intention to connect popular sovereignty and human rights – into a *political* and a *constitutional* component. This enables him to slip an identitarian conception of democracy, which is tailored to a homogeneous population and its shifting moods, as a 'basis' underneath the constitutional superstructure. The law, at any rate, places only loose fetters on politics. According to Schmitt, any state of emergency shows that the claim of politics to rule in accordance with the 'rule of law' can be subordinated to the actual self-assertion of the people. Ultimately the leader and the nation must decide 'whether the adversary intends to negate his opponent's way of life and therefore must be repulsed or fought in order to preserve one's own form of existence' (Carl Schmitt, *The Concept of the Political*, trans. George Schwab, expanded edn [Chicago: Chicago University Press, 1996], p. 27). However, the meaning of the political resides not in the fight itself but in the 'correct political distinction between friend and enemy' (Carl Schmitt, *Political Theology II: The Myth of the Closure of Any Political Theology*, trans. Michael Hoelzl and Graham Ward [Cambridge: Polity, 2008], p. 90 [translation amended]) and in the willingness of the nation to take up the fight to maintain its own way of life in an emergency. Incidentally, Schmitt uses the example of Mussolini to illustrate this talent (ibid.).

This existentialist version still shares certain essential features with the traditional concept of 'the political'. Certainly, the collective identity of the people is defined no longer in the legal terms of a sovereign state but in the ethnonational concepts of political Romanticism. However, the shared features of descent, tradition and language apparently cannot sufficiently ensure the social cohesion of the collective by their supposed organic nature alone. Rather, the political leadership must continually mobilize the nation against external or internal enemies and weld its individual members together so that they remain in political 'condition' to confront life-and-death struggles.

This concept of the political assumed an even more authoritarian profile when Schmitt, a few years after the publication of *Constitutional Theory*, accommodated it to the Nazi regime with his 'concrete order thinking' [*konkretes Ordnungsdenken*].

15 Schmitt, *Political Theology II*, p. 66.
16 Referring to the debate between Carl Schmitt and Eric Peterson, Ruth Groh sees in this a 'myth of the disunited God'; see Ruth Groh, *Arbeit an der Heillosigkeit der Welt: Zur politisch-theologischen Mythologie und Anthropologie Carl Schmitts* (Frankfurt am Main: Suhrkamp, 1998), pp. 156–84. According to this reading, Schmitt anchored the world-historical struggle of the forces of order against the messianic rebels in the dualistic nature of the deity itself: the promise of salvation aroused the restlessness of the idealists and do-gooders who sin against the dictates of the order of creation. On the anti-Semitic assumptions underlying this peculiar conception, see Mischa Brumlik, 'Carl Schmitts theologisch-politischer Antijudaismus', in Bernd Wacker (ed.), *Die eigentlich katholische Verschärfung . . .: Konfession, Theologie und Politik im Werk Carl Schmitts* (Munich: Wilhelm Fink, 1997), pp. 247–56.
17 Thomas Assheuer, 'Zur besonderen Verfügung: Carl Schmitt', *Kursbuch* 166 (2007): 12–19; see also Jürgen Manemann, *Carl Schmitt und die Politische Theologie: Politischer Anti-Monotheismus* (Münster: Aschendorff, 2002).
18 See the commentaries on Schmitt in Jacob Taubes (ed.), *Religionstheorie und Politische Theologie* (Munich: Wilhelm Fink, 1983).
19 See Charles Taylor, 'Die Bedeutung des Säkularismus', in Rainer Forst et al. (eds), *Sozialphilosophie und Kritik* (Frankfurt am Main: Suhrkamp, 2009), pp. 672–96.
20 See Charles Taylor's convincing phenomenological analysis in *A Secular Age* (Cambridge, MA: Harvard University Press, 2007), especially ch. 15, pp. 539ff.
21 John Rawls, 'The Idea of Public Reason Revisited', *University of Chicago Law Review* 64 (1997): 765–807, here pp. 783–4.
22 For a résumé of these objections, see Habermas, 'Religion in the Public Sphere: Cognitive Presuppositions for the "Public Use of Reason" by Religious and Secular Citizens', in *Between Naturalism and Religion*, trans. Ciaran Cronin (Cambridge: Polity, 2008), pp. 114–47.
23 James W. Boettcher attaches too little importance to the differences between my position and Rawls's proposal; see Boettcher, 'Habermas, Religion and the Ethics of Citizenship', *Philosophy & Social Criticism* 35 (2009): 215–38.

24 That is the point of my argument in Habermas, 'Religion in the Public Sphere', pp. 135–47.
25 Habermas, 'Die Revitalisierung der Weltreligionen – Herausforderung für ein säkulares Selbstverständnis der Moderne?', in *Kritik der Vernunft, Philosophische Texte*, Vol. 5 (Frankfurt am Main: Suhrkamp, 2009), pp. 387–407.
26 Thomas Polednitschek, Michael J. Rainer and José Antonio Zamora (eds), *Theologisch-politische Vergewisserungen: Ein Arbeitsbuch aus dem Schüler- und Freundeskreis von Johann Baptist Metz* (Münster: LIT, 2009).
27 Johann Baptist Metz, *Memoria passionis: Ein provozierendes Gedächtnis in pluraler Gesellschaft* (Freiburg im Breisgau: Herder, 2006).
28 Christian F. Rostbøll, 'Emancipation or Accommodation? Habermasian vs. Rawlsian Deliberative Democracy', *Philosophy & Social Criticism* 34/7 (2008): 707–36.

Chapter 8 The 'Good Life' – a 'Detestable Phrase'

1 I am referring to John Rawls, *A Brief Inquiry into the Meaning of Sin and Faith, with 'On My Religion'*, ed. Thomas Nagel (Cambridge, MA; Harvard University Press, 2009). The page numbers in the text refer to this edition.
2 Rawls, *A Theory of Justice*, rev. edn (Cambridge, MA: Harvard University Press, 1999), §79: The Idea of Social Union, here p. 458 (pp. 522–3) (page numbers in parentheses refer to the original 1971 edition).
3 On the method of reflective equilibrium, see ibid., §9, here pp. 42–4 (pp. 48–50).
4 Rawls, *Lectures on the History of Moral Philosophy*, ed. Barbara Herman (Cambridge, MA: Harvard University Press, 2000), Kant ch. VI, §§3 and 4, pp. 238–43.
5 Ibid., Hegel ch. II, §5, p. 366.
6 The brief criticism of pragmatism which Rawls offers in passing (*A Brief Inquiry*, p. 181) betrays the selective instrumentalist reading that was dominant at the time in Europe.
7 'The sin of using people as means only, as Kant would say, can be found in all regions of experience' (ibid., p. 195).
8 Already in the opening sentences of *A Theory of Justice* (§1: 'The Rule of Justice', p. 3 (p. 3)), Rawls commits himself to the analogy between justice and truth: 'Justice is the first virtue of social institutions, as truth is of systems of thought. A theory however elegant and economical must be rejected or revised if it is untrue; likewise laws and institutions no matter how efficient and well-arranged must be reformed or abolished if they are unjust.'
9 The polemic against Greek and medieval ethics finds an echo in the introductory chapter to the lectures on moral philosophy; see Rawls, *Lectures*, Introduction, §1.
10 Even though Adorno (see 'Dedication' in Theodor W. Adorno, *Minima Moralia* [London: Verso, 2005], pp. 15ff.) made room for the

deontological intuition only as part of a more comprehensive critique of alienation founded on a more comprehensive social theory.

11 Rawls, *A Theory of Justice*, ch. 3, §§27–8.

12 In this context Rawls engages in an implicit polemic against Greek thought; he contrasts the fully fledged Christian concept of the 'person', who is individuated through her life history and has shaken off the anonymity of the Roman 'persona', with that of the 'individual'. This makes sense insofar as the corresponding Greek term can be applied to all objects individuated in spatio-temporal terms: 'All persons are individuals, that is separate and distinct units, but all individuals are not persons. Personality is equivalent, perhaps, to what we mean by "spirit". When we speak of spiritual life, it seems that we mean personal life' (*A Brief Inquiry*, p. 111).

13 The contrasting concept to this substantialized notion of an 'elite' is that of the 'loser', a concept which came into vogue only in recent decades; on this, see the fine essay by Ingo Schulze, 'Über den Begriff "Verlierer"', in Schulze, *Was wollen wir?* (Berlin: Berlin Verlag, 2009), pp. 280–86.

14 Rawls, *A Theory of Justice*, p. 514 (p. 587).

15 The transitional path which Rawls himself mentions in retrospect in 1997 with reference to Bodin does not represent a plausible alternative to this continuity:

> If we say that God's will is the source of all being, and of all moral and political values, then the denial of God's existence entails the denial of those values also. But if we say that the ground and content of those values is God's reason or else known to God's reason, then God's will serves only a subordinate role of sanctioning the divine intentions now seen as grounded on reason. In this case the denial of God's existence leads only to the denial of the divine sanctions but not to the denial of values. (*A Brief Inquiry*, p. 267)

Pursuing this path of transforming religious into rational morality would have been an option only under the premise of a Thomistic conception of God; but in fact such an ontotheological concept had already been the target of the young Rawls's polemic.

16 Rawls, *A Theory of Justice*, ch. 20: 'The Nature of the Argument for Conceptions of Justice', here p. 104 (p. 120).

17 The instructive essay by Robert M. Adams ('The Theological Ethics of the Young Rawls', in *A Brief Inquiry*, pp. 24–101) describes the theological context within which the graduation thesis was written. The primary influence on the young Rawls was – via Emil Brunner – dialectical theology and Martin Buber's philosophy of dialogue. Both traditions develop theological propositions based on the existential-religious experience of the communicative encounter with the other or others. Rawls appeals to this performatively present background when he frees God's personality from all ontological connotations and postulates Him from within the horizon of ethical experience in inter-personal relations: 'As to what sort of being God is – that is, whether

He possesses all the metaphysical attributes assigned to Him – we do not presume to know. It is doubtful whether natural theology can tell us very much' (p. 111). This same postmetaphysical abstinence from ontological claims without support in reflection on one's own lifeworld background resonates in the polemical remark in the 'Preface' against natural theology, where we read that a 'pound of Aristotle' is not worth an 'ounce of the Bible'.

18 See Rainer Forst, *Toleration in Conflict: Past and Present*, trans. Ciaran Cronin (Cambridge: Cambridge University Press, 2013).

19 See Charles Taylor, 'Die Bedeutung des Säkularismus', in Rainer Forst et al. (eds), *Sozialphilosophie und Kritik* (Frankfurt am Main: Suhrkamp, 2009), pp. 672–96.

20 Rawls, 'Reply to Habermas', *Journal of Philosophy* XCII/3 (1995): 132–80, here pp. 142f.

21 Rawls, *Political Liberalism* (New York: Columbia University Press, 1992), pp. 128f.

22 Habermas, '"Reasonable" versus "True", or the Morality of Worldviews', in *The Inclusion of the Other: Studies in Political Theory*, ed. and trans. Ciaran Cronin and Pablo De Greiff (Cambridge: Polity, 1998), pp. 75–101.

23 The counter-intuitive nature of this move is shown by how the distinction between political and moral justice becomes blurred in §2 of *Political Liberalism* (p. 11): 'The first concerns the subject of a political conception. While such a conception is, of course, a moral conception, it is a moral conception worked out for a specific kind of subject, namely, for political, social, and economic institutions.' Rawls explains this as follows in a footnote: 'In saying that a conception is moral, I mean . . . that its content is given by certain ideals, principles and standards; and that these norms articulate certain values, in this case political values.'

24 Rawls, 'The Idea of Public Reason Revisited', *University of Chicago Law Review* 64 (1997): 765–807, here p. 771; see James W. Boettcher, 'What is reasonableness?', *Philosophy & Social Criticism* 2004/5–6: 597–621, here pp. 604ff.

25 Habermas, 'Religion in the Public Sphere: Cognitive Presuppositions for the "Public Use of Reason" by Religious and Secular Citizens', in *Between Naturalism and Religion*, trans. Ciaran Cronin (Cambridge: Polity, 2008), pp. 114–47.

Chapter 9 Rawls's Political Liberalism

1 Professor of Philosophy, University of Sussex.

2 Lecturer in Philosophy, University of Essex.

3 James Gordon Finlayson and Fabian Freyenhagen (eds), *Habermas and Rawls: Disputing the Political* (New York: Routledge, 2011).

4 The English translation of *Faktizität und Geltung* (1992) appeared only in 1996; at the time of writing my comments in 1992, I could not assume that Rawls was familiar with this book.

5 See my review article 'The "Good Life" – a "Detestable Phrase": The

Significance of the Young Rawls's Religious Ethics for his Political Theory', chapter 8 in this volume.

6 Finlayson and Freyenhagen, 'Introduction: The Habermas–Rawls Dispute – Analysis and Re-evaluation', in Finlayson and Freyenhagen (eds), *Habermas and Rawls*, pp. 1–21.

7 Ibid., p. 15.

8 The continental legal tradition, which places the emphasis on the positivity of law and on justifying general norms from *the perspective of the legislator*, attaches greater importance to this distinction than the common law tradition, which concentrates more on aspects of the development of law – that is, the hermeneutic application of precedents – from the *perspective of the judge*.

9 Professor of Philosophy at the University of California, Santa Barbara.

10 The 'Notes on a Program of Philosophical Justification' alone, which were written over thirty years ago (in Habermas, *Moral Consciousness and Communicative Action*, trans. Christian Lenhardt and Shierry Weber Nicholsen [Cambridge, MA: MIT Press, 1990], pp. 43–115), represent a rather slender basis for a critique of my approach.

11 Rawls understands the 'objectivity' of moral judgements in a similar intersubjectivist sense; see *Political Liberalism* (New York: Columbia University Press, 1992), Lecture III, §5.

12 This convergence is by no means trivial but is the result of the dissolution of substantive conceptions of justice under the conditions of modern religious and metaphysical pluralism; see Habermas, 'Rightness versus Truth: On the Sense of Normative Validity in Moral Judgements and Norms', in *Truth and Justification*, trans. Barbara Fultner (Cambridge: Polity, 2003), pp. 237–76, here pp. 261ff.

13 On what follows, see Habermas, 'A Genealogical Analysis of the Cognitive Content of Morality', in *The Inclusion of the Other*, trans. Ciaran Cronin (Cambridge: Polity, 1998), pp. 3–46, here pp. 39–46.

14 Christopher McMahon, 'Habermas, Rawls and Moral Impartiality', in Finlayson and Freyenhagen (eds), *Habermas and Rawls*, pp. 200–23.

15 The description of the practice of argumentation covers the distribution of roles, the pragmatic presuppositions, and the goal of communication. The goal of argument can be explained in terms of the meaning of moral validity claims; and this goal explains in turn the patterns of argument which are admissible from a logical and semantic point of view. The contingent contents stem from practical conflicts which participants perceive as being in need of regulation. An examination that *a fortiori* attributes to the participants the dispositions and skills required to fulfil the roles in argumentation as structurally described has no need to appeal to additional factors external to discourse.

16 See my introduction to Habermas, *Diskursethik*, *Philosophische Texte*, Vol. 3 (Frankfurt am Main: Suhrkamp, 2009).

17 I tend to avoid this expression in order to guard against the common misunderstanding of interpretation as requiring an act of empathy.

18 Traces of which can also be found in history – for example, in the development of law.

19 Professor of Philosophy, University of Toronto.

20 In the present context, I cannot address his acute and challenging cri-

tique of the foundations of discourse ethics in formal pragmatics; see Joseph Heath, *Communicative Action and Rational Choice* (Cambridge, MA: MIT Press, 2001).

21 Heath, 'Justice: Transcendental not Metaphysical', in Finlayson and Freyenhagen (eds), *Habermas and Rawls*, pp. 117–34. See below, section IV.

22 However, many colleagues have difficulty in understanding the idealizing, and in many cases counterfactual, content of 'unavoidable' pragmatic presuppositions of communication (e.g., the ascription of imputability or truthfulness). See Habermas, 'Communicative Reason and the Detranscendentalized "Use of Reason"', in *Between Naturalism and Religion: Philosophical Essays*, trans. Ciaran Cronin (Cambridge: Polity, 2008), pp. 24–76.

23 But see the differentiations below in note 27.

24 Briefly, I use the term 'reconstructive' to describe theories that seek to explain the implicitly assumed normative contents of empirically established practices – e.g., everyday communication – from the participant perspective, hence in a performative attitude. Thus a reconstructive theory of the constitutional state – whether it adopts an approach that focuses on particular cases or is geared from the outset to ideal-typical generalization – begins with the constitution-making praxis. Its aim is to exhume, as it were, the normative meaning of a democratic constitution out of the differentiated network of the corresponding institutionalized practices (general elections, parliamentary deliberations, judicial procedures, etc.). However, the system of basic rights at which one arrives at the highest level of abstraction is formally almost indistinguishable from a normative political theory. See Habermas, *Sprachtheoretische Grundlegung der Soziologie, Philosophische Texte*, Vol. 1 (Frankfurt am Main: Suhrkamp, 2009), section III, and the related commentary in the introduction, pp. 23ff.

25 Professor of Philosophy at the University of Illinois, Chicago.

26 Anthony Simon Laden, 'The Justice of Justification', in Finlayson and Freyenhagen (eds), *Habermas and Rawls*, pp. 135–52.

27 I leave open whether this is an appropriate interpretation of Rawls's texts. As I understand it, Anthony Simon Laden underestimates considerably the cognitive claim that Rawls associates with his 'reasonable' conception of justice and, in particular, with the universalistic justificatory function of the original position. Even if the circular relation between the reasonableness of a conception of justice and the claim to truth of the comprehensive doctrines leaves questions open, in the end Rawls even requires the backing of a truth claim for the correctness or rightness of the 'political justification'. For he makes the legitimacy and stability of the institutions of a well-ordered society dependent on the possible transfer of truth from at least one of these doctrines to the generally accepted conception of justice: 'The truth of any one doctrine guarantees that all doctrines yield the right conception of political justice, even though all are not right for the right reasons as given by the one true doctrine . . . When citizens differ, not all can be fully correct; yet if one of their doctrines should be true, all citizens are correct, politically speaking' (Rawls, *Political Liberalism*, n. 19, pp. 153–4).

28 Laden, 'The Justice of Justification', p. 137.
29 That certain disciplines are further removed from everyday contexts of communication than others also has to do with their intrinsic relation to practice. The technically exploitable results of research in natural science differ in this respect from the findings of the human sciences or philosophy. The latter cannot be implemented in technologies. They can either find their way into social subsystems via expert opinions or exert a diffuse mentality-forming influence on the general culture along the intricate paths of public communication and hermeneutic appropriation.
30 I do not mean to imply that political philosophers who have something to say about constitutional principles cannot also contribute as experts to solving corresponding legal problems. Otherwise they can at best exercise an indirect influence over the political culture in the more distant role of authors or intellectuals.
31 London School of Economics and Political Science.
32 James Gledhill, 'Procedure in Substance and Substance in Procedure: Reframing the Rawls–Habermas Debate', in Finlayson and Freyenhagen (eds), *Habermas and Rawls*, pp. 181–99.
33 Ibid., pp. 191–2.
34 The procedural dissolution of the concept 'moral justice' does not mean, however, that the 'rightness' of moral judgements, as a dimension of validity, is identical with 'justice'. The substantive concepts of justice of the past are absorbed into the 'moral point of view' from which conflicts of action must be examined if they are to be resolved in a non-violent manner, in particular through an impartial and intersubjective process of judgement and decision-making among the parties to the dispute themselves.
35 Professor of Political Theory and Philosophy, Frankfurt University.
36 Religious conceptions of the world differ from ethical outlooks in virtue of the fact that they involve convictions with which people of faith associate a 'claim to truth'. From the perspective of the philosopher, however, we must ask in what sense, given this special context, one can speak of religious 'truth'. On my analysis, the kind of validity claimed for religious statements must not be assimilated to propositional truth. For theological reflections on this problem, see Edmund Arens, *Gottesverständigung: Eine kommunikative Religionstheologie* (Freiburg: Herder, 2007), pp. 239–65.
37 The domain of values is not transitively ordered as such. Only the moral point of view, from which we examine the universalizability of various values which compete in cases of conflict, makes sharp distinctions within that domain. Because moral norms are the result of the constructive process of coping with value-laden conflicts, they always draw their semantic content from the reservoir of fleeting values provided by the ethical orientations of persons and cultures.
38 Rainer Forst, 'The Justification of Justice: Rawls and Habermas in Dialogue', in Finlayson and Freyenhagen (eds), *Habermas and Rawls*, pp. 153–80.
39 On this two-step conception, see Habermas, 'Constitutional Democracy – a Paradoxical Union of Contradictory Principles?' in *Time of*

Transitions, trans. Ciaran Cronin and Max Pensky (Cambridge: Polity, 2006), pp. 113–28.

40 Social and cultural rights which grant sufficient options to participate in social and cultural life also depend on this legal form insofar as they have the meaning of guaranteeing the equal value of legal freedoms.

41 Habermas, 'The Concept of Human Dignity and the Realistic Utopia of Human Rights', in *The Crisis of the European Union: A Response*, trans. Ciaran Cronin (Cambridge: Polity, 2012), pp. 71–100.

42 Thomas M. Scanlon, *What We Owe to Each Other* (Cambridge, MA: Harvard University Press, 1998).

43 London School of Economics and Political Science.

44 Catherine Audard, 'Rawls and Habermas on the Place of Religion in the Political Domain', in Finlayson and Freyenhagen (eds), *Habermas and Rawls*, pp. 224–46.

45 I dealt with Kant's conception of securing international peace and security early in my career – for example, in 1960 in the context of a discussion of the so-called atomic age at the sixth Deutscher Kongress für Philosophie; see Habermas, 'Über das Verhältnis von Politik und Moral', in Helmut Kuhn and Franz Wiedmann (eds), *Das Problem der Ordnung* (Munich: Anton Pustet, 1962), pp. 94–117. But it was only in the wake of 1989–90, on the occasion of the controversy over the justification of the first Gulf War and the meaning of humanitarian interventions, that I addressed the problem of a cosmopolitan system *which is intended to make global domestic politics possible* in an extensive written interview with Michael Haller; see Habermas, *Vergangenheit als Zukunft* (Zurich: Pendo, 1991), pp. 10–44 (English translation: *The Past as Future*, trans. Max Pensky [Lincoln, NE: University of Nebraska Press, 1994], pp. 5–55). In 1993 I returned to the topic in the afterword to the second edition of the book (Munich: Piper, 1993, pp. 189ff.; *The Past as Future*, pp. 144ff.).

46 Professor of Philosophy and International Relations, Washington University, St Louis.

47 Although in an essay published to mark the 200-year anniversary of the appearance of Kant's work on peace I referred to such proposals by Daniele Archibugi and David Held, I immediately added: 'The foregoing reflections are conventional in taking their orientation from the organizational components of national constitutions. The implementation of a properly clarified conception of cosmopolitan law evidently calls for somewhat more institutional imagination.' See Habermas, 'Kant's Idea of Perpetual Peace, with the Benefit of Two Hundred Years' Hindsight', in *The Inclusion of the Other*, pp. 165–201, here p. 188.

48 Habermas, *The Postnational Constellation*, trans. Max Pensky (Cambridge: Polity, 2001), p. 110 [the alternative translation, 'global domestic politics', is used throughout the present work – *Trans.*]; see also Habermas, 'Euroskepticism, Market Europe, or a Europe of (World) Citizens?', in *Time of Transitions*, pp. 73–88, here pp. 84ff.

49 Habermas, *The Postnational Constellation*, pp. 106–7: 'In view of this *restriction to the basic services of maintaining order*, even the most ambitious reforms of existing institutions [of the United Nations] would not lead in the direction of a world government.'

50 Habermas, 'Does the Constitutionalization of International Law Still Have a Chance?', in *The Divided West*, trans. Ciaran Cronin (Cambridge: Polity, 2006), pp. 115–93.

51 James Bohman, 'Beyond Overlapping Consensus: Rawls and Habermas on the Limits of Cosmopolitanism', in Finlayson and Freyenhagen (eds), *Habermas and Rawls*, pp. 265–82.

52 Habermas, 'A Political Constitution for the Pluralist World Society,' in *Between Naturalism and Religion*, pp. 312–52.

53 Habermas, 'The Constitutionalization of International Law and the Legitimation Problems of a Constitution for Society', in *Europe, the Faltering Project*, trans. Ciaran Cronin (Cambridge: Polity, 2009), pp. 109–30; see also 'European Politics at an Impasse: A Plea for a Policy of Graduated Integration', ibid., pp. 78–105 (Section IV: Scenarios of a Future World Order, pp. 95–101), and 'The Crisis of the European Union in Light of a Constitutionalization of International Law – An Essay on the Constitution for Europe', in *The Crisis of the European Union*, pp. 1–70 (Section III: From the International to the Cosmopolitan Community, pp. 53–70).

54 Professor of Philosophy, Fordham University, New York.

55 Jeffrey Flynn, 'Two Models of Human Rights', in Finlayson and Freyenhagen (eds), *Habermas and Rawls*, pp. 247–64.

56 BVerfG, 1 BvL 1/09 of 9 February 2010. The judgement concerns how social welfare benefits for the unemployed should be calculated (in the wake of the fourth stage of the Hartz reforms of the labour market introduced by the red–green federal coalition government under Gerhard Schröder in 2005).

57 Ernst Bloch, *Natural Law and Human Dignity*, trans. Dennis J. Schmidt (Cambridge, MA: MIT Press, 1987).

Chapter 10 Religion in the Public Sphere of 'Post-Secular' Society

1 Detlef Pollack, *Säkularisierung – ein moderner Mythos?* (Tubingen: Mohr Siebeck, 2003).

2 Hans Joas, 'Gesellschaft, Staat und Religion', in Joas (ed.), *Säkularisierung und die Weltreligionen* (Frankfurt am Main: Fischer, 2007), pp. 9–43. see also Joas, 'Die Zukunft des Christentums', *Blätter für deutsche und internationale Politik* 8 (2007): 976–84.

3 Jeffrey K. Hadden, 'Toward Desacralizing Secularization Theory', *Social Force* 65 (1987): 587–611.

4 Joas, 'Gesellschaft, Staat und Religion'.

5 Peter L. Berger, 'The Desecularization of the World: A Global Overview', in Berger (ed.), *The Desecularization of the World: Resurgent Religion and World Politics* (Grand Rapids, MI: W. B. Eerdmans, 1999), pp. 1–18.

6 Joachim Gentz, 'Die religiöse Lage in Ostasien', in Joas (ed.), *Säkularisierung und die Weltreligionen*, pp. 358–75.

7 See the contributions by Hans Gerhard Kippenberg and Heinrich von Stietencron in Joas (ed.), *Säkularisierung und die Weltreligionen*, pp. 465–507 and pp. 194–223.

8 Pippa Norris and Ronald Inglehart, *Sacred and Secular: Religion and Politics Worldwide* (Cambridge: Cambridge University Press, 2004).

9 José Casanova, *Public Religions in the Modern World* (Chicago: University of Chicago Press, 1994).

10 Habermas, 'Faith and Knowledge', in *The Future of Human Nature*, trans. Hella Beister and William Rehg (Cambridge: Polity, 2003), pp. 101–15, here p. 104.

11 Thus Francis Schüssler Fiorenza, 'The Church as a Community of Interpretation', in Don S. Browning and Schüssler Fiorenza (eds), *Habermas, Modernity, and Public Theology* (New York: Crossroad, 1992), pp. 66–91.

12 Geert Mak, *Der Mord an Theo van Gogh: Geschichte einer moralischen Panik* (Frankfurt am Main: Suhrkamp, 2005).

13 Thierry Chervel and Anja Seeliger (eds), *Islam in Europa* (Frankfurt am Main: Suhrkamp, 2007). English translation: 'The "Islam in Europe" Debate', 22 March 2007, www.signandsight.com/features/1167.html.

14 Margriet de Moor, 'Alarm Bells in Muslim Hearts', 23 April 2007, www.signandsight.com/features/1309.html.

15 For the history and a systematic analysis, see the comprehensive study by Rainer Forst, *Toleration in Conflict: Past and Present*, trans. Ciaran Cronin (Cambridge: Cambridge University Press, 2013).

16 Habermas, 'Religious Tolerance as Pacemaker for Cultural Rights', in *Between Naturalism and Religion*, trans. Ciaran Cronin (Cambridge: Polity, 2008), pp. 251–70.

17 See my debate with Charles Taylor in Taylor, *Multiculturalism: Examining the Politics of Recognition*, ed. Amy Gutmann (Princeton, NJ: Princeton University Press, 1994), Habermas, 'Struggles for Recognition in the Democratic Constitutional State', reprinted in Habermas, *The Inclusion of the Other*, trans. Ciaran Cronin (Cambridge: Polity, 1998), pp. 203–36.

18 On the public use of reason, see John Rawls, *Political Liberalism* (New York: Columbia University Press, 1992), pp. 212–54.

19 Ian Buruma, *Murder in Amsterdam: The Death of Theo Van Gogh and the Limits of Tolerance* (New York: Penguin, 2006), p. 28.

20 Timothy Garton Ash, 'Islam in Europe', *New York Review of Books*, 5 October 2006.

21 Pascal Bruckner, 'Enlightenment Fundamentalism or Racism of the Anti-Racists?', 24 January 2007, www.signandsight.com/features/1146.html.

22 Bruckner, ibid.: 'This is the paradox of multiculturalism: it accords the same treatment to all communities, but not to the people who form them, denying them the freedom to liberate themselves from their own traditions.' On this, see Brian Barry, *Culture and Equality* (Cambridge: Polity, 2001), and Habermas, 'Equal Treatment of Cultures and the Limits of Postmodern Liberalism', in *Between Naturalism and Religion*, pp. 271–311.

23 Buruma, *Murder in Amsterdam*, p. 28.

24 The decisive critique of the incommensurability hypothesis goes back to Donald Davidson's famous 1973 presidential address to the American Philosophical Association, 'On the Very Idea of a Conceptual Scheme',

reprinted in Davidson, *Inquiries into Truth and Interpretation* (Oxford: Oxford University Press, 2001), pp. 183–98.

25 See Anatol Lieven, 'Liberal Hawk Down – Wider die linken Falken', *Blätter für deutsche und internationale Politik* 12 (2004): 1447–57.

26 Buruma, *Murder in Amsterdam*, p. 29. Buruma describes the motivation of the leftist converts as follows:

> The Muslims are the spoilsports, unwelcome crashers at the party ... Tolerance, then, has its limits even for Dutch progressives. It is easy to be tolerant of those who are much like ourselves, whom we feel we can trust instinctively, whose jokes we understand, who share our use of irony ... It is much harder to extend the same principle to strangers in our midst, who find our ways as disturbing as we do theirs ... (ibid. pp. 127–8).

27 See my critique in the essays 'Freedom and Determinism', in *Between Naturalism and Religion*, pp. 151–80, and 'The Language Game of Responsible Agency and the Problem of Free Will: How Can Epistemic Dualism Be Reconciled with Ontological Monism?', *Philosophical Explorations* 10/1 (2007): 13–50.

28 This is the key issue for John Rawls when he calls for an overlapping consensus of groups with different worldviews on the norms underlying the constitutional order; see Rawls, *Political Liberalism*, pp. 133ff.

29 Ian Buruma, 'Tariq Ramadan has an Identity Issue', *New York Times*, 4 February 2007; Bassam Tibi, 'Europeanisation not Islamisation', 22 March 2007, www.signandsight.com/features/1258.html; see also Tariq Ramadan, '"Ihr bekommt die Muslime, die Ihr verdient": EuroIslam und muslimische Renaissance', *Blätter für deutsche und internationale Politik* 6 (2006): 673–85.

30 On the following, see Habermas, 'Religion in the Public Sphere: Cognitive Presuppositions for the "Public Use of Reason" by Religious and Secular Citizens', in *Between Naturalism and Religion*, pp. 114–47.

Index